Egypt's Golden

# Egypt's Golden Empire

## The Age of the New Kingdom

Joyce Tyldesley

**HEADLINE**

Copyright © 2001 Lion Television Limited/Joyce Tyldesley

The right of Joyce Tyldesley to be identified as the Author of
the Work has been asserted by her in accordance with the
Copyright, Designs and Patents Act 1988.

First published in 2001
by HEADLINE BOOK PUBLISHING

10 9 8 7 6 5 4 3 2 1

British Library Cataloguing in Publication Data

Tyldesley, Joyce A.
  Egypt's golden empire : the age of the New Kingdom
  1.Egypt – History – Nineteenth dynasty, ca. 1320-1200 B.C.
  2.Egypt – History – Eighteenth dynasty, ca. 1570-1320 B.C.
  3.Egypt – Civilization – To 332 B.C. 4.Egypt – Kings and rulers
  I.Title
  932'.014

  ISBN 0 7472 5160 6

Typeset by Letterpart Limited, Reigate, Surrey
Printed and bound in Great Britain by Clays Ltd, St Ives plc

Headline Book Publishing
A division of Hodder Headline
338 Euston Road
London NW1 3BH

www.headline.co.uk
www.hodderheadline.com

For the Lightfoot family: Phil (explosives expert), Patricia (writer), Sophie (ballet dancer), Amy (soccer player) and Eugene (hockey player). Thanks for all the e-mails!

# Contents

# Preface

The New Kingdom pharaohs carved Egypt's official history in stone for all to enjoy. Theirs is an epic adventure told on the grandest of scales: a storybook classic of bloodshed and valour, of world domination, golden treasures, powerful gods and beautiful women. As the centuries-long tale unfolds we meet a vibrant cast of characters: Ahmose the liberator, Hatshepsut the usurper, Tuthmosis the warrior, Ramesses the god. Each, in his or her own way, is called upon to defend their land against the dark forces of chaos which constantly threaten Egypt's charmed tranquillity. Each succeeds, for Egypt's pharaohs did not know the meaning of failure.

This book, based on the Lion Television Series *Egypt's Golden Empire*, tells the story of the New Kingdom empire-builders using a traditional, chronological approach heavily dependent upon the written and artistic evidence left by Egypt's scribes and masons. But this royal history can only ever tell a partial tale. What of the ordinary people who lived and died as Egypt struggled to build her empire? Omitted from the monumental inscriptions left by their kings, they form a ghostly, almost invisible background to New Kingdom life. Here, in alternate chapters presented alongside the traditional history, is woven the unofficial story of the New Kingdom, a social history which is largely preserved in Egypt's material (archaeological) remains. Twisted together, these separate skeins of evidence make a compelling historical yarn.

Egyptian chronology can be very confusing for the uniniti-
ated. The Egyptians recorded the names of their kings in lists
(today known as king lists) which they preserved on their
temple walls. These kings are by convention divided into
dynasties which often, but by no means always, represent ruling
families. Usually, as we might expect, one dynasty follows
another. Occasionally, at times of civil unrest, dynasties might
overlap, with rival kings ruling contemporaneously from different capitals; the Hyksos kings of northern Egypt (Dynasty 15),
for example, overlapped with a period of independent Theban
rule (Dynasties 16 and 17). At the same time Dynasty 14, an
ephemeral group of monarchs of little historical significance,
overlapped both the Theban and Hyksos dynasties.

The glorious periods in Egypt's history – the times when
pharaoh reigned over a unified land secure in his god-given right
to rule – are today known as Kingdoms. Separating the Old,
Middle and New Kingdoms are the Intermediate Periods, far
less glorious times of disunity and divided rule. While the
Kingdoms are relatively well documented, the sequence of
events during the Intermediate Periods can often be difficult to
understand. The Egyptians themselves gave no name to these
embarrassing lapses of unity; indeed, ever selective in their
history, they preferred to forget all about the Intermediate
Periods. If they were mentioned at all, they were used to provide
a neat contrast to the order, peace and prosperity of a kingdom
joined under a single pharaoh. Our story starts with the
confusion of the late Second Intermediate Period (c. 1690–
1550BC) and ends with the onset of the Third Intermediate
Period (c. 1070BC).

The New Kingdom, the age of empire (c. 1550–1070BC),
comprises the successive Dynasties 18–20 and includes some

thirty-three individual reigns. Within each reign events may be dated to a particular regnal year (e.g. the epic battle of Megiddo is dated to Year 22 of the reign of Tuthmosis III). This simple system, used by the ancient Egyptians themselves, makes the dating of events within the Nile Valley extremely accurate. The reigns of the New Kingdom pharaohs are listed in the table given on page xii.

# Table:
# The Pharaohs Of The New Kingdom

Our New Kingdom chronology is derived from a number of sources. The king lists recorded by the pharaohs themselves form the basis of the table, but further information has been gathered from monumental inscriptions and from randomly preserved archaeological material such as date-stamped wine-jars. While the sequence of kings is widely accepted as correct, the precise length of their individual reigns is less certain. The table suggests the minimum reign length for each king. All too often we are forced to estimate the length of a king's rule based on his last known regnal year rather than a dated account of his death. For example, as our last recorded date for the 18th Dynasty pharaoh Akhenaten comes from a label whose initial date of Year 17 has been crossed out and replaced by a Year 1, we assume that Akhenaten died during his 17th year on the throne. This system is broadly accurate but by no means foolproof; there is a tendency to underestimate, and we should therefore allow for a margin of error of maybe ten years within the table.

## Pre-New Kingdom
**Late 17th Dynasty** (c. 1560–1550BC)
Sekenenre Taa
Kamose (3 years)

# New Kingdom
## 18th Dynasty (1550–1295BC)
Ahmose (25 years)
Amenhotep I (21 years)
Tuthmosis I (11 years)
Tuthmosis II (1–3 years)
Hatshepsut (22 years)/Tuthmosis III (54 years)
Amenhotep II (26 years)
Tuthmosis IV (8–10 years)
Amenhotep III (38 years)
Akhenaten/Amenhotep IV (17 years)
Smenkhkare (2 years; probably within the reign of Akhenaten)
Tutankhamen (9 years)
Ay (4 years)
Horemheb (20–28 years)

## 19th Dynasty (1295–1186BC)
Ramesses I (1 year)
Seti I (15 years)
Ramesses II (66 years)
Merenptah (10 years)
Amenmesse (2–4 years)
Seti II (5 years)
Siptah (6 years)
Twosret (2 years)

## 20th Dynasty (1186–1069BC)
Sethnakht (2 years)
Ramesses III (32 years)
Ramesses IV (6 years)
Ramesses V (4 years)

Ramesses VI (7 years)
Ramesses VII (7 years)
Ramesses VIII (3 years)
Ramesses IX (18 years)
Ramesses X (9 years)
Ramesses XI (30 years)

# Third Intermediate Period

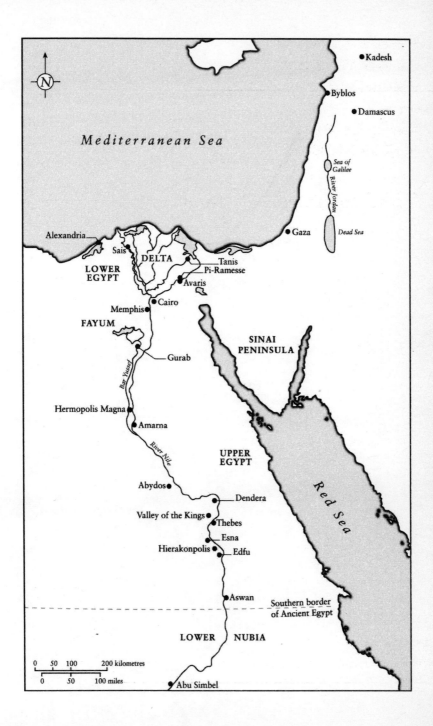

# FOUNDATION

## Thebes, 1560BC:
## The Second Intermediate Period

> Behold, hearts are violent, the land riven by storm, with
> blood everywhere and many dead ... foreign bowmen have
> come to Egypt ...
>
> *The scribe Ipuwer laments the loss of peace and security in Egypt*

K ing Sekenenre Taa brooded in his Theban palace. His
was an unenviable position. Having come to his throne
in uncertain times he was now forced to rule over a
divided land where his own divine authority was restricted to
southern, or Upper, Egypt. To the north the Hyksos, kings of
Canaanite descent, had controlled Lower Egypt for over a
century. To the south the Nubian kingdom of Kush (based in
modern Sudan) was starting to cast an acquisitive eye over
Theban territory. Isolated from the world outside the Nile
Valley, evicted from the Nile Delta and the great city of
Memphis, and uncomfortably trapped between two enemies, the
Theban king was not prepared to accept his lot. The situation
had grown intolerable. The time had come to put his troops to
the test.

Egypt had once been the greatest nation on earth. Her Giza
pyramids, already over a thousand years old, still stood as an

irrefutable testimony to pharaoh's ability to command the labour of a unified land. Now, however, the pyramids were under foreign control, their burials desecrated and their royal mummies lost.

How could Egypt have sunk so low?

# CHAPTER I

## Ahmose:

## The Warrior Pharaoh

Kamose, the mighty ruler of Thebes... is the legitimate king, appointed by Re himself and granted real strength...

*Stela of King Kamose*

Many of the problems of the Second Intermediate Period were rooted in Egypt's unique geography. Egypt is a long, thin country which faithfully follows the progress of the River Nile as it flows from the First Cataract at Aswan northwards into the Mediterranean Sea. For much of its length – over 600 miles – the Nile Valley, bordered by inhospitable sand and impenetrable mountains, protects Egypt from unwanted foreign attention. However, just beyond the ancient city of Heliopolis (modern Cairo), the Nile branches to form the Delta; a broad, flat, fertile plain bound by the Mediterranean coast. To the west the Delta abuts on to Libya, once the home of dangerous nomadic tribes. To the east it links Egypt with the Levant, the 'northern countries', via the sands of the Sinai peninsula.

Throughout the dynastic age the Delta, easily accessible both by sea and land, proved a constant temptation to foreigners eager to escape their own impoverished homelands and make a fresh start in an affluent and well-regulated country. From the end of the Old Kingdom onwards a steady trickle of economic migrants had left the Levant to make a new life in the towns and villages of the eastern Delta.

Egypt had always been wary of foreigners – the Asiatic or easterner, alongside the Nubian and the Libyan, was one of the three traditional enemies recognised and reviled since prehistoric times – but the influx of new workers seems to have been accepted with resignation. Whereas unskilled, unwanted nomads were routinely turned back from the border, urbanised Canaanites – those with a contribution to make to the Egyptian economy – were allowed to settle unchecked in increasing numbers. Asiatics now served as soldiers, as domestic servants and as administrators. Living in peaceful coexistence alongside their Egyptian neighbours, the new arrivals developed their own hybrid cultural tradition, combining elements of Canaanite and Egyptian culture. Never fully integrated, yet never threateningly different, the Canaanites prospered in northern Egypt.

The Middle Bronze Age was a time of increasing turbulence and disruption throughout the eastern Mediterranean. This coincided with a time of weak rule in Egypt; a time when it proved impossible to maintain proper border controls. As the Levantine states themselves came under pressure from eastern migrants fleeing warfare in their homelands, the trickle of foreigners arriving in north-eastern Egypt became a flood. Eventually, as the migrants started to outnumber the native-born Egyptians, the towns of the eastern Delta banded together to form an informal, semi-autonomous Canaanite colony. Thus, gradually and peacefully, foreigners 'conquered' north-eastern Egypt. Under normal circumstances this would have been totally unacceptable; any perceived or real challenge to pharaoh's authority met with a swift armed response. These were not, however, normal times.

Egypt was now a land in full-blown political crisis. The kings of the late 13th Dynasty, a succession of brief and unremarkable monarchs, were slowly but surely becoming impotent. Already they had lost the confidence of the governors who effectively ruled the Nile Valley at a local level. The support of the provinces was essential if Egypt was to function as an efficient unit. Egypt's extreme length and her distinctive settlement pattern – towns and cities ordered single-file along the Nile rather than radiating outwards from population centres – meant that she had a natural tendency to fragment into independent city-states whose citizens were primarily loyal to their own local gods and their own local dynasties.

A series of high Nile floods had done little to help the beleaguered pharaohs. Records recovered from Nubia, and reports of a flood at Thebes, confirm that the Nile flood-level was very high at the beginning of the 13th Dynasty. The Nile Valley was dependent upon the annual inundation, or flooding, which brought water and fertile silt to her fields. Too high a flood, however, could be disastrous; water would damage the mud-brick architecture, ruin the granaries, isolate the cities and indirectly cause famine. At a deeper level, the erratic behaviour of the floodwater might suggest that the gods – those who controlled Egypt – were out of sympathy with their representative on earth. If pharaoh had lost his divine support, he should perhaps be replaced.

When Merneferra Ay, last pharaoh of the 13th Dynasty, fled from his royal palace the Middle Kingdom dissolved. Now Egypt was burdened with two principal courts plus a handful of semi-independent city-states in the Delta region.

In the north the Hyksos, a dynasty of Canaanite extraction, used a limited amount of military force to sack Memphis and proclaim their dominion over the whole of Upper and Lower Egypt. This was an exaggerated claim. Although blocks engraved with the names of Hyksos kings have been recovered from the temple of Hathor at Gebelein, to the south of Thebes, there is no other proof that the Hyksos ever ruled Egypt in her entirety. New Kingdom monarchs shared the (unfortunate, from an archaeologist's viewpoint) habit of moving and reusing inscribed masonry, and we should not necessarily assume that the Gebelein blocks are in their original context. In practice it seems that Hyksos rule extended only as far upstream as Cusae, some twenty-five miles to the south of the Middle Kingdom administrative centre Hermopolis Magna (modern Ashmunein). Here a customs post marked the border between Egypt's two lands. Beyond this border the remnants of the 13th Dynasty had retreated to Thebes to continue the native Egyptian royal line as the ineffectual, ephemeral 16th Dynasty.

The Hyksos kings were to rule northern Egypt for over a century. Although the ancient city of Memphis was to serve as their capital, a new and most splendid city was now being built at the Canaanite Delta town of Avaris (modern Tell el-Daba). Avaris was a well-chosen site. The fertility of the Delta was justly famed throughout the ancient world; now her fields and vineyards would ensure that the royal palace was well provisioned with cereals, vegetables, wine and meat while her marshes and waterways provided an abundant supply of fowl, fish and game. The Pelusiac branch of the Nile allowed ships to sail from the new harbour either northwards into the Mediterranean or southwards via Memphis into the Nile Valley. Links with

Asia were maintained – and could be controlled – via the 'Way of Horus', a 140-mile long roadway which allowed caravans to travel across the inhospitable Sinai peninsula to Palestine and beyond. Desert tracks conveniently bypassing the southern Nile Valley even allowed Avaris to keep in contact with the Nubian kingdom beyond Theban rule.

Avaris, gateway of Egypt, quickly developed into a cosmo-politan, cultured city totally different in character from insular, traditional, inward-looking Thebes. Even the look of the city was different, as for the first time an Egyptian city was protected by exotic, Palestinian-style fortifications. The Hyksos style of government, too, was different. While respecting the ancient traditions of their adopted land (choosing, for example, to write in hieroglyphs, to use Egyptian throne names and to carve Egyptian-style statues and reliefs) the Hyksos opened up Egypt to new ideas. International diplomacy – the exchange of letters, presents and perhaps even brides with brother monarchs – was an important feature of the new regime.

Eastern-inspired architecture, pottery and technology, and such novel innovations as the harnessed horse, now enhanced an Egyptian repertoire which had remained fundamentally unchanged – some might say stagnant – for centuries. Even the pantheon was enriched. While the old Egyptian gods retained their divine attributes, the Hyksos addressed their devotions to Seth or Sutekh – a hybrid mixture of the Syrian weather-god Baal Zephon, the Hittite weather-god Teshub and the Egyptian Seth, evil brother of the good god Osiris, a deity whose many duties also included control over the weather.

As Egypt's strong northern kings reaped the benefits of unrestricted access to international trade routes, her weaker southern rulers quietly consolidated their position. Thebes was

7

a backwater lacking the impressive resources of Avaris. With no access to the fertile Delta farmlands, isolated from the trade routes and with even the traditional royal burial grounds now out of bounds, her rulers embarked upon a conservative, Middle Kingdom-style kingship which placed great emphasis on the development of an efficient military machine.

Relations between the two courts were outwardly amicable and the divided land settled into a superficially peaceful coexistence. However, while the Hyksos kings relaxed, contenting themselves with the fiction that the Thebans had been reduced to the status of insignificant vassals, the Thebans cherished a continuing hatred of Egypt's foreign kings.

The earliest of the southern pharaohs are shadowy, remote figures. While their names survive on the king lists, their deeds go largely unrecorded. A change of ruling family marked the transition between Dynasties 16 and 17 and it is now, with the reign of Intef VII, that we meet the first of the forceful Theban kings. Intef was famed as a builder but would perhaps have preferred to be known as a warrior; although his reign was peaceful his temple dedicated to Min, at Koptos, includes a wistful, highly traditional scene of Nubian and Asiatic captives forced to submit to Egypt's might. Both the Old and the Middle Kingdoms had been started by a southern warrior king marching northwards to reunite his divided land. Could a southern king once again unite Egypt under a New and even more glorious Kingdom?

Intef clung to his dream of unification, and was eventually buried at the new royal cemetery site of Dra abu el-Naga (western Thebes) in a coffin which also contained two bows and six arrows symbolising military might. By now the Theban fortunes were turning. Intef's successor, Sobekemsaf II, was wealthy enough to be buried in some style beneath a small-scale pyramid. When, almost 500 years after his death, robbers breached his tomb they found the king and his queen lying together. Their detailed confessions, recorded in a document today known as Papyrus Leopold II–Amhurst, make fascinating reading. Clearly the robbers had little compassion for their royal victims:

Then [the eight of us] went tomb robbing – this activity had become one of our regular pastimes. But this time we discovered the tomb of King . . . Sobekemsaf, which was in a different league from the pyramids and officials' tombs that we normally went to rob . . . We discovered the king's mummy lying at the back of the tomb. Then we worked out that the burial chamber of his wife, Queen Nebuhaas, must be near by. It proved to be sealed off and protected by a plaster wall and a layer of rubble, but we tunnelled through all the same and found her body lying there too. Then we prised open the sarcophagi and mummy cases they were in, and found the king's noble mummy holding a sword. Around its neck there were lots of *wedjat* amulets and gold jewels, and it was still wearing its gold funerary mask. The king's noble mummy was covered with gold from head to toe. His mummy cases were also lined with silver and gold, inside and out, and were studded with all sorts of precious stones. We tore off the gold which we found on the king's mummy, took the amulets and jewellery that were around its neck and dismantled the mummy cases it was lying in. The queen's body was similarly adorned and we stripped it of whatever we could find in exactly the same way. Then we burned the mummy cases . . .

9

For a century there had been a polite if not exactly cordial relationship between Egypt's two courts, with the Theban kings forced to accept the dominance of their northern neighbours. Now, as the Thebans grew more ambitious and their well-trained army grew more threatening, the Hyksos had reason to feel apprehensive. The new Theban king, Sekenenre (or Senakhtenre) Taa 'The Brave', had enough confidence to challenge the Hyksos rule.

Sekenenre called his country to arms and embarked upon the war of unification which was to claim his own life. His foe was the formidable Hyksos king Apophis (also known as Apepi Aauserra). Two contemporary accounts of this conflict have been preserved; as both were written by the victorious Thebans they can hardly be considered as unbiased histories, but the second at least sheds some light on this otherwise obscure time.

*The Quarrel of Apophis and Sekenenre* is an absurd, wonderful and sadly unreliable tale which tells of the unreasonable demands made by the Hyksos court. The story opens with Egypt suffering under foreign domination. While our hero Sekenenre rules as a prince in the Southern City (Thebes), the avaricious Hyksos king Apophis holds court in the appropriately named Avaris. Here he worships Seth, building a magnificent temple to his god. As the stronger king, Apophis is able to claim tribute from the whole land; a tax which the Thebans bitterly resent. Now Apophis has decided to pick a quarrel with his neighbours. Apophis claims that he is unable to sleep at night; the roaring of the hippopotami at Thebes is keeping him awake: 'Let there be a withdrawal of the hippopotami from the canal ... because they don't let sleep come to me either in the daytime or at night.' Sekenenre is forced to call a council to discuss this outrageous complaint. The stage seems set for a grand battle, but unfortunately the only surviving copy of the story breaks off at this point and the reader is left in suspense.

Of far more historical validity, if less amusing, is an account of the conflict written during the reign of Sekenenre's successor, Kamose, and today preserved on two stelae and an inscribed tablet:

> His majesty addressed his council of advisers in the palace: 'How can I claim to be powerful, when there is a ruler in Avaris and another in Kush? I'm no different from an Asiatic and a Nubian – each of them has his piece of Egypt too, and shares the land with me. Now that Apophis controls Hermopolis, there's no way past him to Memphis, the port of Egypt. [And even if there was], no one lands there now, because of the crippling Asiatic taxes. It's up to me to take him on and rip his belly open. The time has come to liberate Egypt and crush the Asiatics.'

Sekenenre fought at Cusae before falling in battle. The death of a pharaoh at the hands of an enemy was never going to feature prominently in Egypt's official history; historians were expected to skip quickly over the less palatable parts of their past. However, Sekenenre's badly preserved mummy, now stored in Cairo Museum, allows us to recreate the king's final moments in some detail. Surrounded by the enemy, the king had been fatally stabbed behind the ear with a dagger. As he collapsed, dying and covered in blood, two or more assailants armed with a mace and a Hyksos-style round-ended battle-axe launched a savage attack on his head, shattering his skull, nose and eye sockets with a series of blows. Death was inevitable; the king's unmarked limbs and torso confirm that he could not even raise an arm to defend himself. The royal undertakers, working under pressure on the battlefield, were unable to straighten their king's distorted body and to this day Sekenenre's hands remain twisted in agony.

Sekenenre's untimely death provided the Theban cause with a martyr. Prince Kamose — successor and presumed son of Sekenenre — buried his father beneath a small-scale mud-brick pyramid and set out to avenge the dead king. The Kamose stelae confirm that his elderly, rather cowardly advisers cautioned the young king against hasty action. They preferred to take the easy option:

At first the members of his council agreed with him: 'Yes, as far as Cusae is Asiatic territory now.' But then their real views slipped out, all of them speaking at the same time: 'We are satisfied with our share of Egypt. Elephantine is secure and the middle of Egypt is loyal to us as far as Cusae. The best fields there are ours to cultivate and our cattle are free to graze in the marshes; grain is still being sent [to feed] our swine, and our herds have never been seized... Apophis only controls Asiatic territory, *we* control Egypt...'

The Hyksos, content with the status quo and perhaps uncertain of their own fighting prowess, had drafted a peace treaty which would allow the rival kingdoms access to each other's lands. Such a compromise would surely save further bloodshed and would allow both sides to back down with honour. Kamose, however, had the light of battle in his eyes and was determined to test his enemy. He ignored his advisers, launched a surprise attack and, after some fierce fighting in Middle Egypt, advanced as far north as Avaris:

My elite troops flew along the river like falcons, with my golden boat as their flagship, leading from the front... Then I spotted the wives [of Apophis] peering out of the windows at the top of the palace, looking towards the river-bank. Their bodies were hidden as they stared at me; they peeked through the battlements like baby mice [peeping] from their holes. And I shouted out, 'Now that I have arrived, it is time to give up. The odds are on my side – everywhere else is under my control and my cause is just... Watch while I drink wine from your vineyards, pressed for me by Asiatics I have already captured! [Look on] while I demolish your home and chop down your orchards! Your women have already been herded into the holds of my ships, and I am about to take away your horses...

Kamose returned to Thebes, leaving Avaris worried but untouched. His daring raid offered the Thebans little in the way of material reward but was undoubtedly a huge propaganda victory. The seemingly invincible Hyksos were left shocked and demoralised, their vulnerability obvious to all. Furthermore, they had just lost control of the desert routes linking Avaris to her Nubian allies.

This severing of communications between his two enemies was a vital part of Kamose's strategy; already he had firm evidence that the wily Hyksos king was inciting the Nubians to distract the Thebans by attacking them from the south. Again the Kamose stelae take up the tale:

Then I intercepted a message [from Apophis], written on papyrus, on its way south to Kush on the oasis road. And

I found the following on it, in the handwriting of the ruler of Avaris . . . 'The son of Re, Apophis, greets the king of Kush [his] son. Why have you come to the throne and not let me know? Have you seen what Egypt has done to me? Its ruler, Kamose the mighty, has launched an unprovoked attack on me, on my own territory. This is exactly what he did to you before. He has decided to molest [just] two lands – mine and yours – and now he has ravaged them both. So come north! There is no need to worry – he is busy with me here and no one else in Egypt will stand up to you. I will make sure he doesn't leave before you arrive. Then we will divide the towns of Egypt between us and Nubia will rejoice.'

The young king seemed destined for a glorious military career, but this was not to be. Kamose would not sack Avaris, he would not defeat the Hyksos. After a mere three years on the throne Kamose, too, died – probably in battle – and, having no son, was succeeded by his brother Ahmose. Ahmose was still very young; as we know that he was to enjoy a reign of approximately twenty-five years, and can see from his mummy which is now housed in Cairo Museum that he died in his mid-thirties, it seems that he must have been little more than ten years old at his brother's death. His accession was therefore followed by a break in hostilities while Ahmose, guided by his mother Ahhotep, learned his trade.

Ahhotep effectively ruled southern Egypt for over a decade, earning the gratitude of her son and her people. Ahmose was later to honour his mother by presenting her with two highly symbolic gifts; an inscribed ceremonial axe and three flies of valour, large golden flies which represented Egypt's highest military decoration. These artifacts are today housed in Cairo Museum. On a stela at Karnak, Ahmose describes his mother as one who has 'looked after her [Egypt's] soldiers... she has brought back her fugitives and rounded up her deserters... she has pacified Upper Egypt and has hunted down her rebels...' This may be the literal truth.

Eleven years of uneasy peace ended when campaigning resumed in the north, with Ahmose leading a succession of effective strikes against the Delta. He faced a different, and far less confident enemy. The charismatic and astute Apophis had died after a forty-year reign; now the north was ruled by Khamudi, a king fated to rule over a waning kingdom.

Fighting alongside King Ahmose was a soldier also named Ahmose, the son of a woman named Ibana. The commoner Ahmose has left a detailed autobiography on the wall of his tomb at el-Kab. Here we read of the triumphal exploits of Ahmose the King, ably assisted by Ahmose the soldier:

> During the siege of Avaris, the king noticed me fighting bravely on foot [hand-to-hand] and promoted me to his ship 'Rising in Memphis'... Then we took Avaris. I carried off four people there – a man and three women, in total four persons – and his majesty let me keep them as slaves. We went on to besiege Sharuhen and his majesty sacked it after three years. I took my share of the booty there too – two women and a hand. Again, I was awarded the gold of valour and was allowed to keep the people I had captured as slaves.

The reunification of Egypt was no sudden victory but a long, tedious and bloody erosion of Hyksos power. Battle followed battle as the small southern army slowly pushed its way northwards attacking, capturing and burning towns and cities loyal to the Hyksos kings. By Year 22 Avaris had fallen and Ahmose was able to pass through the Delta, sweeping the Hyksos before him, eastwards into Palestine. Here, after an extraordinarily inept three-year siege, Ahmose captured the fortified city of Sharuhen (near Gaza) to establish a Hyksos-free buffer-zone; a foreign area under firm Egyptian control which would prevent the Hyksos or their descendants from reinfiltrating the Delta. In so doing, he established the foundations of Egypt's New Kingdom empire.

With Egypt united from Elephantine (modern Aswan) to the coast, Ahmose quickly turned his attention southwards. Kamose had already recaptured the Second Cataract fortress of Buhen, allowing the Upper Egyptians access to Nubia's valuable resources. Now Nubia, taking advantage of Ahmose's preoccupation with eastern affairs, was preparing to invade southern Egypt. This was, of course, unthinkable. Again Ahmose son of Ibana takes up the tale:

> Once his majesty had slaughtered the Asiatic bedouin, he turned southward to Nubia to crush the tribes there. His majesty slaughtered them all in droves and I managed to carry off two live prisoners and three hands. Yet again, I was decorated with gold, and was given two female slaves. Then his majesty sailed back north, satisfied with the extent of his victories. For he had recaptured both the south and the north.

With his borders secure, the battle-weary Ahmose was faced with two further insurrections: a small rebellion led by the otherwise unknown foreigner Aata, and a more serious rebellion led by the Egyptian-born Tetia. Both rebellions failed, leaving Ahmose the undisputed king of a united land. He had succeeded where his father and brother had failed. Once again a single king wore the crowns of Upper and Lower Egypt.

Ahmose dedicated his final years to the improvement of his own land. Divided rule followed by civil war had left Egypt impoverished, with many of her cities sadly in need of attention. Now the newly unified kingdom, with its eastern and southern territories and wide trade networks, was becoming richer by the day as tribute from the provinces replenished the sadly depleted treasury. Peace and stability meant that the mines and quarries could once more function efficiently and that the royal workshops, now provided with plentiful supplies of raw materials, could again produce works worthy of their monarch and their gods. Workmen, no longer drafted into the army, laid down their weapons and took up their tools, and building works started at many of Egypt's cities, with Thebes, Memphis and Abydos all benefiting from the king's generosity. Unfortunately Ahmose's workmen built mainly in mud-brick; consequently many of his buildings are now lost to us.

While exhibiting a diplomatic loyalty to all the gods and goddesses of the state pantheon, Ahmose made no secret of his particular devotion to Amen, 'the Hidden One', the local god of Thebes. It seemed that Amen must be responsible for the Theban king's success; now he was to receive his reward. Amen was showered with a host of precious offerings (gold and silver vessels, lapis lazuli and turquoise jewellery) while his mud-brick Karnak temple was refurbished in the grandest style. Soon Amen was to become the richest god in the Egyptian empire, while his hitherto insignificant temple was to develop into the largest religious complex in the world. As Memphis continued to serve as the northern administrative centre, Thebes now took her rightful place as Egypt's southern and religious capital.

Avaris, sacked and abandoned at the end of the Hyksos era, was to be resurrected as a trading post and military base. Ahmose set about building an impressive royal city incorporating a fortified palace decorated with Minoan (Cretan) wall paintings, including bull-leaping scenes reminiscent of those found at the royal palace at Knossos. So similar are the scenes in style, that it seems that Ahmose must have been employing Minoan artists to decorate his palace. This raises a host of questions which the Austrian archaeologist Manfred Bietak is endeavouring to answer by painstaking excavation of the sadly denuded Tell el-Daba. Bull leaping was not an Egyptian sport, it was a Cretan ritual strongly connected with Knossos. Why should Ahmose have wished to decorate his palace in Cretan, rather than Egyptian, royal style? Did he have a special reason for celebrating Egypt's link with Crete? Could he even have taken a Cretan bride into the royal harem?

The local governors – those partially responsible for the collapse of the Old and Middle Kingdoms – still held positions of great authority. For the moment they were loyal to the new king, but how long would their loyalty last? Ahmose rewarded the governors who had supported him in battle but then completed the work of the Middle Kingdom monarchs by developing a professional civil service which could provide a suitable support for an expanding empire. Archaeologists have good reason to be grateful to Ahmose; the New Kingdom is characterised by its ever-growing bureaucracy which led directly to the increasing documentation of even the most trivial of matters. Soon the royal archives bulged with accounts, reports, tax returns and copies of all letters sent and received. Scribes — literate men — were suddenly in great demand.

Soldiers, too, would be needed if Egypt was to survive. Ahmose lived in turbulent times; he knew that growing peace and prosperity in the Nile Valley would make Egypt very attractive both to those living in less affluent regions, and to those intent on carving out their own near-eastern empires. An efficient fighting force was essential if Egypt was to avoid a repetition of the unfortunate Hyksos period. And so the somewhat ramshackle and ineffectual Middle Kingdom army structure was revised to produce a professional army which was the envy of the eastern Mediterranean world.

Ahmose died after twenty-five years on the throne, and was buried alongside his brother and his father in a pyramid at Dra abu el-Naga. He now took his place on the continuous king lists maintained in the temples of Egypt, occupying an honourable position between his brother and his son. Over a thousand years later the Greek historian Manetho, the first to divide the Egyptian king lists into dynasties, decided that in recognition of his heroic achievements, and despite his obvious familial links to the 17th Dynasty kings, Ahmose should become the first king of the 18th Dynasty. This tradition has been maintained to this day. Ahmose's reign, which spanned the break between the Second Intermediate Period and the New Kingdom, having started in disruption and ended in unity, therefore becomes the first reign of the New Kingdom.

Amenhotep I, son of Ahmose, is a prime example of a pharaoh who enjoyed a lengthy and strong reign untroubled by civil unrest, invasion or natural disaster and yet who, sandwiched between two outstanding warrior kings, suffers greatly by comparison. As we know surprisingly little about Amenhotep's rule, today's historians tend to condense him into a few paragraphs appended on to his father's story. This is probably appropriate, if a little sad, as Amenhotep's twenty-one years as king were very much a continuation of his father's. Amenhotep proved himself a competent if unspectacular soldier, a worthy guardian of Egypt's borders, and a devoted benefactor to the cult of Amen.

We know that Amenhotep had not been his father's intended heir – some five years earlier Prince Ahmose Ankh had been proclaimed crown prince. As was so often to happen in the New Kingdom royal family, however, the untimely death of an elder son had thrust a younger brother into the limelight. Amenhotep inherited his throne as a relatively inexperienced boy guided by his mother, Ahmose Nefertari. Both mother and son were held in the highest regard by their people, so that even after death they remained linked together, worshipped as gods on the Theban west bank. In marked contrast to the forceful dowager-queen, Amenhotep's sister-wife, Meritamen, makes a fleeting appearance as a pale, shadowy queen.

The new reign saw limited campaigning in Nubia, where the Egyptian position was consolidated and a viceroy was appointed to govern on the king's behalf. There was, however, no attempt to expand the boundaries of the eastern empire. Instead Amenhotep tended to his own land and Egypt, benefiting from her control of Nubia's resources, quietly prospered. Increasing wealth allowed Amenhotep to finish his father's building projects and to start his own. These, as we might expect from a southern king, were centred on Thebes. The Karnak temple once again echoed to the sound of hammer and saw and there was some construction work in Nubia but, as far as we know, little or no building in the north.

Amenhotep died somewhere between forty and fifty years of age, and, although his tomb has not yet been discovered, we may guess that he was buried alongside his predecessors at Dra abu el-Naga. His mummy, moved from its original tomb during the Third Intermediate Period, rebandaged and stored for many centuries in a collection at Deir el-Bahari (Thebes), is today housed in Cairo Museum. It has never been unwrapped.

The king and queen had no living son to succeed to the throne; the respected line of Sekenenre had come to an end. It is a sign of the strength of the 18th Dynasty royal family that Amenhotep's choice of a non-royal successor was accepted without a murmur of dissent. For, free to select his own heir, Amenhotep had looked away from the lesser-born sons of the royal harem. Although his own reign had been relatively peaceful, he was well aware of ominous developments in the Near East and felt that Egypt's needs would best be served by an experienced soldier-king. High born (possibly from a collateral branch of the royal family), both a seasoned cam-paigner and an astute politician, General Tuthmosis had all the qualities required of a New Kingdom pharaoh.

# CHAPTER 2

# The King:

# Lord of the Two Lands

Re himself legitimised me and crowned me with the
crowns of his own head, securing his uraeus on my
forehead ... I was decked with all his glories and filled
with divine wisdom. He crowned me and decided my titles
personally ... He let me accede to the throne of Upper
and Lower Egypt and fixed my forms ... He made the
foreign lands come bowing to my majestic power and
instilled fear of me in the hearts of the nine bows. Every
foreign land is under my feet. He placed victory in all my
actions.

*Coronation Inscription of Tuthmosis III*

Ahmose, scion of the ancient Theban line, had always
believed himself to be the one true king of Egypt.
Now, with Upper and Lower Egypt again united, no
one would dispute his claim to the double crown. Casting off
his individuality, he assumed the time-honoured royal regalia; in
so doing he became one with the long line of pharaohs
stretching back some fifteen hundred years.

The trappings of Egyptian kingship – the ceremonial false
beard, head-cloth, crook and flail, the white crown of Upper

Egypt and the red crown of Lower, are as instantly recognisable today as they were in antiquity. For three thousand years the pharaohs ruled Egypt unchallenged: changes of dynasty there may have been, but no one ever dared to imagine that Egypt could survive without a king on the Horus throne. The essentially unaltering image of the traditional pharaoh was at all times a very powerful one. It was an image strong enough to smooth over irregularities of kingship: as the dynastic age progressed a diverse band of Hyksos pharaohs, female pharaohs, Nubian pharaohs and even Greek pharaohs would each recognise that their adoption of a traditional, Egyptian-style kingship would reinforce their somewhat dubious claims to rule.

The new king ruled a land of some three to four million people. He himself formed the undisputed pinnacle of Egypt's social pyramid. This pyramid – which is best imagined as a well-defined step-pyramid rather than a straight-sided true pyramid – was supported by a base that comprised slaves, servants and the multitude of serfs and tenant farmers who lived in the hamlets and villages of the Nile Valley and the Delta and who farmed the vast estates owned by the king, his nobles and their gods. One step above the peasants came the skilled and semi-skilled artisans; this class encompassed soldiers, sailors and those who worked on the great state projects (the building sites, tombs and temples). Next came the educated professional classes whose ranks included scribes, accountants and doctors. Finally came the select group of inter-related nobility, the two to three thousand elite who controlled much of Egypt's wealth, and who effectively governed the land on their king's behalf. The royal family remained exclusive and aloof, while the king – as far above the peasants as he could be, and as close to the heavenly gods as was humanly possible – was naturally superior to everyone and everything in Egypt.

During the Old and Middle Kingdoms movement between these social steps had been difficult, if not impossible. Heredity meant everything. Education, the key to a dazzling career, was a privilege of the nobility so that less than five per cent of the New Kingdom population (almost all of them male) was literate. Education for the masses, and for women, was considered unnecessary; boys were trained from an early age to follow in their fathers' footsteps and the vast majority, destined for non-professional employment, would have little need of reading and writing. A tradition of marriage within the same social group, often within the same extended family, reinforced the feeling of predestination and, as far as we can tell, few aspired to a life beyond that lived by their parents and grandparents.

Now things were starting to change. New Kingdom Egypt had discovered an insatiable need for educated men. Increased literacy was necessary if the civil service was to keep pace with the demands of the empire, and this increased literacy led directly to an explosion of the professional classes. Alongside the need for scribes ran a demand for effective, professional soldiers who could guard and even expand the empire and its assets. As the effects of Egypt's new-found wealth started to trickle down the social pyramid, Egypt's new 'middle classes' – employees financed by the state and often rewarded for their labours with pensions of land – were suddenly very much in evidence. This was an altogether more materialistic age. The middle classes enjoyed an unprecedented standard of life and (having invested heavily in their funeral plans) death. Only the peasants, still uneducated and firmly tied to the land they worked, continued to live as they had for centuries.

Ahmose, as king, had just one duty, but his was a complex,

lifelong task. He alone was responsible for maintaining *maat* throughout Egypt. *Maat* is a concept which is very difficult to define in modern terms — we have no modern word for *maat* — but it is one which the Egyptians understood to the very depth of their being.

*Maat* was the traditional order which the gods had granted to Egypt when, at the very beginning of time, the land had emerged from the sea of chaos. *Maat* therefore represented the state of rightness, the status quo, order or justice. Chaos (or *isfet*), the opposite of *maat* and perhaps easier for us to understand, was something to be dreaded. The glories of the Old and Middle Kingdoms — times when pharaoh ruled a united kingdom and Egypt flourished in peaceful prosperity — could be attributed to the strong presence of *maat* in the land. The chaotic Intermediate Periods — times of civil unrest, disunity and experimentation — were the ultimate example of what could happen if *maat* was allowed to lapse.

The dynastic Egyptians were a deeply cautious, conservative people who felt it essential that everything should function according to a tried and tested plan. If life proceeded as it had always done, nothing could go too far wrong. This was *maat*. Control and precedent therefore became very important while change or innovation were given a guarded welcome. Change would lead Egypt into the unknown, and there was always a risk that the unknown might prove dangerous. Anyone who doubts this should consider Egyptian art which, although it underwent subtle changes, remained essentially unchanging in repertoire and style for three thousand years. Even today, two thousand years after the end of the dynastic age, the non-expert has little hesitation in recognising an Egyptian tomb scene.

Pharaoh, as the upholder of *maat*, was expected to control

every facet of Egyptian life with a firm hand. He naturally became the head of the judiciary (responsible for law and order), the head of the army (responsible for protecting Egypt's borders against *maat*-less foreigners), the head of the bureaucracy (responsible for managing the land and its resources) and of course the chief priest of every religious cult (responsible for pleasing the gods). This was an excessively centralised system, firmly pivoted on one man. Although he was able to employ deputies to help him in his many tasks, the buck ultimately stopped with the king; he took the praise when things went well, and shouldered the blame when things went wrong.

In theory, the all-powerful pharaoh could have become a despot. After all, he owned the land, its people and all its assets, and was answerable to no man. Fortunately, *maat* provided a check to his actions. *Maat* both kept him in power – it was un-Egyptian and therefore a breach of *maat* not to have a pharaoh ruling over the united land – and controlled him – even pharaoh had to act in accordance with *maat*. He could not, for example, commit murder without justifiable cause. In extreme circumstances *maat* could even destroy a pharaoh; any unavoidable disaster (foreign invasion, flood or famine) might be interpreted as a sign that the king was promoting a *maat*-less reign which had to be stopped.

Ahmose, as upholder of *maat*, now found himself high-priest of all the state cults. He was uniquely suited to this role, for he had become semi-divine at his coronation. Technically, it was the office of king which was divine; the office holder himself remained fully human until his death. However, this technicality was frequently overlooked and, from the very beginning of the dynastic age, it had become accepted that the king of Upper and Lower Egypt was more than mortal. Whatever the history of his birth, the mysteries and rituals of his coronation were powerful enough to transform any man into a godlike being. Pharaoh would then live his life in the limbo between the fully mortal and the fully divine until death brought his transformation to its resolution. Every dead king automatically became a fully fledged god.

The earliest pharaohs, the rulers of the Old Kingdom, had taken their own divinity very seriously. Their formal statues – not portraits, but images carved to represent the very essence of kingship – reveal the aloof, unsmiling faces of a monarchy supremely confident in its own innate power. The Middle Kingdom monarchs, ruling after the hiatus of the First Intermediate Period, were more aware that divine authority alone might not be enough to justify their position. Realising that the monarchy could indeed fail, their formal art takes two very different approaches to kingship; fierce images of warlike sphinxes suggest a monarchy capable of sustaining its position by physical might, while 'portrait' statues show kings whose austere, unapproachable divinity has been mingled with a degree of compassionate humanity.

The New Kingdom pharaohs followed this more practical trend, choosing to reinforce their rule with displays of physical might and national good works rather than relying on divine mystery. Most felt the need to appear as victorious warriors; all felt the need to stress the triumphs and achievements of their reign at every possible opportunity, to the extent that self-justification became one of the less endearing traits of the New Kingdom monarchy. Texts which we see today as unacceptable boasting were to their authors a legitimate means of reinforcing pharaoh's fitness to rule.

I will surpass what was done in the past and I will ensure that the future people say 'how appropriate that she achieved these things.'... [Amen] picked me out because he knew my worth. He knew that I would speak with authority and make you listen... Nothing that I say can possibly fail. If I want something to happen, it happens...

*The walls of Hatshepsut's Deir el-Bahari temple*

Kamose and Ahmose had set a strong military precedent which was to be followed by all successful New Kingdom monarchs. The gods now expected their earthly representatives to triumph over *maat*-less foreigners. Pharaoh needed to prove himself a good soldier; he needed a victory to offer to his gods. While most would be able to comply with this expectation (often enhancing a minor Nubian skirmish to the status of full-blown war), it was to bring problems for those lucky monarchs whose reigns were so secure that they could find no enemy to fight. The image of the warrior pharaoh was to play an increasingly prominent role in religious art as subsequent kings – whether they had fought or not – decorated the outer walls of their temples with oversized triumphal images of themselves.

Most 18th Dynasty reigns were to start with one or more military campaigns before proceeding to a phase of civic improvement which would, it was hoped, allow the king to carve his name deep into Egypt's stone. Divinity seems to have become increasingly important with age, so that whereas a few kings claimed divine birth early in their reigns, it is the longer-lived monarchs, those who lived to celebrate their thirty-year jubilee, who placed the greatest emphasis on their role as a living god.

Pharaoh's semi-divinity was both a great privilege and a great

29

responsibility. He was now the only Egyptian able to communicate with Egypt's gods, the only one who could interpret their wishes. This explains why, in the scenes carved within Egypt's temples, it is only pharaoh who is shown making offerings. Egypt's pantheon did not expect mass mortal worship. Their huge temples were not built to house congregations, but to provide a suitable setting for both the gods' and the king's deputies, the priests who served their cults on a daily basis. This service was interpreted at a very literal level; the gods, or rather their cult statues, enjoyed the spiritual sustenance provided by music, poetry, dancing and incense, but they also required vast quantities of real food washed down with copious draughts of good wine and best beer.

It was crucial that the gods were treated correctly, for the gods controlled Egypt. Today science has given us an insight into many aspects of earthly life. We understand about the circulation of the blood, about the mysteries of conception and birth, and about the transmission and prevention of disease. Outside our own bodies we understand the workings of the solar system, the waxing and waning of the moon, and the advent of day and night. We understand physics, chemistry, biology and geography and so do not worry overmuch that one day the sun will fail to rise.

The New Kingdom Egyptians had no such understanding. To them the world was a mysterious, frightening place. That life had a regular cyclical pattern seemed clear; the rhythms of day and night, birth and death and the swelling and falling of the Nile were obvious to an agricultural community. Even more obvious was the deduction that something, or someone, must be controlling this pattern. Religion therefore developed as a science, providing plausible explanations for what would otherwise have been inexplicable. It must be the gods who caused the sun to rise and the Nile to swell; there was no other possible explanation. However, with this knowledge came the logical realisation that the gods, if unhappy, might also stop the sun from rising. Care of the gods therefore became an important state duty, while neglect of the state cults was a heinous offence against *maat*:

> Whether you are a nobleman or a commoner, pay attention to my words! I did these things on my own initiative. I didn't sleep or lose interest, but repaired what was in ruins. I re-erected [buildings] which had been in ruins ever since there were Asiatics in the Delta at Avaris and nomads roaming around, demolishing what had been made. Right down to my own reign they ruled without Re's support and acted without divine approval. But I am a legitimate ruler, foretold since the beginning of time as a natural conqueror. And now I have appeared like Horus, my uraeus spitting fire at my enemies. I have put an end to sin and the earth has swallowed up every trace of it . . .
>
> *The Speos Artemidos inscription of Hatshepsut*

State religion, heavily focused on the actions of the king, provided little help to a society looking for guidance on how to behave. Only the threat of judgement after death provided a religious check to anti-social behaviour. It was therefore up to pharaoh, in his role as head of the judiciary rather than head of the priesthood, to ensure that his land did not disintegrate into a chaotic *maat*-less sea of crime.

Any criminal act could be interpreted as an offence against *maat*. Pharaoh, however, had developed his own list of priorities.

Murder, today probably considered the most heinous of offences, ranked fairly low on the scale unless the victim was a member of the royal family. The king was not interested in resolving domestic disputes, no matter how violent. Unless they threatened to spill over into civil unrest, it was felt that these were best settled within the local community. He was, however, concerned with crimes that threatened the state; these included theft from royal institutions, theft from the temples and theft from the dead buried in the desert cemeteries. The increasing prosperity and increasing urbanisation of the New Kingdom was to lead to an increase in crimes against property; pharaoh responded with a series of increasingly harsh physical punishments.

With crime kept firmly under control, it was necessary for pharaoh to ensure that his land operated efficiently. Again, the king took technical responsibility for all aspects of rural life and he, via the vizier's office, controlled a vast army of workers all dedicated to making the best of Egypt's abundant resources. Taxation was an important aspect of land management, and vast warehouses were built to house the surpluses collected from the primary producers. This was a prudent move – the rations thus stored not only paid the wages of the state employees, her artisans, bureaucrats, priests and soldiers, but could also prevent disaster at times of famine.

Occasionally a large workforce would be needed for a national project. Under these circumstances the king had the undisputed right to commandeer the labour of his people. The most obvious example of this is the call-up of troops at times of national emergency, but this right could be enforced during times of peace, too. Egypt, lacking sophisticated machinery, relied heavily on simple manpower for the erection of her monuments and the excavation of her irrigation canals. But it did not make economic sense to keep a full complement of labourers permanently on the payroll. While the engineers and artisans who laboured on the New Kingdom construction sites were professional, full-time employees of the state, the vast bulk of the unskilled labour was provided by free-born Egyptians required to donate their labour under the system of temporary call-up, known today as *corvée*. This labour was usually summoned during the inundation season – the time when the Nile flooded the farmland, making farmwork impossible.

> One day his majesty was sitting in his palace... [He] began to make plans for Egypt... His majesty thought long and hard, and considered all sorts of worthy deeds. He was looking for something that would benefit his father Amen, and decided to make him a magnificent divine image out of real electrum. He surpassed all previous attempts, when he made this statue of his father Amen. The image itself was made of electrum, lapis lazuli, turquoise and all sorts of precious stones. Previously the statue of this noble god had been carried on eleven poles, but now it needed thirteen poles.
>
> *Tutankhamen's Restoration Stela*

Building for the gods was a royal prerogative forbidden to mere mortals; the erection of a new temple therefore provided an ideal means of proving royal piety and it naturally followed that the larger the temple, the more pious the king. The monument which ostensibly served as a tribute to the gods thus became a tribute to its royal builder. Only the truly great could contemplate extensive building in stone. While pharaoh had no need to pay for his raw materials, he did have to provide the daily

rations which sustained his workforce and he had to coordinate the necessary supplies of materials and workers. It was therefore obvious to both people and gods that only the wealthy and well organised could afford to build on any large scale.

Building in mud-brick was both cheap and easy; this remained the material of choice for palaces, offices and humble houses well beyond the end of the dynastic age. Mud-brick, however, would eventually crumble and vanish. The New Kingdom pharaohs, intending their temples and their cults to last for ever, began to build in stone. The impressive buildings which started to rise above the low mud-brick houses of Thebes served as a silent, persistent reminder that Egypt was now ruled by kings whose powers exceeded those of all others. Anyone who failed to pick up on this message had only to glance at the stone walls. Here, unable to resist the temptation of a smooth, blank surface, pharaohs carved their exploits for all eternity.

There was always a danger that the remote, godlike king would become isolated from his people. Isolation, and ignorance of provincial happenings, would hamper the king in his mission to maintain *maat*, and could even prove politically dangerous. Ahmose, perhaps bearing in mind the ignominious collapse of the 13th Dynasty which was at least partially the result of over-centralisation, had determined to remain in touch with his roots. Although Thebes and Memphis, the twin homes of the civil service, were cities of obvious importance, the idea of the capital city or cities was now modified. Ahmose adopted a more mobile approach, and spent much of his time travelling up and down the Nile with a small entourage.

So far we have considered only the public aspect – the triumphs, duties and achievements – of the New Kingdom monarch. This is the image of kingship which the pharaohs themselves chose to preserve for us. Should we attempt to peer behind this state propaganda, to seek to find the man beneath the double crown, we immediately come smack up against a blank wall. In spite of her abundant artifacts, her many temples, tombs and papyri, ancient Egypt remains stubbornly silent over the private lives of her rulers. Monumental inscriptions and material remains can only take us so far in our quest for understanding and we are almost completely lacking the personal writings which would help us see the kings as rounded individuals rather than as stereotypes. Perhaps the prime example of this is the young king Tutankhamen who, although world famous many centuries after his death, is still very much an unknown quantity. Thousands of artifacts have been recovered from Tutankhamen's tomb, and yet we know so little of his private life that we are unable even to name his parents with any degree of confidence.

An increasingly helpful means of approaching the pharaohs as people is the study of their mortal remains. Egypt's unique funerary rituals have left us with a series of relatively well-preserved bodies available for modern scientific examination. Whereas Tutankhamen rests in solitary splendour in the Valley of the Kings, many of the other New Kingdom royal mummies are today stored in Cairo Museum. Attitudes towards these royal bodies have undergone a profound change in recent years. While the earliest Egyptologists showed little compunction in desecrating graves and ripping open bandages, it is now accepted that the dead — no matter how long dead — should be treated with an appropriate degree of respect. No responsible Egyptologist would today sanction the stripping of a mummy purely to see the face beneath the bandages and indeed, given the remarkable advances in medical technology over the past century, such a destructive approach is no longer necessary. DNA analysis, X-ray analysis and CAT-scans represent just three non-invasive, exciting new techniques now being applied to Egypt's dead.

Occasionally the superficial examination of a body can provide clues to Egypt's past. We have already seen how Sekenenre's damaged and distorted mummy, for example, has confirmed that the king perished in battle even though we have no written account of his death and no archaeological evidence pointing to a Second Intermediate Period battlefield (battlefields being prone to disappear without trace). At a less obvious level, it is now possible to rehydrate desiccated mummy tissue and, with the aid of microscopic analysis, detect the presence of otherwise hidden illness and parasites. This type of scientific investigation is still very much in its infancy, and access to the royal mummies is understandably restricted, but it seems that the pharaohs will continue to tell their private stories for many years to come.

> Ahmose is her name. She is the wife of the king, Tuthmosis I, and is the most beautiful woman in the land.
> *The walls of Hatshepsut's Deir el-Bahari temple*

Hidden behind the king the royal family, too, are very difficult to reach as individuals. As we might expect, those closest to the king enjoyed the highest possible status and privilege. Their very titles were a constant reminder of their close ties to pharaoh, and so we find the royal court populated by a 'King's Wife', a 'King's Mother', and variable quantities of 'King's Sons' and 'King's Daughters', the products of the royal harem. We have a fair degree of evidence – although none of it intimate – to tell of the official lives of the royal women; queens, dowager queens and princesses who become increasingly important to their fathers as the New Kingdom progresses. Royal sons, however, are something of an enigma and all too often we know of their existence only when they succeed to the throne.

All the kings of Egypt were polygamous; this was something which set them apart from their people. Under normal circumstances, however, the lesser queens of the harem led pampered but relatively insignificant lives away from the bustle of the mobile court while their children had no realistic expectation of succeeding to the throne. Life in the harem, for all but the highest-ranking ladies, was a dull routine of child-care (for those fortunate enough to have met their royal bridegroom) and working in the linen industry.

Each king had a principal queen, a consort whose male children were his acknowledged heirs. It was this abbreviated family which would appear on royal monuments. The consorts of the Middle Kingdom had been allowed little real power; in consequence they now appear as remote beings very much hidden behind their husbands' achievements. With the rise of the Theban royal family this situation had undergone an abrupt change. Even though her status was still derived from her relationship with the king, increasing emphasis would now be placed on the individuality of the queen, so that each consort became a character in her own right.

Strong women were very much a feature of late 17th/early 18th dynasty royal life; we know this because their equally strong husbands were not afraid to acknowledge the debt owed to their wives and mothers. We have already seen Ahhotep and Ahmose Nefertari earning the respect of their people by ruling alongside or on behalf of their young sons; effectively these women were temporary co-regents. Tetisheri, the commoner grandmother of both Ahmose and his wife Ahmose Nefertari, had also been a woman of profound influence who was to be honoured by her grandson after her death:

> The King [Ahmose] said, 'I remember my mother's mother, my father's mother, the Great King's Wife and King's Mother, Tetisheri the justified. She now has a tomb and cenotaph on the soil of the Theban province and the Thinite province. I have said this to you because my majesty wants to have made for her a pyramid estate in the necropolis in the neighbourhood of the monument of my majesty, its pool dug, its trees planted, its offering loaves established...' Now his majesty spoke of the matter and it was put into action. His majesty did this because he loved her more than anything.
>
> *Stela of King Ahmose*

If the queen had become an influential court character, the queen-mother was even more so. Old age was a rare and valued commodity in a land where a fortieth birthday was a rarity and few could realistically expect to live beyond fifty. Women, faced with the very real dangers of pregnancy and childbirth, would be lucky to reach this advanced age; it seems that the remarkably long-lived women of the royal family may perhaps have owed their survival to the institution of the harem which would have spared them the annual pregnancy. Elderly men, those who had outlasted their contemporaries, were treated with great respect and naturally occupied the highest bureaucratic and priestly posts. Older women, too, were valued and respected. This courtesy extended to the royal family, where the Mother of the

King held the most influential female position in the land.

The New Kingdom consort had advanced far beyond the role of breeding machine. She had become an essential part of the kingship. The queen now complemented and fulfilled her husband's role, so that to attempt to rule Egypt without a consort became an offence against *maat*. Like any good Egyptian wife, the queen was expected to support her husband, fulfilling a range of religious and political duties designed to strengthen the right of the royal family to rule. She was rewarded with her own estates which provided an income that gave her economic independence, allowing her to endow her own monuments.

Married to a semi-divine king, mother to the next semi-divine king, and intimate servant of the gods, the queen herself was naturally lit by a faint aura of immortality. As the New Kingdom progressed, as there was less emphasis placed on warfare and an increasing interest in religious matters, the queen developed her own religious regalia, symbols designed to pro-vide a reminder – either conscious or unconscious – of her near-divinity. The vulture crown, for example, suggested a link with the goddess Nekhbet while a crown of tall feathers indicated links with the gods Min, Amen and Re. As the queen started to dress as a goddess, the goddesses started to dress in queenly crowns so that the increasingly fine line between queen and goddess became ever more blurred.

The queen's association with the state cults was a very literal one. The gods, firmly modelled on their creators, had some very human needs. While the king provided them with food, drink and clothing, the queen was required to provide services which only a woman could properly offer. Ahmose Nefertari was the first queen to be granted the title of 'God's Wife of Amen', a position created by Ahmose to allow the royal family to retain a degree of control over the flourishing, potentially threatening, cult of Amen. The duties of the God's Wife are never explained to us, but it seems that somehow the queen was expected to arouse the god sexually so that he would regularly bring forth the seed of creation. As the queen served both the god and the king, the boundary between the temple and the palace imperceptibly narrowed.

> His sister was his guard ... The mighty Isis who protected her brother, seeking him without tiring, not resting until she found him ... She received his seed and bore his heir, raising their child in solitude in an unknown place ...
>
> *New Kingdom hymn to Osiris*

The goddess Isis had married her brother Osiris. She had to; there were very few potential husbands around at the beginning of time. Under the New Kingdom, incest, through choice rather than necessity, had become a regular royal habit. Brother-sister and father-daughter marriages were to occur sporadically throughout the New Kingdom dynasties and, while some of Egypt's most famous and forceful queens, including Tiy (wife of Amenhotep III), Nefertiti (wife of Akhenaten) and Nefertari (wife of Ramesses II) were commoners, many others were themselves born with blue blood in their veins. Outside the royal family incestuous unions were exceedingly rare. Why, then, did the pharaohs choose to marry in this way?

Nothing in Egypt happened by accident, and we can guess that incest offered several advantages to the ruling family. It certainly separated them from the rest of humanity by suggesting a link with the gods. At a more practical level, incestuous marriage solved the problem of finding an acceptable queen consort. Given that the queen might be called upon to act as regent for her young son, this was an important consideration. There could surely be no more suitable queen of Egypt than an Egyptian-born princess.

The incestuous marriage ensured that the immediate royal family remained strong in its exclusivity, its assets kept intact rather than distributed to multiple descendants. This strength might prove important in times of dynastic crisis when it was necessary to have a clear idea of who was (and who was not) in line for the throne. Throughout the New Kingdom there was a tendency to restrict the royal family to the king plus his close female relations; princes, with the exception of the heir to the throne, were not usually allowed to play an important role in their father's reign. Those not in the immediate line of succession were effectively dropped from the nuclear family although they could, following the untimely death of an older brother, be reinstated as necessary.

Finally, the incestuous marriage brought advantages for the royal brides who might otherwise have had difficulty in finding a suitable husband. Old Kingdom princesses had been free to marry into the non-royal elite but by the time of the New Kingdom this was no longer acceptable. Princesses were not expected to marry beneath themselves and as, by definition, all foreigners no matter how high born were inferior to even the most humble Egyptian, this excluded all foreign kings and all non-royals from the marriage stakes. There was therefore no danger that Egypt might – via an aggressive son-in-law – inadvertently fall into foreign hands.

# CHAPTER 3

......................................

# Hatshepsut:
# The Female Pharaoh

The air had become so bad, and the heat so great, that the candles carried by the workmen melted, and would not give enough light to enable them to continue their work; consequently we were compelled to install electric lights . . . As soon as we got down about 50 metres, the air became so foul that the men could not work. In addition to this, the bats of centuries had built innumerable nests on the ceilings of the corridors and chambers, and their excrement had become so dry that the least stir of the air filled the corridors with a fluffy black stuff, which choked the noses and mouths of the men, rendering it most difficult for them to breathe.

*Davis, T. M. (ed.) (1906)*, The Tomb of Hatshopsitu,
London: xiii.

During his 1903–4 season of excavations in the Valley of the Kings, Howard Carter had managed to force his way into a blocked tomb (today known as KV 20) which had been known but inaccessible since the Napoleonic Expedition of 1799. Carter and his men painstakingly cleared the filled corridors and stairways, and inched

43

their way downwards towards the burial chamber. The discovery that this chamber, too, was blocked – packed with rubble fallen from a collapsed ceiling – was almost too much for the hard-pressed workmen to bear.

Carter, not a man to give up easily, persevered with the aid of a patent air-pump. He was rewarded with a curious archaeological puzzle. For here amid the sad debris of a ransacked royal tomb were not one, but two, magnificent yellow quartzite sarcophagi. The inscribed sarcophagus of the female pharaoh Hatshepsut lay open and empty, its heavy lid discarded on the floor. The second sarcophagus had been opened and overturned, its lid left casually propped against the nearby wall. This sarcophagus had once borne the name and titles of Hatshepsut, but had been recarved in antiquity to show the name of her father, the esteemed pharaoh Tuthmosis I.

What had happened? How had Egypt come to be ruled by a woman? And why had Tuthmosis I been buried in his daughter's discarded coffin?

Succeeding to the throne in *c.* 1504BC, the ex-general Tuthmosis knew that he needed to prove himself. He understood that a change of reign could be interpreted as a moment of weakness, the signal for foreigners to chance their arm against their new and inexperienced Egyptian lord. Tuthmosis would have none of that. He was determined to start as he meant to go on. The time had come for Egypt to impose herself on the world's stage.

Years 2 and 3 saw the new king marching southwards to subdue Egypt's oldest enemy, Nubia. Once again the long-serving Ahmose son of Ibana was present to record the triumphal progress as Tuthmosis 'destroyed insurrection throughout the lands and repelled the intruders from the desert region', advancing beyond the Third Nile Cataract to reach the island of Argo. Tuthmosis sailed home in triumph, leaving the shocked and battered kingdom of Kush controlled by the Egyptian viceroy, his authority backed by a chain of Egyptian fortresses. Dangling lifeless from the bow of his ship, the body of a Nubian bowman (possibly the king of Kush) served as a terrible warning to all who might be tempted to resist Egypt's power.

With Nubia cowed, Tuthmosis turned his attention eastwards. Marching from Memphis, he blazed a trail across the Sinai Peninsula and swept northwards through Syria. What happened next is a matter of some debate. Ahmose son of Ibana and a fellow soldier, Ahmose Pennekhbet, tell us that Tuthmosis emerged the victor from an epic battle against Mitanni, the new regional superpower based in the area now occupied by modern Syria, south-eastern Turkey and western Iraq. There is little other evidence to support this view of Tuthmosis as conqueror of the east; a more realistic assessment of his campaign would suggest that he became involved in several local battles but never tested the full might of the Mitannian army. Nevertheless, Tuthmosis had, albeit briefly, reached the River Euphrates. In so doing he had awakened a long-dormant interest in the possibilities of expanding Egypt's eastern borders. Having erected a victory stela on the river-bank, he embarked on his long homeward journey, pausing only to enjoy a celebratory elephant hunt in the Syrian marshes.

Tuthmosis had laid down the foundations of the New Kingdom empire. Back home, things were going equally well. The Theban-born Tuthmosis was happy to follow Ahmose's lead in acknowledging Amen as the inspiration behind Egypt's victories; Amen in turn was happy to receive his share of the battle spoils. As the priesthood of Amen adjusted to their new affluence, the Karnak temple complex was changing beyond all recognition. Tuthmosis completed the work started by Amenhotep I, and then embarked on his own grander schemes. The original mud-brick Middle Kingdom building was now dominated by a sandstone wall while two magnificent gateways (Fourth and Fifth pylons), topped with towers and flagpoles, provided an imposing access to an impressive pillared court. Most amazing of all, twin inscribed red granite obelisks, each standing 19.5m (64 ft) tall, now stood before the main temple entrance, their golden tips glittering in the sunlight.

But it was over on the west bank of Thebes that the most innovative building work was taking place. Tuthmosis had decided to follow the new custom, introduced by Amenhotep I, of building a two-part funerary complex. His tomb, the last resting place of his mummified body, would be physically separated from his mortuary temple, the place where offerings would be made to sustain the dead king for all eternity. This decision had important security implications. While the mortuary temple would remain highly visible (it had to, in order to fulfil its function as a temple), the burial chamber could now be hidden away from prying eyes. Thus there was a chance that the royal graves and their precious contents might remain safe from the thieves who for centuries had haunted Egypt's cemeteries.

Amenhotep had been buried alongside his ancestors at Dra abu el-Naga. Tuthmosis, with no family links to the royal burial ground, was to be buried in a secret rock-cut tomb in a remote valley over an hour's walk away from his mortuary temple. He was the first to excavate in the Biban el-Muluk, the Valley of the Kings.

Tuthmosis I had succeeded to his throne in middle age; he could not realistically look forward to a lengthy reign. Aware that his death might provoke a dynastic crisis, he had taken care to nominate a successor. His consort, Ahmose, had at least one daughter but no living son and so the king announced that the crown was to pass to a young boy also named Tuthmosis, a royal son by a respected lady of the harem, Mutnodjmet. To reinforce the young Tuthmosis' claim to the throne he was married to his half-sister Hatshepsut, the daughter of the king and queen. Hatshepsut, although still young, was already an influential figure at court, bearing the important title of 'God's Wife of Amen'. When, after a highly successful reign of approximately eleven years Tuthmosis died, the young Tuthmosis II started his rule with Hatshepsut by his side.

Tuthmosis II and Hatshepsut were always a totally conventional New Kingdom royal couple. Tuthmosis naturally took the dominant role in the relationship while his sister-wife stood behind her husband to offer him silent, passive support. Things got off to a good start. Egypt's military strength was reaffirmed in Year I with the satisfying crushing of a minor rebellion in Nubia; later came a successful punitive expedition to the Negev (now southern Israel). Tuthmosis made no attempt to expand his empire but he was young, still learning his craft, and he had time on his side. Meanwhile, back home the royal masons continued their life-long work at the Karnak temple.

Queen Hatshepsut, too, was busy building. In 1916, thirteen years after he had explored Hatshepsut's tomb in the Valley of the Kings, Howard Carter had prepared to enter a newly discovered tomb cut high in the face of the Wadi Sikkat Taka ez-Zeida, an isolated ravine approximately one mile to the west of Deir el-Bahari, Thebes. This was a dangerous task; the locals who had already explored the tomb had found that there was only one possible way in. Carter recounted his exploits in an article written for the *Journal of Egyptian Archaeology* (1917: 4):

> When I wrested it [the tomb] from the plundering Arabs I
> found that they had burrowed into it like rabbits... I
> found that they had crept down a crack extending half way
> down the cleft, and there from a small ledge in the rock
> they had lowered themselves by a rope to the then hidden
> entrance of the tomb at the bottom of the cleft: a
> dangerous performance, but one which I myself had to
> imitate... For anyone who suffers from vertigo it certainly
> was not pleasant, and though I soon overcame the sensa-
> tion of the ascent I was obliged always to descend in a net.

This was the tomb which the queen-consort had prepared for
herself during the early years of her husband's reign. Inside,
Carter discovered an impressive quartzite sarcophagus inscribed
for 'The Great Princess, great in favour and grace, Mistress of
All Lands, Royal Daughter and Royal Sister, Great Royal Wife,
Mistress of the Two Lands, Hatshepsut'. The sarcophagus,
however, was empty and the tomb unfinished. Hatshepsut was
never to occupy her lonely grave.

Tragedy struck and Tuthmosis died after a reign of between
one and three years. His was a sudden, unexpected death. His
funerary preparations were not complete, his imposing tomb was
unfinished, and the late king had to be buried in a hastily prepared
uninscribed tomb in the Valley of the Kings. Tuthmosis had
joined the ranks of those pharaohs denied the chance to prove
themselves. The distinguished anatomist Grafton Elliot Smith,
examining the king's mummified body in the early twentieth
century, noted that Tuthmosis' skin was disfigured by 'raised
macules varying in size from minute points to patches a few

centimetres in diameter'; whether these scabrous patches should be taken as proof that the king died of plague, or whether they merely represent some unfortunate side-effect of the mummification process, is not clear.

Now the wheel of fate was about to turn full cycle. Once again the king and queen of Egypt had a daughter – Princess Neferure – but no son. The crown therefore passed to the infant Tuthmosis III, a son born to Tuthmosis II by Isis, an otherwise anonymous lady of the harem. It seems likely, but is unproven, that the young Tuthmosis would have been married to his stepsister Neferure as a means of emphasising his right to rule. As the humble Isis was considered unsuited to act as guardian for her son, Hatshepsut prepared to follow in the footsteps of Ahhotep and Ahmose Nefertari. She would now rule Egypt as a queen regent. The right of the widowed queen to act as regent for her son was an age-old precedent which could be traced back to the Old Kingdom. Hatshepsut, however, was being asked to rule on behalf of a stepson.

Inscriptions carved at the Semna Temple in Nubia, dated to Year 2 of the new regime, confirm that Hatshepsut accepted her new role with becoming queenly reticence. Here we can see an adult-looking Tuthmosis III, 'King of Upper and Lower Egypt and Lord of the Two Lands', being presented with the white crown of Upper Egypt. He is clearly the acknowledged, and sole, pharaoh of Egypt and Nubia. A mere five years later there had been a dramatic change. Now Hatshepsut was recognised as Egypt's dominant king.

The seemingly impossible had been achieved. Somehow Hatshepsut had persuaded her people – or more significantly, she had persuaded Egypt's ruling elite – that she should be recognised as a legitimate monarch alongside Tuthmosis III.

Tuthmosis, too young to object, would be allowed to continue with his rule, but he was now very much Hatshepsut's junior partner. How this came about we shall probably never know. Could there have been a crisis which required an adult king on the throne? Or had this been a carefully planned, slow but sure usurpation of power? Is Hatshepsut a hero, or a villain?

Throughout her reign Hatshepsut was to show a strong devotion to the goddess Maat, the personification of the concept of *maat* or 'rightness'. She was determined, through her building works, her art and above all her monumental inscriptions, to convince her people and her gods that *maat* truly filled every corner of her land. To emphasise this she chose as her throne name, the name by which she was known to her people, Maat-ka-re (*Maat* is the soul of the sun-god Re). How then could Hatshepsut square her assumption of a male role with her strong belief in the force of *maat*? Surely the king of Egypt was intended to be a man? Hatshepsut, following the modern adage, 'never apologise, never explain', remains obstinately silent on this matter.

We are left to speculate that Hatshepsut perhaps did not see her gender as any real affront to *maat*. She did not have to look far back in her own dynastic history to see that a queen-regent could rule Egypt as effectively as any man. There was no specific prohibition on female pharaohs. Indeed, during the Middle Kingdom, there had even been the short-lived reign of the female king Sobeknofru whose rule had seen the end of the turbulent 12th Dynasty. Nor was there any ban on co-regencies; the joint reign had long been a feature of dynastic royal life.

Hatshepsut was both the daughter of the previous king and, through her mother Ahmose (probably the daughter of Amenhotep I) a descendant of the venerated Ahmose and Ahmose

Nefertari. No one, in terms of blood, had a stronger claim to the throne. As long as she did not displace the rightful king – an unforgivable offence which certainly would have been contrary to *maat* – Hatshepsut would have been able to justify her reign as the logical extension of the role of queen-regent. She may even have convinced herself that she would renounce her power once Tuthmosis came of age.

Now Hatshepsut, conveniently forgetting her somewhat insignificant late husband-brother, set out to prove herself a worthy successor to her father's throne. This meant that she needed to demonstrate her ability to defend Egypt's borders. Historians once argued that Hatshepsut must have been a pacifist, either because of her natural 'womanly' qualities (a view much discredited since the world has experienced a succession of strong, even aggressive female rulers) or because she was reluctant to allow the army to assume too much power. However, we now have enough evidence to confirm that, while she held no great dream of empire, Hatshepsut was not averse to fighting. She accomplished her mission early in her reign with a minor but pleasingly successful Nubian skirmish; small stuff when compared with the military achievements of Tuthmosis I and III, but certainly comparable to the victories of Tuthmosis II and more than enough to prove to her people that *maat* was being maintained.

Content with protecting rather than expanding her borders, Hatshepsut was interested in the economic benefits of empire. Egypt was rich in natural resources and would never run out of food, but she had a growing need for wood, for luxury goods and for the scented incense which could be burned in the temples. Foreigners were now to be exploited rather than subdued and Hatshepsut's reign was to see a series of highly successful foreign trading missions plus increasing development of the copper and turquoise mines in Sinai. Most remarkable of all was her expedition to the land of Punt. This mission, which she regarded one of the highlights of her reign, was to be recorded in a series of scenes carved into the wall of Hatshepsut's mortuary temple at Deir el-Bahari. Here it took the place of the battle-scenes which a more conventional pharaoh might have carved.

> The king himself [Hatshepsut] made an inquiry at the podium of the Lord of the Gods [Amen]. And an oracle was received in the inner sanctuary, a divine command from the god himself: 'Search out the roads to Punt and open up paths to its incense groves. Lead an expedition over land and sea to bring back the exotic produce of the God's Land ...' The god's command was followed exactly, because her majesty was eager to obey it.

Punt, a far-away almost legendary kingdom situated somewhere along the Eritrean/Ethiopian coast, had long been known as a source of desirable exotica. Here precious resins, ebony, ivory, gold and much, much, more were available for those pharaohs who had the daring and the wherewithal to organise a successful expedition. No one had visited Punt in living memory; some even doubted its existence. Now Hatshepsut determined to prove her worth. Dedicating her fleet to Amen, she sped her envoy Neshi off on his great adventure.

Five impressive Egyptian sailing ships, manned by marines and loaded with trinkets, arrived safe and sound in Punt. Disembarking, Neshi found himself in a small village of curious round houses raised on stilts, set amid a flourishing tropical forest. Here he was greeted courteously by the slender, bearded chief and his overweight wife and daughter. Trading commenced. After some hard bargaining the Egyptians happily accepted a vast mound of valuables – everything that Amen and Hatshepsut might have wished for. Meanwhile the Puntites expressed polite delight with the trivia offered by their guests (remember, Hatshepsut's account is not guaranteed accurate or even truthful, and her envoy travelled with an armed guard).

> Look, they are already returning peacefully to Karnak. And they have brought something truly amazing – all the fine products of God's Land, which your majesty sent them for: piles of incense gum and trees heavy with fresh incense, ready to plant in the festival hall, in the sight of the Lord of the Gods. You shall cultivate them personally in the orchard next to my temple, so that I can relax among them. Just as my name is pre-eminent among the gods, your name will be pre-eminent among humans, forever.

Neshi returned home in triumph, his ships groaning under the weight of their spoils. The people gathered to watch the sailors disembark, heavily burdened with gold, ebony, ivory, a menagerie of exotic wild animals and even living trees carefully suspended from carrying poles, their roots protected by baskets. Incense could now be grown in the garden of the Deir el-Bahari temple. Hatshepsut was delighted and offered thanks to Amen. The success of her mission made it obvious to even the most hardened of sceptics that the gods were not offended by the female monarch. *Maat* was indeed present throughout the land.

Increasing trade brought increasing wealth. As her coffers filled, Hatshepsut was able to indulge her passion for building, financing an ambitious programme of public works which included both the establishment of new temples and the repair of monuments damaged during the civil war. An inscription preserved on a small rock-cut chapel at Beni Hassan, Middle Egypt, known today as the Speos Artemidos, makes her policy clear:

Since my reign began, roads which were blocked in both directions are in use again. The army, which had been neglected, has now been properly equipped. The temple of the Lady of Cusae had fallen into ruins – the earth had swallowed up its holy shrine, and children played on the sanctuary roof. Because royal authority was no longer respected, crooks had embezzled its funds and no one was celebrating the night-time services. [But] I rebuilt and reconsecrated it, and fashioned a new divine statue out of gold ... May my inscription be as solid as the mountains and may the sun-disk cast its rays over my royal titles. May the falcon stand tall on my royal standard forever.

Hatshepsut is probably correct in her claim to be the first to build in Middle Egypt since the Second Intermediate Period. Undoubtedly, Middle Egypt, as a border zone between the Theban and Avaris courts, had suffered greatly; it seems likely that many of the monuments would indeed have been in need of restoration. But Hatshepsut, a mistress of propaganda, is here deliberately exaggerating the traumas of Hyksos rule and the *maat*-less civil war so that they form a direct and pleasing contrast with the stability, prosperity and rightness of her own reign. In the absence of an actual enemy to loathe she now promotes hatred of the long-departed Hyksos as a means of uniting her own people behind her rule.

The Karnak temple was once again changing form. Hatshepsut built an imposing new sandstone gateway (the Eighth Pylon), a suite of rooms around the barque or boat shrine of Amen, and a mud-brick royal palace for her own use. Her new red granite barque shrine, known today by its French name, the Chapelle Rouge, was to be dismantled during the solo reign of Tuthmosis III when its blocks were used as filling material in other building projects. Today, however, it has been substantially retrieved and is being slowly reassembled in the Karnak Open-Air Museum.

> I swear, as Re lives for me, and as . . . Amen loves me . . . I made each of these two monolithic obelisks for my father, Amen, from a single block of granite, and plated them with electrum, to ensure that my name lasted for ever in his temple. Their stone was flawless and needed no patching!

Like her father before her, Hatshepsut raised gold-tipped obelisks to the glory of Amen. Lest we should be in any doubt over their origins, their inscriptions celebrated the female king as their author. The obelisk symbolised the first rays of the sun at the time of creation. Glittering in the strong Karnak sun, they were an awesome sight.

We should not underestimate the skill and planning involved in the dedication of an obelisk. The work in the granite quarry was both labour intensive and mind-numbingly dull, as each obelisk had to be 'cut' using hard-stone hammers repeatedly bounced against the rock surface, but it was the transport and erection of the roughly cut piece which caused the real logistical headache. Although we know that the obelisks were moved on an immensely long barge towed by an armada of rowing boats, and can guess at various methods of up-ending the monument within the temple precinct, no one has yet been able to demonstrate convincingly how this prodigious feat might have been achieved. Hatshepsut's tallest surviving obelisk tops 29.5m (over 96 ft) in height, while her unfinished obelisk, abandoned in its Aswan quarry after developing a fatal crack, would have stood an impressive 41m (135 ft) tall and weighed an estimated 1,000 tons.

It is for her beautiful mortuary temple at Deir el-Bahari, (Djeser-Djeseru, or Holy of Holies) that Hatshepsut is best remembered. The temple complex, set in tiers in a natural bay in the Theban cliff, has long been considered one of the most beautiful buildings of the dynastic age.

Here Hatshepsut built a temple where she hoped that she and her father would be remembered for all eternity. Here their souls would receive the perpetual offerings of food, drink and incense made by the living. Included in the temple were shrines dedicated to a variety of gods. Hathor and Anubis had their own chapels, there was a shrine devoted to the memory of the royal ancestors, and there was a solar temple, open to the sky, dedicated to Re-Herakhte. Hidden at the very heart of the building, cut into the Theban rock face, was the dark shrine of Amen–Holy of Holies, the variant of Amen with whom Hatshepsut expected to become one after death.

Hatshepsut soon abandoned her unfinished tomb in the Wadi Sikkat Taka ez-Zeida. Solitude, and a good view, were appropriate for a queen but as a pharaoh she preferred to be buried alongside her father in the more prestigious Valley of the Kings. This decision was taken very literally; rather than build a new tomb, Hatshepsut had decided to expand, and then share, her father's last resting place. Tuthmosis I was to be taken from his original wooden sarcophagus and reinterred in a splendid, albeit second-hand, quartzite sarcophagus alongside the even more splendid new sarcophagus which awaited his daughter.

Hatshepsut consistently stressed her devotion to her father, a devotion that went far beyond simple filial love. For Tuthmosis I was Hatshepsut's reason for claiming the throne. She had followed him as the god Horus had followed his dead father King Osiris, her gender being an irrelevance which she believed her father would have been happy to overlook. Indeed, glossing over her time as consort to Tuthmosis II and rewriting history to suit her needs, Hatshepsut (falsely) tells us that her father had taken the unusual step of proclaiming her co-regent before his death: 'This is my daughter. I put her in my place. She is my successor on the throne...'

Yet the endorsement of an earthly father, no matter how exalted, might not have been enough to excuse her assumption of power. Hatshepsut therefore revealed herself to be the daughter of a divine father. As the child of Amen, patron god of the Egyptian empire, she surely had a pre-determined right to rule his land.

The walls of the Deir el-Bahari mortuary temple preserve the story of Hatshepsut's divine nativity in a series of images and descriptive passages. Amen comes to Egypt to visit the beautiful Queen Ahmose:

He found her asleep in the depths of the palace, but his divine fragrance woke her and she smiled at him. He was aroused and came to her immediately. He gave her his heart and revealed his true divine form. And as he came towards her, she saw his beauty and rejoiced. Then his love flowed through her body and the palace was filled with a heavenly smell, with all the fragrance of Punt...

Once Amen had fulfilled his desire for her, he told her: 'It is up to you to declare that Khenmet-Amen Hatshepsut [The One who is joined with Amen, the Foremost of Women] is the name of my daughter, whom I have placed in your womb. One day, she will be the rightful king and will rule over the whole of this land...

In heaven we see the new baby and her identical soul being moulded on a potter's wheel by the ram-headed god of creation, Khnum. Nine months later the pregnant Ahmose is being led to the birth bower by Khnum and Heket. All goes well, and Hatshepsut is born. Amen takes his daughter, kisses her and speaks to the assembled gods:

> Come to me in peace, daughter of my loins, beloved Maatkare [Hatshepsut], you are the king who takes possession of the diadem on the Throne of Horus of the Living, eternally.

The naked infant Hatshepsut, and her soul, both appear as male figures; to anyone unable the read the accompanying hieroglyphic text, Egypt's newborn king was male.

> Her body was covered with the finest incense. Her scent was a divine shower, her odour was just like Punt. Her skin was plated with electrum and glittered in the sight of the whole land, like the stars in the festival hall.
>
> *Deir el-Bahari Inscription*

Hatshepsut had once been content to appear as a typical, beautiful but bland Egyptian queen. Now, just as she had reinvented her past, so she would successfully reinvent her appearance. Recognising the power of the image of the traditional pharaoh, she took the decision to adopt this image in all her official representations. The public Hatshepsut was routinely depicted wearing the kilt, crown or head-cloth, collar and false beard which had from the days of the very first pharaohs defined Egyptian kingship. Very occasionally, towards the beginning of her rule, she appeared as a woman dressed in king's clothing but more usually she had the breastless body of a man. The more private, smaller-scale Hatshepsut, the Hatshepsut who appeared deep within her own temple, retained a more feminine appearance.

Hatshepsut had started her reign with a cabinet of ministers inherited from her father and her brother. As she grew more confident in her judgement she made new appointments, selecting men of relatively humble birth who might be expected to have a personal loyalty to her alone. These ministers had a vested interest in keeping Hatshepsut in place. If she fell, they would fall with her. Included among these arrivistes was Senenmut, a humble-born courtier who was to enjoy a meteoric rise to power. Senenmut was to play a major role during the first three-quarters of her reign. He, once the guardian of the princess Neferure, has been credited with either building or designing the Deir el-Bahari temple. However, it is Senenmut's more personal involvement with his mistress which has caught the attention of modern historians.

Senenmut's image has been preserved in at least twenty-five hard stone statues; these, almost certainly intended to be placed in the courtyard of the temple of Amen, reveal a serious, unsmiling

individual solemnly going about his official duties. Far less flatter-
ing are graffiti scribbled on the wall of an unfinished Middle
Kingdom tomb at Deir el-Bahari. During the New Kingdom this
tomb was used as a workmen's hut and, like workmen the world
over, the Theban labourers decided to improve their rather basic
accommodation with a display of pornography. Amid a collection
of crude scribbles we can today distinguish a tall, fully clothed
male (tentatively identified as either Senenmut or Hatshepsut)
who is being approached by a smaller, naked man with a very large
erection and unmistakable intentions. Near by on the same tomb
wall we can see an anonymous naked couple enjoying either
'doggy-style' intercourse, or buggery. The dominant figure is
obviously male. His large companion has a dark pubic triangle but
no penis and no breasts. She is wearing what may be a rough
depiction of a royal headdress, and has therefore been tentatively
identified as Hatshepsut. The male figure is therefore assumed to
be Senenmut.

Senenmut's image has also been discovered within the dark
recesses of the Deir el-Bahari temple. This was unheard of;
although it was possible for commoners to appear on the outer,
or public, temple walls only the king and the gods should appear
on the inner, hidden surfaces. And yet Senenmut left over sixty
small representations of himself concealed behind the wooden
doors of the temple shrines and statue niches. This is not a case
of mistaken identity; the accompanying texts confirm that these
are Senenmut worshipping both Amen and Hatshepsut 'on
behalf of the life, prosperity and health of the King of Upper
and Lower Egypt, Maatkare living forever'. Even worse, although
he already had a conspicuous, almost complete tomb perched
high on top of the Sheik el-Gurna hill, Thebes (TT 71),
Senenmut now started to excavate a tomb hidden beneath the

sacred precincts of Hatshepsut's mortuary temple (TT 353).

Senenmut vanished abruptly from court and his body has never been found; there is no evidence that it was buried in either of his tombs. The obvious explanation is that he died a natural death and was given a respectful burial, perhaps in a third tomb, which was later plundered by tomb robbers. More fanciful is the suggestion that he was banished by an angry Hatshepsut, furious at the temerity of a man who would presume to violate the precincts of her most sacred temple.

After two decades on the throne Hatshepsut followed the precedent of the Middle Kingdom pharaohs and entered into semi-retirement, allowing her co-ruler and intended successor to step into the limelight. Tuthmosis had been trained as a soldier and was already commander-in-chief of the army. Now, faced with growing discontent among his eastern vassals, he was forced to commit his troops to the first of the series of military campaigns needed to reimpose firm control on the Levant.

A single stela carved at Armant, Upper Egypt, tells us of the death of the female pharaoh on the 10th day of the 6th month of Year 22 (early February 1482BC). His twenty-two-year joint reign now over, Tuthmosis III buried Hatshepsut alongside Tuthmosis I in KV 20. Finally he was free to rule as an independent king.

# CHAPTER 4

# The Woman:
# Mistress of the House

She has no enemies in the south and no opponents in the north; all the foreign lands which the gods created work for her. They approach her in terror, their leaders bent double, carrying their gifts on their backs. They hand over their children, hoping to get the breath of life [in return] . . .

*Deir el-Bahari Punt inscription*

Against all the odds Hatshepsut had succeeded in a man's world. Hers was not, however, an unprecedented success. Already several New Kingdom queens had played an important role in affairs of state with Tetisheri, Ahhotep and Ahmose Nefertari each proving themselves confident, resourceful women capable of taking control as and when necessary. The Middle Kingdom had provided a more obvious parallel; Queen, or more correctly King, Sobeknofru had ruled her land as pharaoh at the very end of the failing 12th Dynasty. Sobeknofru had made no attempt to appear to her people as a traditional male pharaoh, yet was recognised as a genuine king, the last of her line. All these queens had the active support of the men around them, and Sobeknofru's brief reign (3 years, 10 months and 24 days) was included in the official list of kings of Egypt.

Two things seem obvious. Firstly, there was no legal or theological bar to a woman becoming king. Sobeknofru's reign proves that, under appropriate circumstances, a female monarch could be acceptable and the historian Manetho confirms this by recording a 2nd Dynasty King Binothris during whose reign 'it was decided that women might hold kingly office'. Secondly, it is clear that the New Kingdom allowed its highest-ranking females access to both political and religious power. This power was very much a by-product of their close links with the king: it is only those women with the closest of ties to the crown (queen mothers, queen consorts and royal daughters) who are given the chance to exercise any form of authority. The royal women do not have their own power, they acquire it by deputising for the king.

> The favourite daughter of Amen, his special child who was created in his presence, the glorious image of the Lord of the Universe, whose beauty was created by the souls of Heliopolis; who seized the lands like the primordial god and was specially created to wear his crowns... Amen himself places her on his throne in Thebes. He selected her to guard Egypt, to inspire awe among the nobles and the common people; the female Horus who protects her father...
>
> *Obelisk inscription of Hatshepsut*

In front of every successful Egyptian woman there was an equally if not more successful man who gave her power. Even Hatshepsut felt the need to justify her actions by making constant references to the two fathers who supported her reign, the heavenly Amen and the more earthly Tuthmosis II. As British Egyptologist John Ray has commented:

> Hatshepsut can be seen as the Queen Elizabeth I of ancient Egypt. She comes from a very proud but rather upstart dynasty, and one of the strongest features in her life is her relationship with her father Tuthmosis I. Her father appears in all sorts of contexts and it is quite clear that she used her dynastic position to remind people of who she was. She may be a woman, she may be somebody whose claim to the throne is rather shaky, but do not ever forget that she was the daughter of Tuthmosis I. Queen Elizabeth used to interview ambassadors underneath a portrait of Henry VIII. The message was the same: I am my father's daughter.

Elizabeth, of course, had inherited the throne under the terms of her late father's will. We do not know what caused Hatshepsut to extend her totally legitimate period as queen regent.

Egypt's highest-born women might be given the chance, via their fathers, husbands or sons, to exercise absolute power. More humble women, too, might deputise for their menfolk. From the very beginning of the dynastic age it had been recognised that a wife could represent her husband in matters of business, the wife rather than the father or brother being recognised as man's closest companion and support. Egyptian art emphasises this point; family sculptures routinely show women physically supporting their husbands with their right arm wrapped protectively around his shoulder or waist.

This acceptance of the woman deputising for her husband

could have unforeseen results. A curious court case dated to the 19th Dynasty reign of Ramesses II is preserved on a broken ostracon. Here we read of an anonymous government official who has started to steal from the storehouses belonging to the temples of Thebes. The thief prospers, until he is transferred to a new job in the Delta region. Loath to give up his unearned income, the thief instructs his wife and daughter to remain in Thebes so that they might carry on where he has left off. This they do with great success; it seems that no one ever questions the wife's right to enter the storehouse and help herself to its contents. Eventually, however, the pair are caught; a vigilant scribe complains that the wife is acting without proper authority. She is eventually charged with stealing a vast array of goods. The trio are summoned to appear before the court, but unfortunately the end of the case is lost.

We know that a woman could legally serve as her husband's representative. What else do we know of the lives, hopes and expectations of the women of the New Kingdom empire? The women who, almost invariably illiterate and preoccupied with domestic duties, provided a back-up to the more public lives of their menfolk. History tends to overlook these silent Egyptians, and our evidence for their existence is through necessity derived from indirect sources. From archaeology, a handful of legal documents, and a wide selection of chance references in the male-dominated literature.

It was hard to be female in a Bronze Age world where biology and social expectation combined to provide all too many women with a brief, hard and painful existence. Egyptian women, however, were luckier than most. Egypt did not practise legal sexism and her women were allowed the same legal rights as men. Indeed, Egyptian women, married or single, enjoyed rights which many western societies have only matched in the past century or so. Why this should be we do not know, although it seems probable that the relaxed abundance of life in the Nile Valley was at least partially responsible. With no pressure on land or resources, with almost everything owned by the king and the gods, there was little need to exert strong controls over family life.

> The Egyptians in their manners and customs seem to have reversed the ordinary practices of mankind. For instance women attend the market and are employed in trade while men stay at home and do the weaving... Sons need not support their parents unless they choose, but daughters must, whether they want to or not... The men wear two garments each, the women one...
>
> *Herodotus*, Histories II: 35

Egyptian women were entitled to own, buy, sell and inherit property. In a society which lacked money and relied on barter, the right to trade surplus produce on the open market was an important one which guaranteed the industrious woman an income. Although most women lived with their husbands or fathers, this was not a legal requirement; they were free to live alone, could work outside the home and could testify as witnesses in the civil court. They might even act as guardians to their own children; an extremely important right for Egypt's widows and divorcees.

However, it would be a serious mistake to imagine that their legal equality left dynastic women free to act as they pleased. The theoretical right to own property meant very little to those – the vast majority – too poor to own anything beyond a couple of garments and a cooking pot. The right to work did not carry with it an entitlement to a highly paid career or even an education, it simply meant that those not worn out by child-care and domestic duties were allowed to supplement the family income by working at a level appropriate to their station in life. For most this meant back-breaking toil in the fields, or in the heat and gloom of the weaving sheds.

> Do not control your wife in her house when you know she is efficient . . . There are many men who do not realise this, but if a man desists from strife at home he will not find it starting. Every man who establishes a household should hold back his hasty heart.
>
> *A New Kingdom scribe offers his readers good advice*

While many women did work outside the home, this was not considered ideal. From the very beginnings of the dynastic age it had been accepted that women should be indoor creatures responsible for the home and the family, while their menfolk led outdoor lives interfacing with the non-domestic world. Their roles complemented each other and, together, husband and wife were considered a team. The good husband would shelter and protect his wife; the good wife in turn would give her husband support and provide him with a comfortable home. Again Egyptian tomb art makes this distinction very clear. While upper-class women appear as frail, pale beings dressed in impractical semi-transparent white garments, their men are hearty, robust and browned by the sun's rays. Only in the Amarna Period was this convention overturned for the royal women who were temporarily allowed to assume a masculine red-brown colour.

Time and time again Egypt's poets and artists show us the ideal New Kingdom family; husband, loving wife and, eventually, one or more miniature children. We find this ideal in royal art, in statuary and even in divine art, where the gods themselves married goddesses to beget divine offspring. Amen, for example, was known to be married to the goddess Mut and the couple had a son, the moon god Khonsu. Osiris, god of the dead, was married to his loyal sister Isis. When Osiris was killed and dismembered by his evil brother Seth, it was the good wife Isis who rescued the pieces and resurrected her husband. Reunited, Osiris and Isis conceived the god Horus, forming a divine family of god, wife and child.

It would be hard for us to overestimate the importance of this basic family unit. The Egyptians lived in a harsh, frightening environment, threatened not by extremes of climate – famine and flooding were relatively rare calamities – but by the more humdrum dangers of disease, incapacity, childbirth and accident. The state had little interest in the welfare of individuals; there was no health service, welfare system or national police force and only when there was a perceived threat to the well-being of the nation as a whole would pharaoh step in to dispense aid or justice. Similarly, the state gods offered little in the way of protection or comfort to those in physical or mental distress. Denied any form of official support, the people pinned their hopes on the semi-official religious cults, their local gods and the family. These, it was hoped, would provide insurance in times of need.

At a more practical level, the family formed the basic working unit. As we have seen, boys followed in their fathers' footsteps; in consequence, brothers, fathers, sons, uncles and cousins all worked together. Contracts, and employment, depended not so much upon what, but whom, one knew. Officials routinely offered the best posts to their relations; no one saw any wrong in this, as the family had to look after its own.

> My sister is unique – no one can rival her, for she is the most beautiful woman alive. Look, she is like Sirius, which marks the beginning of a good year. She radiates perfection and glows with health. The glance of her eye is gorgeous. Her lips speak sweetly, and not one word too many. Long-necked and milky breasted she is, her hair the colour of pure lapis. Gold is nothing compared to her arms, and her fingers are like lotus flowers. Her buttocks are full but her waist is narrow. As for her thighs – they only add to her beauty ...
>
> *Papyrus Chester Beatty I*

We might therefore expect the New Kingdom wedding, the achievement of the family unit, to have been a time of great celebration. Doubtless it was, but it was an informal celebration which goes unrecorded in the state and temple archives. Occasionally a couple blessed with possessions might sign a pre-nuptial agreement but this was the exception rather than the rule. On her wedding day the bride would simply leave her parents' house and move into her husband's home (or his parents' home). Co-habitation was all that was needed to signal marriage.

After marriage wives were expected to remain faithful to their husbands, a measure, given the lack of effective contraception, presumably designed to ensure that her children were indeed the children of the father who was working hard to feed and clothe them. However, it was a popular male belief that married women were insatiable temptresses, eager to take advantage of inexperienced young men who would then face the wrath of the cuckolded husband:

> Do not fornicate with a married woman. He who fornicates with a married woman on her bed, his wife will be copulated with on the ground.
>
> *The Late Period scribe Anksheshonq*

In the *Tale of the Two Brothers*, a 19th Dynasty fictional account of infidelity and betrayal, the adulterous wife who attempts to seduce her brother-in-law is killed and her body thrown to the dogs. This is the ultimate punishment; the wife is denied a proper burial, and will never live beyond death.

Men did not have to meet such high standards of behaviour and Egypt's flourishing brothels offered opportunities for dalliance without recrimination. It was never, however, acceptable for a married man to flaunt his infidelity as this would threaten the ideal of family life. In a late New Kingdom letter recovered from the workmen's village of Deir el-Medina, Thebes, we can read the cautionary tale of Nesamenemope, a married man who for many months has been sleeping with a woman who is not his wife. Everyone in the village knows what is going on. The wronged wife's family are not prepared to put up with such an insult, and they have the support of their community. Everyone blames the woman, the temptress, rather than the weak man. One night an angry mob gathers to march to the mistress' house, shouting 'We are going to beat her, together with her people.' Luckily, an official manages to stall the rabble, sending a warning message to the couple. Nesamenemope should sort out his household. He must divorce his wife – providing her with maintenance and freeing her to marry again — before he recommences his affair.

> My sister has arrived — my heart is bursting, my arms spread wide to hug her... My heart is in its element, as happy as a fish in the breeding ground. O night, if only you could last forever, now my mistress is here!
>
> *Love song*

Married women spent much of their lives either pregnant or breast-feeding. The Egyptians were first and foremost farmers. They fully understood that intercourse would lead to pregnancy, and allowed sex to play a vital role in the divine tales of creation which sought to explain the existence of mankind. However, although Egypt trained the best doctors in the Mediterranean world, and despite unique mortuary practices which allowed an unrivalled insight into the intricacies of the human body, there was little understanding of the processes of conception and birth.

There was therefore little effective help for those wishing to avoid pregnancy: sour milk douches and crocodile dung suppositories were only slightly more effective than prayers and magic spells. Children were in any case welcomed; the more the merrier. There is a general feeling that boys were more welcome than girls, as boys were best suited to earning a living and performing their parents' funerary rituals, but nowhere in the male-dominated literature do we meet the strong anti-female bias found in ancient Greece and Rome. Egyptian girl babies were not found abandoned in the streets.

Infertility was a tragedy which could not be cured by prayers, petitions to the dead, or medical means: even feasting off vast mounds of lettuce, a plant strongly associated with fertility, was unlikely to produce the desired result. Barren marriages were therefore often 'cured' by divorce or adoption, with the wife receiving the blame for the failure to conceive.

Childbirth was a frightening time; a time when the uncontrolled forces of nature would enter the home to create a new life. It was therefore logical that the mother-to-be would require both medical and ritual or spiritual assistance. This would be provided by a female midwife trained as much in the recitation of spells as in the delivery of babies. Throughout the dynastic age birth remained a female-dominated rite of passage; one with no obvious role for men. In consequence, the surviving literature is not particularly informative in this area and only one story, *The Westcar Papyrus*, written during the New Kingdom but set in the Old Kingdom court of King Khufu, includes anything resembling a detailed description of childbirth. Even here the messy facts are delicately veiled for the male readers. We meet the lady Reddjedet who is delivered of triplets by four goddesses disguised as travelling midwives. Reddjedet squats on a birthing stool (a stool with a hole in the seat designed to let gravity assist at the birth) while one midwife stands in front of her, another behind. The babies are delivered, washed and placed on a cushion. The new mother then gives the midwives a payment of corn for their services and they depart for their next case.

Outside the fictional world, our information is meagre. We know that as the time drew near the midwife would prepare her tools. These, to modern eyes, were a worrying mixture of the practical and the quaint. The birthing blocks where the mother-to-be would crouch, and the sharp obsidian knife which would be used to cut the umbilical cord, had obvious medical uses and yet were imbued with deep superstitious meaning. Amulets and charms bearing the figures of the pregnant hippopotamus goddess Taweret and the dwarf demi-god Bes were purely ritual items used to protect both mother and unborn child. The curious boomerang-shaped batons carved out of hippopotamus teeth used during the Middle Kingdom had no obvious purpose but may have been employed to draw a protective magic circle around mother and baby.

The mother prepared for the birth simply by removing her clothing and loosening her hair. In a wealthy household she may have retreated to a specially constructed birthing hut set apart from the house; this, however, was a privilege available to few. If all went well, the child would be delivered into the arms of the midwife who squatted in front of the labouring mother. The mother would then name her child. If things went badly, if the baby got stuck, there was very little that could be done.

Most mothers had no option but to breast-feed their babies. Royal women, however, employed wet-nurses, recruiting not servants but the wives of top government officials. These nurses developed a great and lasting influence over their young charges. Hatshepsut was nursed by the lady Sitre who was also known as Inet. As king she commissioned a sandstone statue showing herself as a miniature pharaoh sitting on Sitre's knee, her feet resting on the 'nine bows', the symbolic representation of the traditional enemies of Egypt. Unfortunately the statue inscription is now damaged but, in an inspired piece of archaeological detective work, the American Egyptologist Herbert Winlock was able to reconstruct its lost message. Writing in the *Bulletin of the Metropolitan Museum of Art, New York* (1932: 32.2: 5–10), Winlock recalled an inscribed limestone flake which he had seen in Vienna:

... on which an ancient scribe had jotted down an inscription in vertical columns. Comparing this inscription with the one on the statue, I have little doubt that the ostracon gives the preliminary draft for the statue inscription, drawn up by the scribe who was directing the sculptor. On the statue the inscription is incomplete, and it gives us a curious feeling to find ourselves filling in the gaps from the original rough draft after a lapse of thirty-five hundred years.

The text was translated by Winlock as follows:

May the king Maatkare [Hatshepsut] and Osiris, first of the Westerners, [the great god] Lord of Abydos, be gracious and give a mortuary offering [of cakes and beer, beef and fowl, and thousands of everything] good and pure, and the sweet breath of the north wind to the spirit of the chief nurse who suckled the Mistress of the Two Lands, Sit-Re, called Yen [Inet], justified.

During his 1903 season in the Valley of the Kings Howard Carter had explored a small, robbed, non-royal tomb (KV 60) which still housed two female burials plus a number of mummified geese and a leg of beef. One mummy lay in a wooden coffin inscribed with the name of In or Inet; presumably this is Sitre, accorded the unusual privilege of burial in the Valley of the Kings. The second mummy, found lying on the floor, was that of an unusually fat woman with red-gold hair and worn teeth. She is so far unidentified but some experts have suggested that she might be Hatshepsut herself.

New mothers were allowed fourteen days of rest and

75

seclusion to recover from the birth before resuming their normal routine. It is difficult to calculate the hours worked by the average New Kingdom housewife, as circumstances would obviously vary from family to family. However, comparison with pre-mechanical Britain would suggest that while household cleaning would have relatively low priority (the houses being small, dimly lit and essentially furniture-less and the desire to eliminate all dirt down to the level of the invisible germ being a comparatively modern obsession), clothing and feeding the family would be arduous tasks.

Let them bring all sorts of beer, and every type of bread. [Let them bring] piles of vegetables, those which are in and out of season, and all kinds of tasty fruit. Come and devote today to pleasure, tomorrow and the next day too – for three days sit in my shade . . .

*Papyrus Turin 1996*

Egypt had abundant natural resources, and under normal circumstances no one needed to go hungry. Food could be home-grown, earned in the form of government rations, hunted, fished or bartered at market. Water could be obtained from wells, from canals or the Nile. The conversion of these raw materials into a palatable meal, however, was a time-consuming process. Grain was the staple food and principal source of carbohydrate. Ground on a stone saddle quern, sieved, and mixed with water and salt, the grain could be made into simple flat bread which could be cooked on the sides of the dome-shaped clay ovens. The addition of yeast allowed the production of leavened loaves, while eggs and honey could be added to make cakes. Finally the bread could be crumbled and added to water to ferment into beer; a thick, slightly sweet, soupy beverage best drunk through a filtering straw. This mild beer was the main drink of the masses, consumed at every meal. Wine made from grapes grown in the Delta was reserved for the elite.

Everyone ate vast quantities of bread, even the gods, whose temples received offerings of hundreds of loaves each day. Vegetables and fish, too, were widely available. Meat, however, was very much an upper class treat. The typical peasant family ate an essentially healthy but extremely limited diet rich in bread, fish, onions, lettuce and pulses supplemented by occasional small game and home-raised fowl.

Clothing and laundry were also the responsibility of the Mistress of the House. When imagining our 'typical' New Kingdom family we should abandon all thought of the gleaming white, intricately pleated garments seen on the elite tomb walls. Most women dressed throughout the year in practical, plain, sleeved dresses similar in style to the galabiyahs worn by modern Egyptian villagers. These were made from lengths of linen or occasionally wool; cotton and silk being unknown. Woven sandals, and perhaps a shawl for warmth, completed the outfit. Men wore a similar wardrobe, although the long outer garment would be removed and replaced by a kilt when working in the fields. Washing was done by hand in the canal or the Nile; those fortunate enough to employ laundrymen were in the minority.

Elite women, freed from mundane household duties, enjoyed the leisure to conduct an elaborate toilette which started with the washing, shaving and oiling of the body, and ended with the donning of white garments, glittering jewellery and an intricate wig made of human hair. The total effect could be examined in a polished metal hand mirror. Mirrors were, however, a great luxury and most women would only ever see their own faces reflected in water.

There is little doubt that the ability to be clean – to remove the ever-present dust and sand and dress in pristine garments – provided an obvious, immediate distinction between the rich and the poor. Cleanliness was intensely desirable, even erotic:

> I love to go down and wash, while you look on. I will let you see me in all my beauty, in a fine robe of royal linen, impregnated with perfumed oil ... Then I will step into the water near you and bring you back a red fish, which fits my fingers perfectly. I will lay it down in front of you, as you look on ... My brother, come and watch me!
>
> *Love poem*

Sweet smells could be equally enticing; we have already seen the god Amen seducing Queen Ahmose with wafts of exotic perfume. The medical papyri include various recipes for masking more unpleasant odours with mouthwashes, deodorants and scents. These fragrances had to be strong – they had to battle against the combined effects of poor personal hygiene, a regrettable lack of soap and the unfortunate side-effects of a diet rich in onion, garlic and beans.

# CHAPTER 5

## Tuthmosis:
## The Egyptian Napoleon

[The statue of Amen] began wandering through the colonnade ... And the men leading it did not understand that it was looking everywhere for my majesty. When it reached me, it stopped ... I threw myself on my belly before him, I grovelled in the dust, I bowed down in front of him ... He opened the gates of heaven for me, he unlocked the doors of the horizon and I flew up to heaven like a divine falcon. I saw him in his heavenly guise and I worshipped his majesty ...

*From the coronation inscription of Tuthmosis III*

Egypt had been passive for far too long. There had always been a danger that foreigners might confuse Hatshepsut's desire for peace with weakness; now, as had happened before, the death of a strong pharaoh had inspired rebellion among her vassals.

Nubia posed no threat to the status quo; Ahmose, Amenhotep I and Tuthmosis I had each put a considerable amount of effort into destroying the Kushite kingdom, leaving Nubia firmly squashed beneath the mighty Egyptian thumb. It was to the east that the danger lay. The king of

Kadesh, an influential Syrian city-state situated on the River Orontes, was spreading discontent. Some reports maintained that he was even preparing his troops for war.

Tuthmosis, adult and well-prepared for his role but with little practical experience of leadership, was astute enough to realise that he could not afford to relax his grip on his eastern territories. Whoever controlled the Levant and her seaports would dominate the trade routes which formed the life-blood of the Bronze Age economy. More importantly, a controlling interest in Syria and the Levantine states would halt the expansion of Egypt's enemies who might otherwise grow powerful enough to threaten Egypt herself.

Pharaoh needed no excuse to call his country to arms. 'Asiatics' had always been included among Egypt's traditional foes, and Hatshepsut's recent promotion of the Hyksos as hate figures had been well calculated to unite the Egyptian people in their fear and loathing of foreigners. The New Kingdom Egyptians lived in constant dread that their eastern enemies would reinvade the Delta. It seemed entirely reasonable – almost self defence – to strike the first blow.

The political map of the Near East – never particularly stable – was undergoing rapid change. The coastal cities of Byblos, Beirut, Tyre and Sidon retained a long-standing loyalty to Egypt. To the north, however, in the lands now occupied by modern Turkey, the Indo-European Hittites had developed into a well-established entity whose natural route of expansion would eventually bring them into conflict with Egyptian interest in north Syria. Also interested in this region were the Hurrians, an ethnic group whose power-base was the nation-state of Mitanni. It was now over thirty years since the Mitannian army had faced Tuthmosis I in battle; years which had been spent

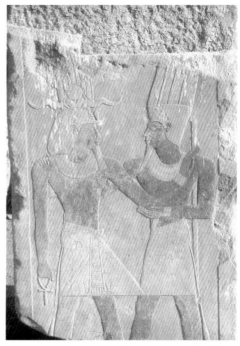

THE RIVER NILE BRINGS PROSPERITY TO
AN OTHERWISE ARID LAND
(ALEX LAY/LION TELEVISION)

ONE OF THE TUTHMOSIDE KINGS GREETS
THE THEBAN GOD AMEN
(STEVEN SNAPE)

PHARAOH AHMOSE PURIFIED WITH SACRED WATER OF GODS AMON RA AND RA ON A
GOLD ENAMEL PECTORAL FROM QUEEN AHHOTEP TREASURE C.1550BC
(THE ART ARCHIVE/EGYPTIAN MUSEUM CAIRO/DAGLI ORTI)

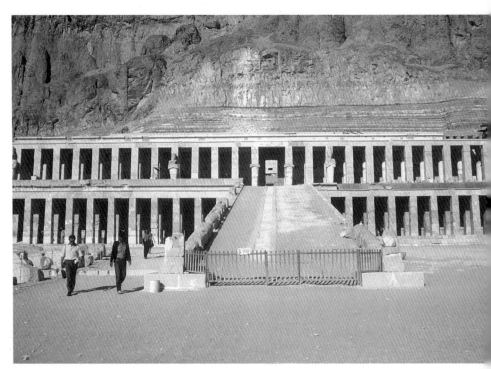

THE DEIR EL-BAHARI MORTUARY TEMPLE
(STEVEN SNAPE)

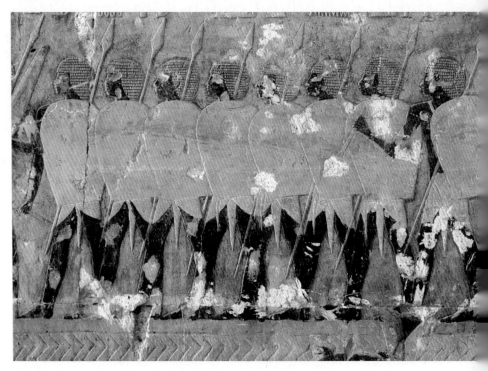

EGYPTIAN SOLDIERS ARRIVE IN PUNT
(STEVEN SNAPE)

QUEEN AHMOSE MERITAMEN SISTER AND WIFE
OF KING AMENHOTEP I, 1525-1504BC
(ᴇ ART ARCHIVE/EGYPTIAN MUSEUM CAIRO/DAGLI ORTI)

HATSHEPSUT'S IMAGE CHISELLED OFF
HER TEMPLE WALL
(STEVEN SNAPE)

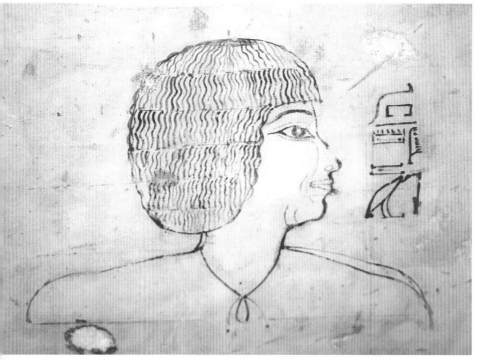

SENENMUT, HATSHEPSUT'S RIGHT-HAND MAN
(LION TELEVISION)

AMENHOTEP III, THE GOLDEN PHARAOH
(STEVEN SNAPE)

ONE OF THE COLOSSI OF MEMNON –
AMENHOTEP III
(STEVEN SNAPE)

THE KARNAK TEMPLE
(LION TELEVISION)

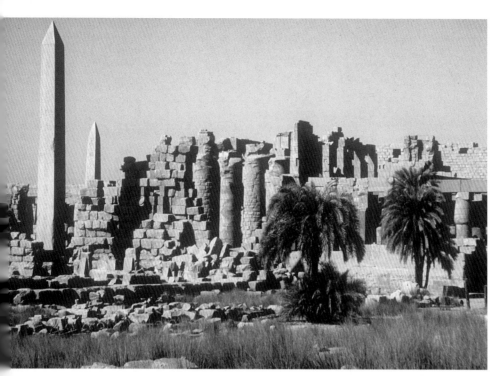

THE KARNAK TEMPLE OF AMEN
(STEVEN SNAPE)

THE AMARNA ROYAL FAMILY SHOWN ON A BOUNDARY STELA
(STEVEN SNAPE)

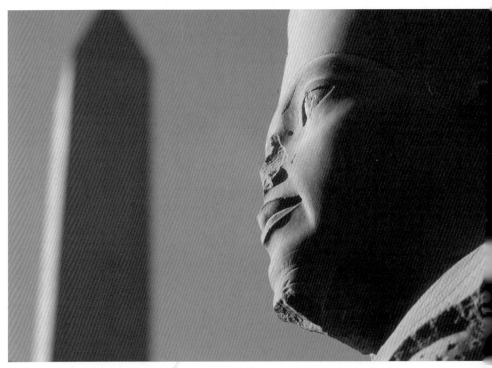

STATUE OF THE GOD AMEN, CARVED IN THE IMAGE OF TUTANKHAMEN
(ALEX LAY/LION TELEVISION)

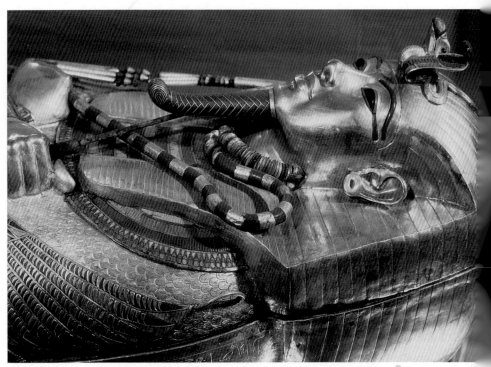

GOLD COFFIN OF TUTANKHAMEN, WHO REIGNED 1347-1337BC
(THE ART ARCHIVE/EGYPTIAN MUSEUM CAIRO/DAGLI ORTI)

HOREMHEB

(STEVEN SNAPE)

SETI I WITH OSIRIS, GOD OF ABYDOS

(STEVEN SNAPE)

THE GREAT TEMPLE OF ABU SIMBEL

(STEVEN SNAPE)

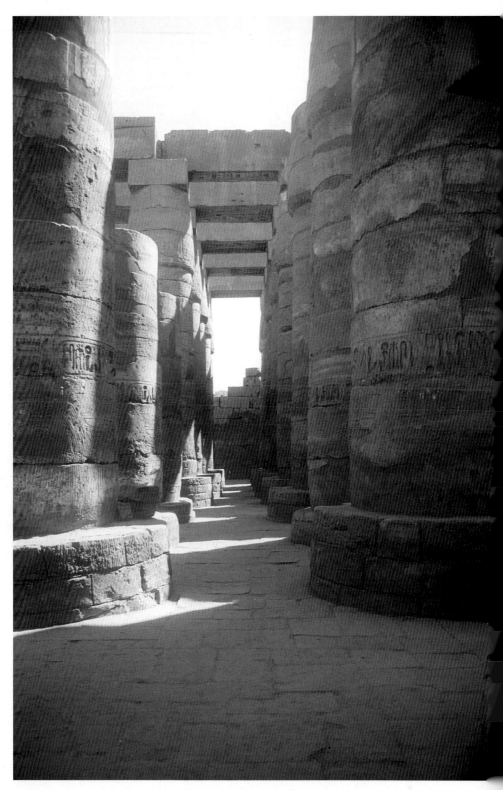

THE HYPOSTYLE HALL, KARNAK
(STEVEN SNAPE)

consolidating Mitanni's hold on north Syria and Mesopotamia. Now, with the independent, ambitious city-states of Kadesh and Tunip as friends, the Mitannian alliance posed the most immediate threat to Egypt's imperialist plans.

Tuthmosis set out to prove himself. In his own words, his intention was to 'overthrow that vile enemy and to extend the boundaries of Egypt in accordance with the command of his father Amen-Re'. He was to invest seventeen years in this mission, his seasonal campaign trail leading him from one fortified city-state to the next in a totally predictable pattern. After a battle or siege Tuthmosis would overcome the enemy, gather his spoils, sack the town and finally appoint a local pro-Egyptian ruler who would govern on his behalf. Occasionally one important step could be omitted; the might of the Egyptian army was starting to be feared across the near east, and some city-states found it prudent to concede without fighting, effectively paying Tuthmosis and his men to go away. As he collected taxes and tribute from an ever-growing number of vassals, the Egyptian treasury grew richer and richer.

Nubia, like Egypt a long, thin geographical unit focused on the River Nile, had effectively become Egypt's southernmost province. She was governed by an Egyptian viceroy and, although there remained a chain of Egyptian forts built during the more turbulent Middle Kingdom occupation, the main instrument for Egyptian control was now a series of fortified towns filled with Egyptian colonists who regulated economic and political life in the region. Her officials were a mixture of expatriate Egyptians and elite Nubians who had so adapted to the new regime that they took Egyptian names, enjoyed Egyptian lifestyles and were ultimately buried in Egyptian-style tombs. The people were encouraged to recognise the supremacy of the Egyptian gods although a few Nubian gods were in turn absorbed into the flexible Egyptian pantheon.

Such close control was not possible in the more disparate east, which had no unifying geography, religion, language or culture but had a history of semi-independent, fundamentally hostile fortified settlements dotted about the landscape. Recognising this fundamental difference, Tuthmosis never attempted to absorb his eastern territories into the wider Egypt. Instead he allowed local traditions to continue under his control – a control made obvious by the Egyptian garrisons – while developing a strategy of appointing local rulers to govern on his behalf. Lest they should falter in their loyalty, he sent the children of the local aristocracy back to Egypt where they would be educated in Egyptian ways. While foreign daughters effectively became hostages in the royal harem, sons were taught in the palace schools alongside Egypt's elite. After many years of indoctrination they returned home fully Egyptianised and totally loyal to pharaoh.

Year 22, fourth month of winter, day 25. His Majesty passed the fortress of Sile on his first victorious campaign to crush the people who were assaulting Egypt's borders.

Now Tuthmosis was on the move. Crossing the Sinai Peninsula he made first for the city of Gaza, loyal to Egypt since Ahmose's reign. From there he attacked Yehem, a fortified city occupied by a consortium of enemies headed by the king of Kadesh. Victory at Yehem allowed him to advance eastwards across the Carmel mountain range to the fortified city of Megiddo. We know all this, because Tuthmosis travelled with a band of military scribes who recorded his every move in a 'day book'. Later the glorious details of his triumphs, and the impressive booty collected, would be inscribed on the walls of the Karnak temple. They make stirring reading:

> His majesty conferred with his army... saying, 'That wretched foe of Kadesh has come and gone into Megiddo. He is there right now and has got the support of the chiefs of all the areas which used to be loyal to Egypt as far as Naharin... What is your opinion about this?' And they replied to his majesty, 'What will it be like to go on this path which keeps getting narrower? We have received reports that the enemy is waiting on the other side and that their numbers are constantly increasing. Won't our horses have to go in single file and our army and people likewise? Won't our vanguard have to fight while our rearguard is still standing here in Aruna unable to fight. There are two other paths here. One of them is ideal – it comes out at Taanach. The other goes north of Djefti – we would end up north of Megiddo. Our lord should go on whichever of these seems best, but do not make us march along that difficult path.'

In a display of tactical brilliance, and contrary to the advice given by his over-cautious, risk-averse generals, Tuthmosis decided to avoid the two long, relatively easy routes to Megiddo, leading his troops instead in single file along a narrow, winding mountain pass. This daring move allowed him to creep up on his unsuspecting enemy who had camped outside the city walls.

The surprise was everything which Tuthmosis could have hoped. As dawn broke over the mountains, the king of Kadesh and his rebellious followers could hardly believe their eyes. The sun was rising, illuminating the high ground which bristled with the flashing armour, the chariots and weapons of a massive and impeccably prepared Egyptian army. At the head of his troops stood pharaoh himself. He was an awesome sight:

> ... in his electrum chariot, dressed in his battle array, strong-armed like Horus the lord who achieves things, like Montu of Thebes, his father Amen strengthening his arms. The southern wing of his majesty's army was at the southern hill of Kina and the northern wing was north-west of Megiddo. And his majesty was in the middle. Amen was protecting his body, the blood-lust and strength of Seth were flowing through his limbs.

The Egyptian army divided into two wings, and swooped. The battle was easily won, but then things started to go wrong. Tuthmosis temporarily lost control of his men. Contrary to orders, the jubilant Egyptians paused to loot the abandoned enemy camps, and to cut the hands from the dead so that they might be counted. As the Egyptian army was otherwise occu-pied, the city gates were shut fast. They would not be opened for anyone and the enemy troops now trapped outside the city wall had to abandon their chariots and flee. Tuthmosis watched in disbelief as princes and generals were rescued with knotted cloth: 'and sheets were lowered down to lift them up into the town'. The Egyptians were notoriously bad at dealing with sieges (we have already seen Ahmose spend an astonishing three years trying to capture the Hyksos outpost of Sharuhen), but Tuthmosis knew that all he had to do was to build a stockade around the city and then sit tight and wait. Seven long months later, hungry Megiddo surrendered.

Megiddo had been a wealthy, sophisticated city, and Tuthmosis reaped a vast reward. A slow-moving caravan now wound its way back to Memphis, burdened with chariots, armour, weaponry, gold, goods, livestock and, of course, the unfortunate prisoners-of-war, both soldiers and civilians, men, women and children, now destined to live their lives as Egyptian slaves. The king of Kadesh, severely humiliated, escaped the debacle; his allies were captured and forced to swear an oath of loyalty to Egypt.

This was indeed a famous victory; an epic battle which would linger in the folk memory for centuries. Over a millennium later, when the writer of the Biblical Book of Revelation spoke of the last battle of doomsday, he would set it here, at Megiddo:

And he gathered them together in a place called in the Hebrew tongue Armageddon.

*Revelation 16: 16.*

Tuthmosis had developed a taste for victory and the spoils of war. He would not now be content until he had total control of the Near East. In Year 29 he captured the Tunip-controlled coastal towns of Ullaza and Ardata before, in Year 30, attacking Kadesh herself. Once again the king of Kadesh experienced humiliation at Egyptian hands, but the fortified city, protected by the curve of the River Orontes, survived substantially intact to fight other battles. Finally Tuthmosis turned his attention towards his arch rival Mitanni. There was to be a direct confrontation.

Year 33 saw the Egyptian army sailing to the friendly Lebanese port of Byblos. Here the army struck camp and waited as the carpenters of Byblos — making good use of the world-famous Lebanese wood — built a series of flat-pack boats.

These were to be loaded in pieces on to carts, and trundled along behind the troops as they made their way over the mountains, along the Orontes valley and past the subdued Kadesh and Tunip. Aleppo, occupied by the king of Mitanni, was the target. Here Tuthmosis enjoyed three fierce, wholly satisfactory confrontations. His enemy retreated in disarray, and Tuthmosis soon found himself standing on the west bank of the River Euphrates at Carchemish, facing the Mitannian army who now occupied the east bank.

The Mitannians had naturally commandeered or scuppered all the available boats; it should have been impossible to follow them across the river and the Mitannians, believing themselves to be totally safe, lowered their guard. Tuthmosis, however, had had the foresight to bring boats with him. Assembling his prefabricated vessels, he crossed the Euphrates and continued his rout, seizing property and burning enemy towns as he went. The Mitannian high command, fleeing before the Egyptians, were forced to hide ignominiously in caves. It was another famous victory. Tuthmosis erected a celebratory stela alongside that of his grandfather, and paused on the long march home to enjoy an elephant hunt in Syria.

> His southern frontier is to the horns of the earth, to the southern limit of the land. His northern to the marshes of Asia, to the supporting pillars of heaven.
>
> *Gebel Barkal Boundary Stela*

Tuthmosis now ruled over an empire whose borders, marked by boundary stelae, stretched from Gebel Barkal beyond the Third Cataract in Nubia to the banks of the River Euphrates in Syria, and whose sphere of influence spread much further afield. The

might of the Egyptian army was universally feared; Egypt was
the ancient world superpower. Tuthmosis found himself inun-
dated by gifts from 'brother kings'; the monarchs of Babylon,
Assyria and Hatti (the Hittite capital) who prudently wished to
be his friend. Meanwhile tribute and taxes were donated by the
lesser states who wished to earn pharaoh's protection. Mitanni
was not totally vanquished, and was soon to re-emerge as an
important power-base, but she was temporarily subdued and
very wary of Egypt.

Back in Egypt Tuthmosis was rich enough to attempt to
outbuild Hatshepsut. Building sites sprang up all along the
Nile, in Nubia, Thebes, Middle Egypt, Heliopolis, Memphis
and the Nile Delta. Amen, in particular, as the inspiration
behind Tuthmosis' victories, benefited from Egypt's hard-won
wealth. The Karnak temple experienced extensive remodelling
which was to see the removal of the limestone chapels built by
Amenhotep I and their replacement by sandstone shrines. There
were two new gateways and a new temple dedicated to Ptah.
Eventually, in Year 42, the central area was decorated with the
*Annals*, the stirring story of Tuthmosis' eastern triumphs which
we have used in our reconstruction of his military campaigns.

Much of his Karnak building work was concerned with the
preparations for the celebration of the royal *heb-sed*, or thirty-
year jubilee. For Tuthmosis III had become the first New
Kingdom monarch legitimately entitled to such a celebration.
Thirty years on the throne was a remarkable achievement which
few would attain. Although Hatshepsut had celebrated a jubilee
her reign had lasted for no more than twenty-two years.
Tuthmosis, however, inheriting his throne as an infant and
counting from the start of his joint reign, was to rule Egypt for
an impressive 53 years, 10 months and 26 days.

The proclamation of a jubilee was a cause for nationwide celebrations – it was the clearest possible sign that the gods were happy with their pharaoh, and that *maat* was flourishing in Egypt. The *heb-sed*, an ancient ceremony of regeneration, had been celebrated in Memphis since the days of the first kings of the unified Egypt. Originally it was a public ritual designed to reinforce the king's powers after each successive thirty years on the throne; the ageing king would prove his continuing fitness to rule by performing a gruelling series of tasks including a race around a ritual arena. By the New Kingdom the *sed*-festival had evolved into a religious ceremony rather than a display of physical strength. It would now be celebrated after the first thirty years of rule and then every three or four years until the death of the king.

Workmen were also busy across the river on the Theban west bank. Medinet Habu benefited from a new temple dedicated to Amen and a new mortuary temple dedicated to the cult of Tuthmosis II. The king's own mortuary temple, Djeser-Akhet (Holy Horizon), was under construction at Deir el-Bahari, directly to the south of Hatshepsut's mortuary temple, Djeser-Djeseru. Djeser-Akhet, today little more than a ruin, was similar in plan to Djeser-Djeseru and, as it was built on higher ground, was designed to dominate Hatshepsut's monument.

Hidden in the Valley of the Kings, work on Tuthmosis' own tomb (KV 34) was well under way. Meanwhile, in KV 20, Hatshepsut now rested alone. Tuthmosis I had been taken from his daughter's side and transferred to a new tomb (KV 38); the lid of his empty sarcophagus had been left propped against the wall of KV 20, where Howard Carter was to find it over three thousand years later. Both Tuthmosis III and Hatshepsut were eager to stress their relationship with Tuthmosis I while glossing over their relationship with the short-lived Tuthmosis II; proof, if proof is needed, of the high regard which all the Tuthmoside rulers had for their illustrious forebear. Tuthmosis III occasionally took this to extremes by claiming to be the son, rather than the grandson, of Tuthmosis I: a claim which was to cause intense confusion to modern Egyptologists.

Towards the end of Tuthmosis' solo reign Djeser-Djeseru, Hatshepsut's mortuary temple, once again resonated with the sound of hammer and chisel. The monument was covered in scaffolding; there were workmen everywhere. Now, however, the royal masons were engaged in destruction rather than creation. An attempt was being made to remove all evidence of Hatshepsut's reign from her monuments. This was a very personal attack. Her name was to be hacked very precisely from her temple walls, her carved and painted image was to be carefully erased – often leaving a very obvious gap in the middle of a scene – and her statues and sphinxes were to be torn down, smashed or defaced, and discarded. Some statues, the more public ones, were undoubtedly recarved into the image of the reigning king. At Karnak even Hatshepsut's obelisks – far too large to move – were to be walled up so that they were hidden from view. The female pharaoh would effectively vanish from the history of Egypt.

This was a very serious matter. Not because it falsified history – as the living representative of the long line of past pharaohs, Tuthmosis III was fully entitled to rewrite his own and his country's past – but because it threatened to deny Hatshepsut the chance of eternal life. The elimination of Hatshepsut's name and image was a direct assault upon her spirit.

Since the beginning of the dynastic age the Egyptians had believed that it was possible for the spirit to live beyond death;

this would happen, however, only if some trace of the deceased remained on earth. Ideally the body should survive to house the spirit, but it was also possible to live on through the preservation of an image, a name or even a memory. If all evidence of a dead person was lost the spirit too would die and there would come the much dreaded 'Second Death': total, irredeemable, endless obliteration.

Was Tuthmosis truly intending to condemn his co-regent to eternal oblivion? Or was he simply intending to tidy up the history of his own lengthy reign, eliminating all evidence of his period as a junior king and demoting Hatshepsut to her more acceptable female roles of king's wife and, following the precedent of Ahhotep and Ahmose Nefertari, queen regent?

For a long time archaeologists – posing as amateur psychologists – believed that they knew the answer. Tuthmosis, they argued, must have hated the stepmother who for over twenty years had denied him his birthright. Publicly humiliated and seething with resentment, Tuthmosis had been forced to watch, impotent, as the usurper enjoyed a glorious, lengthy reign. Who could condemn the new king for indulging in one vindictive, cathartic act of violence against Hatshepsut? However, we now know that this may be too simple an answer.

Recent analysis of the architecture of the Karnak temple has shown that the attack on Hatshepsut's memory, far from being Tuthmosis' top priority, probably did not start until relatively late in his reign. The Karnak temple was Tuthmosis' most prominent monument; here, if nowhere else, we should expect to find the royal commands being carried out promptly and efficiently. The hall of annals, whose walls tell the glorious tale of Tuthmosis' eastern triumphs, could not possibly have been decorated before Year 42; the year when these triumphs occurred. However, the hall concealed a few inscriptions and illustrations relating to Hatshepsut which should, had the attack on her name and image started at the beginning of Tuthmosis' solo reign (Year 22 or 23), not have been there.

Other examples of 'desecration' at Karnak may turn out to be nothing of the sort. The dismantling of Hatshepsut's inconveniently sited Chapelle Rouge, for example, should probably be seen as a part of the impersonal remodelling of the temple precincts rather than as a persecution of Hatshepsut's memory. As we have already seen, this rather drastic type of 'restoration' occurred with relative frequency at Karnak, and Tuthmosis was already guilty of destroying chapels built by Amenhotep I. Even the walling up of the obelisks may simply have been an attempt to incorporate them into Tuthmosis' new plan rather than a rather pointless attempt to hide them.

At the same time, the thoroughness of the attack on Hatshepsut must be questioned. The Deir el-Bahari temple underwent the most thorough purge, yet even here it was still possible to read some of the 'erased' inscriptions. Hatshepsut's name was preserved at Armant, on some of the blocks of the Chapelle Rouge, at the Speos Artemidos and in her tomb (KV 20) where the workmen who removed Tuthmosis I made no attempt to deface Hatshepsut's own inscribed sarcophagus.

This evidence suggests that we are looking at a rather haphazard, incomplete attack on Hatshepsut's name and image conducted towards the end rather than the beginning of Tuthmosis' lengthy reign. This fits badly with the idea of Tuthmosis as a man driven to instant destruction by a silent hatred nurtured for over twenty years. In any case, this 'anger theory' does not sit well with what we know of either Hatshepsut or Tuthmosis. It is clear that Hatshepsut herself did not perceive Tuthmosis as an immediate threat; she had ample opportunity to remove him from the succession and yet, rather than kill her infant co-regent, she actually encouraged him to train as a soldier. Similarly, Tuthmosis was no shy and retiring Cinderella-like character dominated by a forceful step-mother; he came to the throne with enough vigour and determination to challenge and defeat the ruler of Kadesh.

What evidence we have – and we must always remember that this evidence is almost certainly biased towards its author – suggests that both Tuthmosis and Hatshepsut were more or less happy with their joint rule. If Tuthmosis could have altered anything, he would perhaps have wished that his co-regent did not enjoy such an unexpectedly long life. If this is the case, the incomplete 'attack' on Hatshepsut's monuments is best inter-preted as an impersonal attempt, as Tuthmosis neared death, to rewrite history by removing the unnecessary and possibly even *maat*-less period of double rule and so claiming all of Hatshepsut's works and triumphs as his own.

Whatever Tuthmosis' motives, the results were as we might expect. Hatshepsut's name was excluded from the king list preserved in the temples of Abydos and Sakkara, so that the revised succession passed from Tuthmosis I to Tuthmosis II and then Tuthmosis III. Similarly, she was to be omitted from the celebration of the festival of Min shown on the wall of the Ramesseum. Thus Hatshepsut effectively joined the list of queens who ruled Egypt on behalf of infant pharaohs, but whose work was preserved in folk memory rather than official records. Manetho, writing his history of the kings of Egypt in approximately 300BC, made use of this memory to include a female pharaoh as the fifth king of the 18th Dynasty.

By Tuthmosis' own account he was the ideal pharaoh. Not

only was he a brave warrior in the mould of Ahmose, he was a scholar whose wide-ranging interests included botany, religion and history. His portraits show him to be fit, handsome and, at the beginning of his reign, virtually indistinguishable from Hatshepsut; both were depicted with the distinctive Tuthmoside facial features, also seen in Tuthmosis I, which included a long nose and a wide mouth pulled over prominent front teeth. Many members of the 18th Dynasty royal family were burdened with buck teeth. By the end of his reign he had developed a more individual appearance with a heavier, more muscular upper body.

Fortunately, thanks to Egypt's unique rituals of death, we are able to compare the idealised images devised by the royal artists with Tuthmosis' actual remains. Since his death, Tuthmosis has had a disturbed history. Stripped of his bandages and robbed in antiquity, rewrapped and stored in a royal cache for centuries, his mummy was rediscovered and plundered by modern tomb robbers in 1871, unwrapped and examined by Emile Brugsch in Cairo Museum 1881, rebandaged, and reopened by Gaston Maspero in 1886.

Beneath its neat bandages the mummy had suffered badly at the hands of the tomb robbers and 'restorers'. The head, hands, feet and limbs were detached and the undertakers who rescued the desecrated corpse had found it necessary to include four wooden splints as stiffening within the linen bandages. The king's face was, however, undamaged, and Tuthmosis emerged from his wrappings a relatively short man (5ft tall; just over 1.5 m) whose stature has led to repeated comparisons with the equally short French emperor Napoleon Bonaparte. Tuthmosis, in his fifties when he died, was almost completely bald, with a low forehead, narrow face, delicate ears and, of course, the family buck teeth.

Today the Egyptian authorities impose strict controls on the treatment of their mummies, and destructive investigative techniques are totally forbidden. The most recent study conducted on the body of Tuthmosis III involved the extraction of a minute sample of loose tissue suitable for DNA analysis. This sample, taken by a team from Brigham Young University, Utah, has been used to prove Tuthmosis' blood relationship to the rest of the 18th Dynasty royal family. As Tuthmosis has now been sealed in a state-of-the-art nitrogen case, designed to protect him from further decay, it is unlikely that he will be subjected to further scientific investigation in the near future.

Tuthmosis had died after a reign of nearly 54 years. His son, Amenhotep, buried his father in the Valley of the Kings and assumed the Horus Throne of Egypt. The new Amenhotep II inherited a generous legacy. In just under a century, a dynasty of ambitious Theban rulers had transformed Egypt from a struggling kingdom into an imperial power.

# CHAPTER 6

············································

# The Soldier:
# Most Valiant of Men

Then I sent a strong unit of Medjay troops ahead, but
held myself back, so that we cut off Teti, son of Apophis,
inside Nefrusy. I did not let him get away. And I also
trapped the Asiatics who were overrunning Egypt, as he
had turned Nefrusy into a swarming nest of Asiatics. I
spent the night in my ship, satisfied. And when the next
day dawned I swooped down on him like a falcon. By
breakfast time, I had already defeated him. I demolished
his stronghold, killed his men and made his women come
down to the riverbank. My soldiers were like lions after a
kill, as they carried off slaves and cattle, wine, fat and
honey. They revelled in dividing up the loot.

*Kamose defeats the Hyksos*

The Egyptian army was, by the end of Tuthmosis' reign,
the most efficient — and the most feared — fighting
machine in the Ancient World. This had not always
been the case.

The united Egypt had been born out of internal warfare and
strife. In 3000BC the southern warrior king Narmer had
marched northwards to conquer the Delta lands and consolidate

his country. This was to become a repetitive pattern. A thousand years later southern kings were again moving northwards, ending the civil unrest of the First Intermediate Period and inaugurating the peaceful Middle Kingdom. Finally, as we have just seen, the end of the disrupted Second Intermediate Period witnessed the Theban Ahmose marching northwards to expel the Hyksos and reunite Upper and Lower Egypt in 1550BC.

The propaganda of the successful warrior was important from the very earliest of times. Our first image of an Egyptian king is found on the 'Narmer palette' a pre-dynastic carved stone tablet now displayed in Cairo Museum. Here we can see Narmer about to kill a representative enemy. Pharaoh, impassive beneath the white crown of Upper (southern) Egypt, raises a club in his right hand. The enemy grovels ignominiously at his feet and, apparently resigned to his fate, prepares to have his skull smashed. On the reverse of the palette we see Narmer wearing the red crown of Lower Egypt as he reviews rows of decapitated men; presumably his defeated enemies. We can therefore date this ancient piece to a time when Narmer was entitled to wear both the white and the red crowns; the very dawn of the unified land.

This potent image of the king personally executing an enemy, known to Egyptologists as a 'smiting scene', was to persist in various forms for some three millennia. The details might vary: pharaoh might use a club, a scimitar or a sword to perform his grisly task, and the enemy might be a stereotypical Nubian, Libyan or Asiatic, or even be an unidentified foreigner. But even after five thousand years the meaning of the scene remains crystal clear. Pharaoh – the living representative of *maat*, Egypt and her gods – will always triumph over his *maat*-less, non-Egyptian, worthless enemy. In the New Kingdom, with its acres of stone temple walls, this set-piece image was joined by larger scenes showing pharaoh victorious in battle. Now the king, appearing at a far larger scale than his fellow soldiers, rides in his chariot and tramples his miniature fleeing foes. Even those who, as far as we know, never set foot on a battlefield were keen to exploit the symbolism of the warrior pharaoh.

It therefore seems very curious — given this history of civil war and bloodshed, this centuries-long identification of specific foreigners as enemies, and the constant emphasis on the military supremacy of the Egyptian king — to find that soldiers played a very low-key, almost negligible role in Old and, to a lesser extent, Middle Kingdom life. Indeed, Egypt did not develop a fully professional army until the early New Kingdom.

Strongly feudal, Old Kingdom Egypt had been served by a series of local, privately controlled armies plus a haphazard system of national draft. While pharaoh's immediate interests were protected by his own company of professional body-guards, the highly influential provincial governors maintained their own troops whose primary loyalty was to their region and to the governor who paid them rather than to their country. Pharaoh could commandeer these private troops as and when needed. If there was ever a need for a larger force — to defend Egypt's interests in Nubia, perhaps, or to protect the workers who laboured in the mines and quarries — unskilled men would be called up under the *corvée* system of compulsory labour. Unsurprisingly, the army had little social prestige and few upper-class men chose to make their careers in the military. Anyone who was anyone at this time trained as a scribe and then served their king either as a priest or a bureaucrat.

When His Majesty fought against the Asiatic Sand Dwellers he made an army of many tens of thousands of men from all of Upper Egypt ... His majesty put me at the head of the army ...

*From the Old Kingdom autobiography of the courtier Weni*

This flexible system must have been effective. Throughout the Old Kingdom Egypt's borders remained secure, and there was even military expansion in the south. However, it was unwieldy, unreliable and potentially dangerous. The local governors were not always the most loyal of subjects; it was unwise to allow them too much power.

The more outward-looking Middle Kingdom pharaohs, intent on subduing Nubia and dreaming of eastern expansion, were interested in developing a more efficient military machine. As the provincial governors were slowly but surely stripped of their hereditary powers they lost their private armies; now pharaoh alone controlled Egypt's troops. At the same time the increasing number of foreign campaigns, and the establishment of a chain of Egyptian forts in Nubia, called for the services of a large number of full-time soldiers. More permanent soldiers in turn called for a more structured system of command. Time was, however, running out and the Middle Kingdom collapsed before this new-style army could be fully developed.

New Kingdom Egypt emerged fully integrated into the turbulent near eastern Late Bronze Age world. Her kings, haunted by the memory of recent foreign rule, well understood the need for reliable, well-trained soldiers who could defend their land against potential invaders. Indeed, their new imperialistic ambitions hinged on the abilities of the revamped Egyptian army to dominate the Near East. The army now had the seal of royal approval. Pharaoh had transformed himself into an invincible warrior-king and the humble soldier had become a respected member of the community.

Suddenly it was acceptable – even desirable – to enlist. For the upper classes, fighting alongside the king was a sensible, rewarding career move; one which would generally be followed by a more relaxing stint in the priesthood or the civil service. Meanwhile the ambitious but uneducated, those who could not become scribes, were for the first time offered a viable alternative to following their father's trade or profession. It was perhaps inevitable, given Egypt's traditions, that the more important army positions would become hereditary, and we soon find son following father into the ranks.

The vast list of known New Kingdom army titles – over fifty ranks, ranging alphabetically from adjutant and assault officer to standard-bearer and valiant man – gives some inkling of the complexity and sophistication of the military machine at this time. Meanwhile the old system of conscription had not been entirely abandoned. Although there was now a permanent standing army, there was also a reserve list of trained men which would be called up and armed at times of national emergency.

The king, as we would expect, remained nominal head of the whole army; he, assisted by an experienced war-cabinet, would make all the tactical decisions and to him would go the credit for all of Egypt's glorious victories. Both Kamose and Tuthmosis III make this aspect of their role clear when, in their inscriptions, they tell us how they override the cautious advice of their ministers and lead their troops to glorious victories at Avaris and Megiddo respectively. This theme of the king being proved an expert tactician is one that was to be adopted by subsequent kings; in ancient Egypt, pharaoh always felt free to 'borrow' his predecessors' achievements.

Immediately below the king came the commander-in-chief, often the heir to the throne. The troops were split into a northern and southern corps; within each corps there were divisions of some five thousand men, named after regional gods. The divisions were further broken down into companies (250 men; 5 platoons), platoons (50 men; 5 squads) and finally squads (10 men). Throughout the New Kingdom the army consistently betrayed its bureaucratic origins, with a great deal of attention being paid to — some might even say wasted on — managerial rather than combat duties. The correct provision of rations, weapons, clothing and furniture, the measuring of routes, registration of troops and construction of duty rotas were never considered unimportant.

For many centuries Egypt's soldiers had battled with relatively primitive weapons: simple bows and arrows, copper-headed battle-axes, flint or copper-tipped spears and clubs or maces. They wore no helmet and no armour, but fought bare-chested in a short kilt, relying on the protection of a cumbersome, rectangular cowhide shield. This was all very well when fighting the Nubians whose weapons were equally primitive. Egypt's eastern enemies, however, were far better equipped. Without the new technology introduced by the Hyksos during the Second Intermediate Period, Egypt would have struggled to build her empire. The Theban kings observed, learned and copied. Soon the Egyptian army was fighting with the most technologically up-to-date weapons in the world.

The unwieldy shields were quickly replaced by shorter, lighter versions while the old-fashioned self- or long-bow gave way to the more efficient composite bow, a bow with twice the effective range of its predecessor. There was a new-style metal dagger which eventually evolved into a short sword, and body armour made from small bronze leaves riveted on to jackets. While the majority of his troops remained bare-headed, the king himself started to wear a distinctive leather helmet known today as the blue crown. Thus, he would always remain obvious in the confusion of the battlefield. Pharaoh, of course, showed consummate skill in handling the new weapons:

> When His Majesty was still a young prince he adored horses and delighted in them ... the King's son was put in charge of the horses of the royal stable ... He, above all, understood the management of the chariot and its horses ... His Majesty rode in his chariot ... he grasped his bow and four arrows and [shooting at the targets] his arrows emerged from the back of the first as he aimed at the next. It was a remarkable feat, one never before seen ...
>
> *From the Giza stela of Amenhotep II*

Amenhotep II was, in his own opinion, one of Egypt's greatest sportsmen. Not only was he a champion archer and a master horseman, he also rowed and hunted with an amazing degree of success. His presentation of himself as an all-round sporting hero is one which subsequent pharaohs were to copy. In times of relative peace it seems that sporting and hunting triumphs went some way towards compensating for a shortage of battlefield glories. More fortunate kings were able to prove their worth in battle:

> Then His Majesty prevailed over them at the head of his army. And when they saw that his majesty was defeating

them, they started fleeing headlong towards Megiddo, with fear written all over their faces. They even abandoned their horses and their golden and silver chariots . . .

*Annals of Tuthmosis III*

The horse, and the horse-drawn chariot, had been introduced to Egypt by the Hyksos. Egypt, a country more used to dealing with boats than horses, would never develop a cavalry of horse-riding soldiers. Chariots, however, were quickly recognised as an important weapon. They were to play an increasingly significant role in New Kingdom military life so that while Tuthmosis III fought at Megiddo with a large complement of foot soldiers supported by a few chariots driven by the army elite, two centuries later Ramesses II fought at Kadesh with an army now more formally divided between infantry and chariotry.

At Megiddo, Tuthmosis' charioteers faced an unusual threat. The wily king of Kadesh, part of the enemy alliance, had developed a cunning plan. He would release a mare in heat to disturb the Egyptian stallions and cause havoc among the Egyptian troops. The autobiography of the foot-soldier Ahmose-Mahu, recorded on the wall of his Theban tomb, tells how disaster was narrowly averted: 'I ran after her on foot, carrying my dagger, and I killed her and cut off her tail . . .' Tuthmosis, of course, went on to win the battle and returned home with an impressive 892 captured enemy chariots.

Then His Majesty set off at a gallop, charging right into the doomed Hittite troops. He was utterly alone – no one else was with him. Then His Majesty turned and looked over his shoulder and realised that 2,500 chariots had trapped him and blocked his escape route – all the

doomed Hittite chariot drivers . . . And there were three of
them to a chariot, all working together as a unit. But I
[Ramesses II] had no officer with me, no chariot driver, no
warrior and no shield bearer. My infantry and chariotry
had fled rather than fight them. Not one of them stayed
to fight.

*The Kadesh Poem of Ramesses II*

Ramesses' chariots would find themselves pitted directly against
the Hittite charioteers. This was unusual. Egypt's two-wheeled
chariots should not be viewed as the ancient equivalent of our
armoured tanks, and all thoughts of the chariot race in *Ben Hur*
should be dismissed. At first sight the Egyptian chariots
appeared impressive – easily fulfilling their function of striking
fear into the hearts of those daring to challenge pharaoh's might
– but they had severe practical limitations, being light and
ill-protected. Rather than being used to charge the enemy – an
enemy whose long spears and arrows might well have proved
devastatingly effective against the chariot, its horse and its crew
– chariots served as mobile platforms used for launching
weapons. Their agility also made them valuable for chasing and
dispersing fleeing foot soldiers.

Each chariot was manned by a driver who controlled the two
horses and a fighter equipped with a bow or, more unusually, a
lance. These soldiers, the 'Young Heroes' recruited from the
nobility, were quickly recognised as the glamorous army elite –
perhaps the ancient equivalent of our wartime fighter pilots.
Pharaoh, naturally, fought in a chariot and, whatever the realities
of the battlefield, New Kingdom temple walls display a series of
kings standing tall, unafraid and alone in their chariots amid the
heat and dust of battle.

The Egyptians, as we might expect from a people whose domestic life was centred on the River Nile, were extremely adept at handling small boats. They were never, however, comfortable with long sea voyages; Punt was about as far as the Egyptians were prepared to sail. Although, as we have seen from the military exploits of Tuthmosis III, the army was happy to employ boats, there was no attempt to develop a separate, specialised navy. The Egyptian marines, although occasionally asked to repel sea-borne invaders and pirates, were more often used to transport troops and equipment for relatively short distances. Ahmose son of Ibana, the ubiquitous battlefield companion of Ahmose, Amenhotep I and Tuthmosis I, had started his army career in such a ship:

> I spent my formative years in the town of El-Kab, because my father fought for the late king Sekenenre – his name was Baba, son of [the lady] Ra-Inet. During the reign of King Ahmose, I joined up myself to replace him on the warship 'Wild Bull'. I was still only a child at the time – I was unmarried and slept alone in a hammock. Later, after I had started a family, I was drafted on to the warship 'Northerner' because of my consistent bravery. It was my job to follow the king on foot, walking in the tracks made by his chariot.

Egypt's geography offered her a natural protection which her more exposed Near Eastern neighbours must have envied. The cataracts to the south, the deserts to the east and west and the Mediterranean Sea to the north each provided a degree of security against invasion by those attracted by Egypt's affluence. These natural boundaries were not now considered enough and, from the Middle Kingdom onwards, forts were built to protect both the southern boundary and the vulnerable Nile Delta. By the reign of Tuthmosis III the southern border was academic; as we have already seen, Nubia had effectively been annexed and was now a part of southern Egypt. However, the Delta defences were to be maintained and strengthened throughout the New Kingdom: memory of the unfortunate Hyksos episode was still very strong.

Along the north-eastern Delta ran the Walls of the Prince: a string of forts, probably sited one day's march apart, established during the Middle Kingdom reign of Amenemhat I. A similar system of forts protected the Way of Horus, the desert road which crossed the Sinai peninsula giving access to the Levant. Unfortunately the Walls of the Prince forts are now lost, although contemporary writings tell us that they provided protection and acted as trading posts for those passing on legitimate business between Canaan and Egypt. Sile, the most westerly fort, was the customs office: here everyone crossing the border was required to register with the authorities, and undesirables were invariably turned away.

By the 19th Dynasty the north-western Delta frontier was also well protected. Today the ruins of three Ramesside forts are known to lie to the west of Alexandria, with a further two in the western Delta at Tell Abqa'in and Kom el-Hisn. These probably represent the remains of a more substantial network of forts stretching from ancient Memphis to the modern Libyan border. These forts guarded against possible Libyan incursions while serving as landmarks for boats crossing the Mediterranean Sea from Crete to Egypt. The most westerly of these forts, Zawiyet Umm el-Rakham, is currently being excavated by a team from Liverpool University, England, under the direction of

Dr Steven Snape. El-Rakham lies at the very edge of the Egyptian empire. The extraordinary size of the fort (almost 20,000 square metres in area) and its massive thick mud-brick wall indicates that the Libyans were now perceived as a serious threat to national security.

According to its excavator, a posting to Zawiyet Umm el-Rakham was something to be dreaded:

Being posted to Zawiyet Umm el-Rakham, 300 km to the west of the Nile Delta, must have seemed like being sent beyond the edge of the world. Placed on a narrow sliver of land, between the hostile desert to the south and the dangerous sea to the north, with only terrifying Libyan nomads for company, the garrison at Zawiyet Umm el-Rakham must have felt very alone indeed.

Foreign postings, to the garrisons in Nubia and the Near East, were never going to be appreciated. It was a basic tenet of state propaganda that Egypt, the gods' own country, had no equal. Like all true Egyptians, the soldiers instinctively knew that home is best, and life outside the predictable security of the Nile Valley – indeed, in many cases, life outside the home town – was seen as a challenge to be overcome rather than an opportunity to be enjoyed:

Let me tell you the woes of the soldier ... He is called up to go to Syria. He is not permitted to rest. There are no clothes and no sandals. The weapons of war are assembled at Sile. He has to march uphill, through the mountains. He only drinks water every third day, and even then it is tainted and smells of salt. His body is racked with sickness. The enemy comes and surrounds him with weapons, and life ebbs away from him... His own wife and children are back home in the village. He dies and does not reach it...

*The New Kingdom satirical Papyrus Anastasi (also known as Papyrus Lansing)*

In reality, most foreign postings were not too bad. Nubia was so thoroughly Egyptianised that the soldiers would have received all their home comforts, while many of the eastern fortresses were sited in sophisticated Levantine cities. However, a principal cause of concern, for the upper classes at least, was the possibility of dying away from home. While Egypt's lower classes were buried, unmummified, in simple pit graves dug in the desert sands, her elite viewed it as essential that their bodies received the prescribed funerary rituals. Death and burial in a foreign field might well mean forfeiting the chance of eternal life.

The vizier brought three youths, saying, 'Put them to be priests...' but they were seized and taken away to the north, it being said, 'They shall be infantrymen.'

*Papyrus Bologna 1094*

Some had chosen to be soldiers. Others had military life thrust upon them, being recruited under national call-up or on the field of battle. The army was generally happy to accept mercenaries even, on occasion, absorbing entire groups of defeated enemies. Whole contingents of Nubians now enlisted. The Sherden, once a notorious pirate gang who menaced the Delta coast, were eventually to be found fighting alongside Ramesses

II, still dressed in their distinctive horned helmets and brandishing straight swords, but now totally under Egyptian command.

The Medjay, too, were a good example of assimilation into the armed forces. Originally hostile nomads dwelling in the Nubian Eastern Desert, Medjay mercenaries fought alongside the Theban kings at the start of the New Kingdom. This led to the Medjay settling in the Nile Valley where they worked as private guards. As more and more native Egyptians chose to work alongside the Medjay, and as more and more intermarriages occurred, the term Medjay lost its original meaning. Soon the Medjay was the recognised name for Egypt's nearest equivalent to our own police force. Unlike our own force, however, the Medjay were employed to protect the interests of the state, not the individual.

> Come, I will tell you the woes of the foot soldier . . . He is brought as a child and is imprisoned in a barrack. A painful blow is given to his body, a glancing blow to his eye and a splitting blow to his brow. His wounded head splits open. He is flung down while he is beaten like a piece of papyrus . . .
>
> *Papyrus Anastasi III*

Raw recruits, many still boys, started army life in training camps where experienced officers taught the basics of drill and weaponry. Physical punishments were an accepted part of this training, but the trainee soldier was no worse off in this respect than many another apprentice as Egypt's mentors believed in regular beatings. Newly trained, equipped with staff, sandals, clothing and weapons, the fledgling soldiers set off on their first posting either to an Egyptian garrison or a foreign fort. This almost invariably involved a long and tiring walk.

The full Egyptian army on the move was a spectacular sight, one carefully calculated to strike fear into the hearts of rebellious locals. The army oozed confidence. Rows of disciplined troops marched in measured ranks, their colourful standards fluttering in the breeze. Plumed horses pulled gleaming chariots driven by the army elite. In a startling golden chariot pharaoh himself appeared, dressed in full armour and wearing his distinctive crown. Slowly but surely the army marched by, with the chariots travelling at the same, slow speed as the infantry and the support waggons. No sensible pharaoh would risk separating his forces as the two functioned together as one fighting machine.

The army cared for its men as well as it could; after all, fighting on foreign territory was a stressful business and success in battle was to a large extent dependent upon the health, morale and discipline of the troops. Good food was considered important. Within the fort the soldier could expect to receive a decent ration of grain augmented by local produce: bread, vegetables, fowl, beer and even wine. Out on the campaign trail, however, he had to carry his own ration of bread and water in his pack, supplementing this as he could along the march. Hunting and foraging were encouraged and, as we saw at Megiddo, looting was considered a perk of the job.

Life in the army was harsh but, by Egyptian terms, fair; it certainly compared well with life in the quarries or the mines and the potential rewards far outweighed the risks. Many upper class males took commissions for a brief period before transferring to high-ranking administrative posts. Those who persevered with army life, and who lived to become respected veterans, could expect a generous pension from their grateful monarch.

Ahmose son of Ibana was regularly rewarded for his valour; he eventually retired a relatively rich man, having received 'gold seven times in the presence of the entire land, and male and female slaves, and many fields'. Alongside the riches went enhanced social position. Ahmose was a man of relatively humble birth, yet he had worked alongside his pharaoh. His son and his grandson, benefiting from this royal connection, went on to become royal tutors. Even greater was the reward offered to the successful general Tuthmosis I (and later Horemheb and Ramesses I); in the New Kingdom it was by no means impossible that a soldier would become king of Egypt.

For those who could not stand army life, desertion offered the ultimate solution. Desertion, however, was a grave offence and, if the fleeing soldier managed to remain at large, he knew that his family would be punished in his absence. Escape meant exile from family and home; an exile which the Egyptians found hard to bear.

The tale of the Middle Kingdom courtier Sinhue makes obvious what every right-thinking Egyptian would have known. For no obvious reason Sinhue ran away from court following the assassination of the Pharaoh Amenemhat I when 'my senses were disturbed, my arms spread out and I trembled all over'. Sinhue lived as an exile among the Asiatics for many years, but longed to return home to die in the comfort of his home land. Eventually he appealed to pharaoh's mercy. Sinhue's story has a happy ending; forgiven by pharaoh, the sand of the desert was washed from his body, he was dressed in Egyptian clothes and provided with a house, garden and stone pyramid. The moral of the story is clear: without doubt, Egypt is the best place in the world.

# Thebes 1353BC:
# The Late 18th Dynasty

O living Aten, may you rise beautifully from the horizon. Life begins as soon as you rise in the east, after you have filled every land with your beauty. For you are beautiful and great, glinting high above the whole world. Your rays embrace the lands, to the limit of what you have made.

*The Great Hymn to the Aten*

The newly crowned Amenhotep IV was planning his country's future. His father's death had made Amenhotep the most influential man in the Mediterranean world. He had inherited an empire – the greatest empire ever known – whose unprecedented peace and prosperity offered boundless possibilities. With his beautiful consort, Nefertiti, by his side, and with a treasury filled with gold, Amenhotep seemed set for a glorious reign.

Amenhotep, however, was not a conventional pharaoh. His thoughts, his beliefs and even his appearance set him aside from other men. He had the vision, or the folly, to think the unthinkable and the power and wealth to implement his dreams. Under his chosen name, Akhenaten, Amenhotep IV was set to challenge the established order of *maat*, bringing Egypt and her empire from supremacy to the brink of disaster.

# CHAPTER 7

# Amenhotep III:
# The Golden Pharaoh

His majesty had this stela carved and erected in this
temple... following his return from his first victorious
campaign in eastern Syria, where he had killed all his
enemies and extended the borders of Egypt. His Majesty
approached his father Amen happily, after personally
clubbing to death the seven princes who had previously
ruled the land of Takhshi and hanging their corpses
head-down from the prow of his royal flagship... Six of
these corpses he hung from the city wall at Thebes, along
with their severed hands. The one remaining corpse he
transported south to Nubia, and hung it from the enclosure wall of Napata, so that his victories would be
remembered forever throughout the land of Nubia. He
has seized the southerners and crushed the northerners as
far as the ends of the earth, wherever the sun shines. He is
free to fix his borders where he chooses, because his father
Amen-Re has decreed that no one can oppose him...

*Amada Stela of Amenhotep II*

Egypt's empire, born out of insecurity and established by bloodshed, had been maintained through a well-judged mixture of fear and diplomacy.

Amenhotep II had determined to carry on where his father and co-regent, Tuthmosis III, had left off. He too would be a warrior pharaoh, a king physically capable of humbling foreigners and upholding *maat*. Amenhotep's reign, however, was destined to be very different in style from that of his immediate predecessors. Warfare was slowly giving way to peace and Egypt, an acknowledged military superpower, now had few enemies left to subdue.

Amenhotep the would-be soldier, a victim of his country's military success, was called to defend his empire just twice. Few dared to rebel openly against Amenhotep's might; those who did faced punishments of stark brutality designed to serve as a clear warning to others. Naturally, Amenhotep's campaigns were both successful. The awful fate of the rebellious prince of Takhshi was broadcast in Egypt and Nubia, the grim message reinforced by the presence of decomposing Syrian bodies swaying from the high temple walls.

Amenhotep's reign was essentially a tranquil one, a reign that used the taxes and tribute offered by the vassal states to good effect. There was monumental building at all the principal Egyptian and Nubian sites while Karnak, now purged of all obvious references to Hatshepsut, was made ready for Amenhotep's *heb-sed* celebrations with the erection of a splendid new festive pavilion. Here the carved decorations betrayed a developing interest in traditional sun cults and the northern falcon-headed deity Re-Herakhte who had once inspired the pyramid-building pharaohs of the Old Kingdom, but who had been forced into the shadows by Amen's rapid ascent.

Amen remained the most prominent New Kingdom god, his Karnak temple the world's greatest religious monument and his priesthood the richest Egyptian cult; but the more ancient deities were, with the king's help, slowly starting to challenge his supreme authority. At Giza Amenhotep built a temple dedicated to the sphinx, the human-headed lion which guarded the causeway to Khaefre's already ancient pyramid. The sphinx was now to be recognised, and revered, as a form of the sun god Re-Herakhte.

Unfortunately Amenhotep was not fated to reach his jubilee and his *heb-sed* pavilion was to be dismantled during the late 18th Dynasty reign of Horemheb. The king died after twenty-six solid years of rule when his throne passed to his son, Tuthmosis IV.

Amenhotep II was interred in a magnificent tomb (KV 35). Here he was to remain for over three thousand years. Although his burial was robbed in antiquity, when the king's mummy was desecrated by thieves searching for jewellery and amulets, the priests who converted KV 35 into a storehouse for rescued royal mummies were careful to replace the rebandaged Amenhotep II in his own stone sarcophagus. Thus Amenhotep became one of just two pharaohs to be discovered in modern times lying in his own tomb in the Valley of the Kings.

In 1898 Victor Loret rediscovered the forgotten tomb, its shattered funerary equipment and its curious assortment of royal bodies. Amenhotep II still lay in splendour in his sarcophagus; Tuthmosis IV, Amenhotep III, Seti II, Siptah and Ramesses IV–VI rested in labelled coffins stored in a walled-up side-room; three anonymous, coffinless mummies lay side by side in an open side-chamber. Most peculiar of all was the discovery, in the passageway leading to the burial chamber, of a blackened male body firmly glued to a wooden funerary boat. This unfortunate mummy, an as yet unidentified royal prince, had been attacked by thieves so soon after his funeral that the resins within and beneath his bandages had not yet set. Snatched from his coffin, stripped of his wrappings, amulets and jewellery and then carelessly dropped on the boat, he had been stuck for well over two thousand years.

The Egyptian government attempted to keep the tomb and its precious contents intact. However, it proved impossible to guard Amenhotep and all too soon the inevitable happened. The prince in the boat vanished and Amenhotep lay once again stripped of his bandages. It was left to Howard Carter, then Inspector General of the Monuments of Upper Egypt, to play detective and follow the trail of footprints leading away from the tomb. The footprints were proved to be those of the notorious tomb-robber Mohammed abd el-Rassul. Mohammed stood trial for theft but, in the teeth of the evidence, was acquitted. In 1931 Amenhotep was sent by train (first-class) to the security of Cairo Museum. Here he remains today; a well-preserved male of approximately fifty years of age at death, unusually tall, 1.8m (6 ft) and with greying brown hair.

The new pharaoh, Tuthmosis IV, knew that he had been lucky. As a younger prince he could never realistically have expected to become king. The gods, however, had made their own plans. One day, weary after a hard morning's hunting in the Giza desert, the young prince had sought refuge from the hot noonday sun. Lying in the cool shadow of the sand-covered sphinx, he fell quickly into a deep sleep. In a vivid dream a version of Re-Herakhte appeared before Tuthmosis. Speaking as his 'father', the god implored his son to restore the neglected sphinx. This Tuthmosis did, first employing labourers to clear away a small mountain of sand and then repairing the sphinx's broken paw and chest. Re-Herakhte, suitably grateful, rewarded his son by making him king of Egypt. This remarkable tale was carved on a magnificent 'dream stela' and set between the paws of the newly restored sphinx so that all might read it and marvel.

The truth behind this fantastic tale is, of course, difficult for us to assess. Why did the king need to cite an oracle to justify his accession? This was by no means a unique occurrence — Hatshepsut and Tuthmosis III had both made judicious use of the oracle — but we know that Tuthmosis had brothers. Is this a hint that there was a rival, possibly stronger claimant to the throne? One thing is clear. From this time on Tuthmosis regarded Re-Herakhte rather than Amen as his own personal patron.

Although a relatively young man, Tuthmosis was already married and enjoying the pleasurable amenities of the royal harem. Soon there were eight baby princes and princesses filling the royal nursery. The Great Royal Wife Nefertiry, however, played a relatively insignificant role in her husband's reign and it was his mother, the formidable Dowager Queen Tiaa, who was routinely depicted alongside the new king. It was Tiaa rather than the non-royal Nefertiry who now served as God's Wife of Amen. This was not unusual; Amenhotep II, too, had chosen to share his reign with his mother rather than his wife, and we are left wondering whether Hatshepsut's unconventional rule may have made subsequent kings wary of allowing their spouses too much independent power. Eventually Nefertiry disappears, presumably dead, and is replaced by Tuthmosis' sister Iaret.

Tuthmosis was to rule for a mere eight to ten years, dying at somewhere between twenty-five and forty years of age. This was long enough to campaign in Palestine, suppress a Nubian rebellion, contract a diplomatic marriage with a princess of Mitanni and raise an obelisk (an obelisk which had already been cut by his grandfather, Tuthmosis III) at the Karnak temple, but not long enough to make a profound impact on Egypt's landscape. Many of Tuthmosis' over-ambitious projects were eventually to be completed by his son.

Long-lived pharaohs spent many years excavating their tombs and gathering their grave goods together. Tuthmosis' preparations for death were incomplete. He had started two tombs; now the most impressive (WV 22) had to be abandoned and the Valley workforce had a mere seventy days, the period of embalming, to make the more humble KV 43 ready. Here, after an appropriate display of pomp and circumstance, Tuthmosis was buried alongside the two children, Prince Amenemhat and Princess Tentamen, who had pre-deceased him. Again, Valley security failed. Less than a century after the funeral, the tomb had been ransacked by the ruthless thieves; eventually Tuthmosis was rescued, rebandaged and stored for safety in his father's tomb. KV 43 was eventually excavated by Howard Carter who discovered, amid the smashed desolation, the stiff, stripped body of the young Prince Amenemhat standing propped against a wall.

His spindly body, recovered from the Amenhotep II cache, confirms that the unfortunate Tuthmosis may have suffered from a debilitating wasting disease. The anatomist Grafton Elliot Smith conducted a hasty post-mortem on the king in the early twentieth century. Writing in *The Royal Mummies*, his 1912 account of the autopsies performed on all the royal mummies housed in Cairo Museum, he reports his findings:

The body is that of an extremely emaciated man, 1.646m in height. It shows no sign of any ante-mortem injuries ... The skin is very dark and discoloured, so that it is not possible to form any accurate idea of its original colour ... The head has a very effeminate appearance. The face is long, narrow and oval, the chin being narrow, prominent and somewhat pointed. The forehead has a marked slope. The nose is small and straight, and narrow and aquiline in shape. The lips are thin ... Toutmosis [Tuthmosis] IV presents a striking resemblance to Amenothes [Amen-hotep] II, but the latter had a more virile appearance and was considerably older.

As the twelve-year-old Amenhotep III was crowned at Memphis, his mother, Mutemwia, a lesser wife of Tuthmosis IV, emerged from the seclusion of the harem to act as regent for her young son. Amenhotep had inherited the most secure throne in the Ancient World. The 18th Dynasty was now some two centuries old and the age of the warrior pharaoh had gone. Routine brutality was no longer necessary; all effective rebellion had ceased and there were no more wars to fight, no more pretenders to the throne. Egypt was at peace; rich, respected and ready to enjoy the magnificent fruits of empire.

The trader Hatshepsut, rather than the soldier Tuthmosis III, served as a role model for Amenhotep III. The new king was to be celebrated as a builder and a thinker rather than a warrior. Nevertheless, we should not underestimate Amen-hotep's willingness to defend his empire. He was not averse to taking punitive action in Palestine when needed, and he is known to have personally conducted two Nubian campaigns. The best recorded of these, in Year 5, ended with the victorious Amenhotep acquiring some 740 prisoners of war and 312 hands cut from the enemy dead. This victory was to be celebrated on stelae erected throughout Nubia, allowing Amenhotep to take his rightful place among the defenders of *maat*.

In peaceful times it was, however, far easier to prove bravery on the hunting field. In the absence of a foreign enemy the slain bull, or any slaughtered animal, could represent chaos tamed by *maat*. At the same time the bull symbolised royal strength and power, so that the death of a bull at pharaoh's hands served as symbolic confirmation of that pharaoh's fitness to rule. Like his grandfather before him, the young Amenhotep was a keen big game hunter, eager to tackle the bulls and lions which roamed wild in Egypt's deserts and marshland. His daring exploits were recorded for all to read, in this case on a scarab which was issued throughout the realm:

One of His Majesty's most amazing achievements. Word reached His Majesty that wild bulls had turned up in the desert around the Lake District [probably the Faiyum, but possibly the Delta plains]. That night His Majesty sailed north in the royal ship 'Rising in Truth'. He set out successfully and reached the Lake District safely at dawn [the next day]. Then his majesty mounted his chariot, followed by the whole of his army. The officers and privates of the whole army, every last one of them, and even the children tagging along were ordered to keep a look out for wild bulls. Then His Majesty ordered them to trap the bulls inside an enclosure fence and a ditch. He proceeded to hunt all of the bulls. Out of a total of 170 bulls, His Majesty bagged 56 in a single day. For the next four days he did nothing, so that his horses could recover. Then His Majesty mounted his chariot again. Total number of bulls which His majesty bagged this time – 40 bulls, making a grand total of 96 bulls.

This scarab is dated to Year 2, when the already-married king can have been no more than fifteen years old. However, as the scarab implies, the royal hunt was less dangerous than we might imagine. Egypt's animals were not expected to fight back; they were rounded up and penned before a hunt, providing the royal marksmen with the easiest possible 'wild' target.

Forced to lay down his sword, Amenhotep took up instead his pen (or rather, as he wrote in ink on papyrus rolls, his paintbrush and palette). Diplomacy was the lifeblood of the empire, and Amenhotep corresponded regularly both with his near equals, the 'brother' monarchs of Mitanni, Babylon, Assyria, Hatti, Arzawa (western Anatolia) and Alashiya (Cyprus) who controlled the Near East, and his inferiors, the vassals whose constant petitions kept the Egyptian foreign office busy. Foreigners were, of course, by definition inferior beings; but to his brother monarchs at least, Amenhotep was polite if not effusive.

At a time when tribes in northern Europe could neither read nor write, Amenhotep's messengers were carrying diplomatic letters for hundreds of miles by boat and horse. Written not in Egyptian but in Akkadian, the language of Babylonia which had become the international *lingua franca*, these letters united the ancient world. We would know nothing about these letters, however, were it not for a single chance discovery.

In 1887 a Middle Egyptian peasant woman was conducting a clandestine excavation at the ancient site of Amarna, looking for *sebbakh* – decayed ancient mud-brick which was valued not as an antiquity but as a fertiliser. As she dug downwards she came across a series of hard-baked clay bricks covered in lines of tiny marks. Curious, and hopeful that her find might prove valuable, she took the bricks home. Eventually she started to sell them on the illegal antiquities market.

The anonymous peasant woman had made one of the world's greatest archaeological discoveries. By inadvertently digging up the Amarna diplomatic archive, she had uncovered not bricks but copies of official correspondence written to and by the kings of Egypt on clay tablets. The tiny marks were the wedges of the cuneiform script used when writing Akkadian. Unfortunately, Egyptologists were fatally slow to appreciate the importance of her find. The tablets were initially dismissed as fakes, and by the time their true value was realised the collection had been split up, with many of the tablets lost or damaged. Today we have just over 350 tablets and tablet-fragments, whose dates stretch from the later part of the reign of Amenhotep III to Year 3 of Tutankhamen. From these we may reconstruct life at the courts of Amenhotep III and his son Akhenaten.

The letters reveal the extent to which gift exchange played an important role in dynastic diplomacy. Some 'gifts' were obligatory; Amenhotep expected his vassals to shower him with tax and tribute in exchange for his protection. Others were presents between near equals; the kings of Babylon and Mitanni sent extravagant offerings of clothing, chariots, horses, slaves and precious iron jewellery. Iron was a new metal, a real rarity, and the bracelets which now made their way to Egypt were greatly prized. In return the givers expected – and occasionally demanded – copious gifts of precious Egyptian gold. The newly crowned King Tushratta of Mitanni, for example, was not too proud to send what was essentially a lengthy, repetitive begging letter. After extensive greetings to his 'brother' and the extended royal family, and a reminder of the good relationship between the two courts during his father's reign, he continued in a less than subtle fashion:

> I asked my brother for a great deal of gold, saying 'May my brother give me more than he gave to my father and send it to me.' You sent my father vast quantities of gold. You sent him large gold jars and gold jugs ... May my brother send me great quantities of unworked gold, and also much more gold than he did to my father. For in my brother's country, gold is as plentiful as dirt ... May the gold that I ask for not become a cause of distress to my brother, and may my brother not cause me distress. May my brother send me large quantities of unworked gold ...
>
> *Amarna Letter 19*

Even allowing for the fact that pharaoh had occasionally to return the compliment, these incoming taxes, tribute and presents brought Egypt more, and far easier, wealth than the booty of any war. Among the most valuable gifts were royal women. Foreign brides arrived with magnificent dowries, bringing ties of kinship which bound the brother monarchs even closer together. Amenhotep set out to collect a wife from each of his fellow monarchs. The grasping Tushratta already had a sister and a daughter in Egypt. Soon there were so many foreign princesses housed in the royal harem that it proved difficult to keep track of them. King Kadeshman-Enlil of Babylon was driven to write inquiring about the whereabouts of a sister who appeared to have vanished without trace:

Now you are asking for my daughter as your bride, but my sister was given to you by my father and is there with you although no one has seen her and no one knows whether she is still alive or dead.

*Amarna Letter 1*

All kings were expected to offer a daughter to Amenhotep, this being the closest possible link between two monarchs. Thus, although Kadeshman-Enlil already had a sister in the Egyptian harem, a sister sent during his father's reign, Amenhotep now expected him to provide one of his own daughters to reinforce their personal bond. Kadeshman-Enlil, at first reluctant, eventually agreed:

As for the girl, my daughter, about whom you wrote to me concerning marriage. She has become a woman: she is ready. Just send a delegation to collect her...

*Amarna Letter 3*

Kadeshman-Enlil, however, as King of Babylon considered himself the equal of the king of Egypt. He expected a reciprocal bride. Amenhotep would have none of this:

When I wrote to you about the possibility of my marrying your daughter you wrote to me as follows: 'No daughter of a king of Egypt has ever been given to anyone.' Why not? You are a king and you can do what you like.

*Amarna Letter 4*

Although Kadeshman-Enlil urged Amenhotep to send him a princess – after all Amenhotep was a powerful king, and could presumably do as he liked – Amenhotep would not be swayed. He had no wish to see his position challenged by a grandson sired by a rival king. Kadeshman-Enlil was in no position to bargain. His final desperate plea for any woman whom he could pretend was an Egyptian princess – 'Send me a beautiful woman as if she was your daughter. Who will be able to say, "This is not the king's daughter?" ' – fell on deaf ears.

It seemed that Amenhotep could do no wrong. His Egypt was blessed with a series of bumper harvests, his storehouses were piled high with grain and his treasury was filled with Nubian gold. Amid this peace and prosperity, new ideas flourished. Egypt was no longer a conservative nation, she was eager for progress and change. Her people, adjusting to their new wealth and influenced by the relaxed cosmopolitan climate, abandoned their simple, dignified linen garments, adopting instead frivolously pleated diaphanous robes and elaborately curly wigs. Arts and literature flourished, and the palace workshops surpassed themselves in producing exquisite items in glass, pottery, faience and stone. To draw a parallel between late 18th Dynasty Egypt and swinging Sixties London may be a parallel too far, but the same excitement – the buzz of the new – seems to have infused both.

The traditional artistic approach now seemed old-fashioned and somehow out of touch with the new, vibrant Egypt. The royal artists, who had for so long followed conventions developed during the Old Kingdom, started to experiment with different styles so that the king that we see at the end of Amenhotep's long reign appears very different from the stereotypical pharaoh glimpsed at the beginning. Gone is the rigid adherence to convention; in its place is a more fluid, relaxed style and the emergence of a king who appears both informal and undisciplined. The intention is perhaps to show Amen-hotep as a free-spirited young man – a man transformed by his revivifying *heb-sed* – but many early Egyptologists, unaware of the complexities of Egyptian art, were deeply unimpressed by visions of Amenhotep in what they interpreted as relaxed, louche and even decadent poses. Some published the view that Amenhotep had entered into a premature senile decay brought about by sexual excess, and that the still-strong Queen Tiy was now effectively ruling the country on her husband's behalf. There is, however, no archaeological or textual evidence to support such an assumption.

Ever since the days of Tuthmosis III Egypt had been ruled from Memphis. Situated at the apex of the Nile Delta, linked by river to the south, by sea to the Mediterranean and by land to the eastern empire, the ancient port made a sensible choice of capital for pharaohs wishing to monitor foreign affairs. Now, with long-term stability in the Near East, and with a growing interest in religious matters, Amenhotep planned to move his principal royal residence back to Thebes, leaving Memphis as the northern administrative centre. It was at Thebes (known to the Egyptians as Waset, or 'The Sceptre'), rather than Memphis, that he was to celebrate his three *heb-sed* festivals.

A royal jubilee needed a suitably imposing setting. On the Theban west bank, well away from the hustle and bustle of the city, Amenhotep founded his 'Palace of the Dazzling Aten and House of Rejoicing', an extensive complex known today as the Malkata Palace. Here was everything a king would ever need; private royal apartments, audience chambers, a splendid festival hall and even a temple of Amen. There were luxurious bath-rooms, harem quarters, a suite for the queen, rooms for officials and servants and, of course, extensive storage facilities, while a nearby workmen's village housed the artisans who would service the palace. A large artificial harbour was excavated to provide easy access for goods, and a suitable setting for the water-borne pageantry of Amenhotep's *heb-sed*.

The palace, in its heyday, must have been a wondrous sight. Mud-brick may have been cheap, but it was certainly not viewed as a crude building medium. The thick, cool mud-brick palace walls were smoothed with plaster and then either tiled or painted with vibrant, colourful frescoes showing scenes of nature and the gods. Amenhotep himself slept in a room whose walls were decorated with an enchanting frieze featuring the naked Bes, a demi-god associated with fertility, and whose ceiling displayed stylised vultures with outstretched wings. Doorways and windows were reinforced with valuable stone and wood. Even the floors were ornamental; the audience chamber, used for Amenhotep's official business, was decorated with images of bound captives which would of necessity be trampled by anyone walking across the room. Once decorated, the palace rooms were filled with the best the empire could offer; luxurious gilded furniture, rich textiles and everyday objects made by a master craftsman.

Today, Malkata presents a very different appearance. In the Nile Valley there is a very sudden cut-off between the fertile soil which borders the river and the arid desert beyond. For many centuries visitors have marvelled that it is possible to stand astride this natural boundary with one foot in the fertile 'black land', one in the desert 'red land'. The Malkata palace complex originally straddled this line; now the parts which once lay on the damp soil have vanished, dissolved back into mud and lost beneath modern fields, while the parts built on sand have fared somewhat better. Even here, however, it takes a great leap of the imagination to reconstruct the stunted, corroded and collapsed remnants of mud-brick walls into Amenhotep's stunning palace.

Splendid though it was, the Malkata Palace was never intended to be a permanent structure and, indeed, it was to be abandoned soon after Amenhotep's death. From the very beginning of his reign Amenhotep had planned immortal works in stone. From the Delta in the north to the southern limits of Nubia, the vast resources of the Egyptian empire were turned to building. The newly reopened Tura limestone quarries echoed to the incessant sound of the mason's hammers as vast rocks were hewn and dispatched by barge to Thebes. No earlier pharaoh had been able to commission such an ambitious and extravagant programme of monuments.

Included in the building programme was the commissioning of royal and divine statuary. We have over a thousand surviving statues of Amenhotep, many of which have been carved on a truly colossal scale. It is daunting to think that these are likely to represent only a fraction of the number originally carved. The erection of a statue – the excavation of the stone, its roughing-out and transport to the royal workshop – was an expensive and time-consuming business; not surprisingly, many pharaohs took short-cuts and 'borrowed' from their predecessors. The chief vandal was the 19th Dynasty king Ramesses II who habitually recarved Amenhotep's statuary into his own likeness so that, although they were unrelated, Ramesses often bears a distinct resemblance to Amenhotep III.

Amen, now united with his northern solar rival to form the composite god Amen-Re, benefited enormously from Amenhotep's generosity. During his reign the Karnak complex was extensively redesigned, with many earlier structures now dismantled and used as filling or foundations for new works.

Much of residential Thebes, too, was flattened as the Middle Kingdom mud-brick town made way for the glorious ever-expanding New Kingdom temple. The redesigned city, built on lower level ground, is today lost beneath the ground-water.

Karnak was to be blessed with two splendid gateways: the massive Third Pylon was to be 'a very great gateway before Amen-Re, covered in gold throughout...' while the unfinished Tenth Pylon, its walls decorated with scenes of Amenhotep triumphant, made a suitable background for two colossal statues of the king. Amenhotep, when it came to statuary, definitely believed that bigger was better; the huge quartzite feet of one of these statues still stands beside the remains of the pylon; it has been estimated that the whole statue would have stood an astonishing 21m (70 ft) tall.

The Theban calendar was dominated by two religious festivals, the Opet festival when the statue of Amen-Re was carried in great ceremony from his Karnak sanctuary to the Luxor temple, and the Festival of the Valley when Amen, his wife Mut and son Khonsu crossed the river to visit Hathor who resided in Hatshepsut's mortuary temple, Deir el-Bahari. On high days and holidays Amen now sailed from Karnak in a magnificent new boat, a cedar-wood barque lined with silver and decorated with gold. Carried high on the shoulders of his priests, Amen in his boat was able to travel along the new processional way, an avenue lined with ram-headed sphinxes, to the Luxor temple. Hatshepsut and Tuthmosis III had built at Luxor; now their limestone temple was demolished to make way for Amenhotep's more magnificent sandstone edifice.

Across the Nile on the west bank directly opposite the Luxor temple, work was under way on the construction of Amenhotep's mortuary temple. This, situated at Kom el-Hetan, was to be even larger and more impressive than the Karnak temple. It seemed that the mortuary temple was being built by a god, for a god. A stela housed within the temple precincts told of its glories:

> He made it as his monument for his father Amen, a monument of eternity and everlastingness, of fine sandstone worked with gold throughout. Its pavements were made pure with silver, all its doors with fine gold. It is very wide and great and decorated to endure ... It resembles the horizon of heaven when Re rises in it.

In front of the eastern gateway to his great temple Amenhotep placed two gigantic seated statues of himself. These, named the 'Ruler of Rulers', were versions of the god Amen, provided as objects of worship for the local population who were denied access to the temple precincts proper. If those who brought offerings to the statues grew muddled and started to worship their king, Amenhotep would merely have smiled. It was no coincidence that Egypt's gods were starting to look like their royal creator.

Now almost the entire temple has vanished – much of its masonry and statuary has been detected in the monuments of later pharaohs – leaving only the colossal statues behind. For many centuries one of these statues emitted a hair-raising moan at daybreak; repair work by the Roman emperor Septimus Severus eventually put an end to this curious dawn chorus. Today, seated in forlorn isolation beside the busy road that allows coachfuls of tourists access to the mysteries of the west bank, the Colossi of Memnon are ranked among the world's most famous and impressive monuments.

To broadcast Amenhotep's greatness to his empire his court published a series of propaganda scarabs. Smaller-scale scarabs – faience and semi-precious stones carved into the shape of the dung beetle, the earthly representative of the god Khepre who rolled the sun across the sky, and engraved with magical spells – had long been valued as amulets. Now they were to be put to a new use. Much larger, and mass produced in their hundreds, their undersides were inscribed with news of Amenhotep's latest adventures before the scarabs were distributed throughout the empire. In this way his far-flung people knew when their king had acquired a new foreign bride, killed a magnificent 102 wild lions, or commissioned the excavation of a pleasure lake.

It is from one of these scarabs, known today as the 'marriage scarab', that we learn of Amenhotep's unconventional choice of chief wife:

King of Upper and Lower Egypt, Nebmaatre, son of Re, Amenhotep ruler of Thebes, given life, and the king's chief wife Tiy, may she live. The name of her father is Yuya and the name of her mother is Thuyu . . .

The marriage scarab is tantalisingly brief – there is, after all, a limit to the amount of news which can be crammed on to a scarab – but it clarifies what might otherwise have been a confusing situation. Amenhotep, himself the son of a secondary queen, knew just how important it was that his intentions be understood. Although Tiy is not of the royal blood, it is she who has been chosen as consort, and it is her children who will eventually inherit the throne. We are never told how Tiy was selected for this important role. It is tempting to fantasise about a romantic royal love match between a prince and a pauper but, given that bride and groom were little more than twelve years old at the time of their marriage, it seems more likely that the forceful Mutemwia had a hand in their union.

Queen Tiy was not in the slightest bit daunted by her humble birth. She set out to challenge convention and Amenhotep, realising the value of an effective consort, was happy to comply. Setting a new precedent, Tiy was, from the first days of her marriage, mentioned in official dispatches alongside her husband; indeed, she was even mentioned in the scarab published to proclaim the marriage of Amenhotep and Princess Gilukheppa of Mitanni, a union which Tiy may well have celebrated with mixed feelings. Soon even the most traditional of foreign rulers were writing to Tiy – a mere woman, and a woman of humble birth at that – as if she were an equal. In statuary and reliefs the queen rapidly grew in size until she was depicted alongside, and frequently at the same scale as, Amenhotep. This set her far above other mortal women and far closer to the gods.

Tiy's family, her father Yuya, mother Thuyu and brother Anen, reaped enormous material benefit from their daughter's marriage, but did not consider it seemly to boast about their royal connections. During his lifetime Yuya held a mixture of sacred and secular titles including 'God's Father', 'Priest of Min', 'Master of the Horse' and 'Lieutenant Commander of the Chariotry', while Tiy's brother Anen became the influential Second Prophet (or Second Priest) of Amen. In death all three enjoyed expensive burials, with Yuya and Thuyu sharing a small but well-equipped tomb excavated at the entrance to the prestigious Valley of the Kings (KV 46). It is here that Thuyu indulges in a restrained boast about her children, claiming the title 'King's Mother of the Great Royal Wife' and twice mentioning her son Anen. The beautifully preserved bodies of

Yuya and Thuyu are today housed in Cairo Museum. Curiously, for Egyptian-born residents of Akhmim, they both have yellow hair; we do not know if this is a natural blonde, or evidence of dye applied either before or after death.

As Amenhotep grew older, as death loomed ever nearer, his thoughts turned to religion. Egypt offered a vast choice of gods; her eclectic, flexible pantheon provided a deity for every possible taste and occasion, and to modern observers it can sometimes seem that nothing was too weird or too humble to have a religious significance. Colours, all types of animals, royal regalia, even mirrors and birthing-bricks; all were capable of conveying a religious message to the initiated.

While continuing to acknowledge Amen as the patron god of the empire, Amenhotep, a cosmopolitan sophisticate rather than a Theban warrior, felt little personal need for Amen's practical support. Egypt had been at peace for decades, times had moved on. Besides, thanks to the generosity of the earlier New Kingdom pharaohs, the cult of Amen was becoming enormously, threateningly, rich. With riches went power; as a major landowner, Amen controlled people's lives. When Amen processed through the streets of Thebes he now put on a show which rivalled or even (if Amenhotep dared to admit it) eclipsed the royal procession. It was perhaps time for some of the other gods to share the limelight. Although he was to build extensively at both Karnak and Luxor, planning his own burial under Amen's auspices in the Valley of the Kings, Amenhotep was not prepared to allow Amen to dominate religious life.

Away from Thebes the old gods had retained their local influence. They too had benefited from the spoils of empire, and Ptah of Memphis in particular now inhabited a temple which rivalled and possibly even surpassed Karnak in its

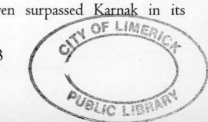

grandeur. Unfortunately the temple of Ptah is now entirely destroyed and we can only imagine its splendours. Materially, the traditional gods were wealthier than they had ever been. Politically, however, they had been forced to take a back seat to the southern upstart Amen. Now, following the trend set by his father Tuthmosis IV and his grandfather Amenhotep II, Amenhotep developed an increasingly deep interest in the old, northern solar cults.

The falcon-headed Re-Herakhte was to a large extent rehabilitated, while an old but rather obscure deity named the Aten became a quiet but persistent presence. The Aten was unusual among Egypt's human- and animal-headed gods as it was a faceless, genderless deity; it too had once taken the form of a falcon but from the time of Amenhotep II onwards the royal artists depicted the Aten as a blank sun's disk fringed by long human arms tipped with hands which were capable of holding religious symbols, most often the *ankh* which signified life. Suddenly the Aten was everywhere, and even the king's barge was known as Aten-tjehen, 'The Aten Dazzles'.

The northern animal cults, too, were back in vogue. These were cults which revered the power of animals; not animal worship, but worship of the god's power expressed through the animal. The heir to the throne, Prince Tuthmosis, left school and was sent to Memphis where he could train with the army, study with the civil service and serve as High Priest and *sem*-priest of Ptah. Tuthmosis also worked with the Apis bulls, taking particular responsibility for their burials. The Apis bull, identified by his distinctive markings, was treated as a living god. In fact he enjoyed a lifestyle not dissimilar from that of the king; he lived in a palace, had servants, enjoyed the best food and drink and amused himself with a harem of cows. At death he was given a state funeral, with mummification and burial in a dedicated bull cemetery. Tuthmosis was to die soon after his move to Memphis – his tomb remains undiscovered, but it seems likely that he was buried in the ancient Sakkara cemetery.

At the same time Amenhotep was starting to explore his own divinity. The story of Hatshepsut's divine birth, mutilated but still readable on the wall of the Deir el-Bahari mortuary temple, fascinated Amenhotep. Hatshepsut had been a woman determined to prove the legitimacy of her reign. Amenhotep could not have been more different; secure in his masculinity, his crown and his wealth, he had no need to justify himself either to his people or his gods. There was only one possible chink in his armour, one potentially sensitive subject; Amenhotep had not been born to a King's Great Wife.

Now Amenhotep enlisted Amen's help. In order to promote his own divinity, and perhaps to provide a retrospective boost to his mother's status, Amenhotep 'borrowed' Hatshepsut's fantastic tale, reproducing it, suitably amended, on the wall of the newly refurbished Luxor temple. Luxor made an ideal setting for such a tale as it was a temple dedicated jointly to Amen, to the ithyphallic fertility god Min and to the celebration of the royal soul, or Ka. Now it is Queen Mutemwia who is seduced by the overwhelming perfume of Amen, and the infant Amenhotep who is acknowledged as the son of a god.

His *heb-sed* marked a turning point for Amenhotep. Before he was clearly a man, albeit a man with divine attributes. Afterwards he was less obviously human, his identification with the Aten or sun disk more obvious. The cult of the Aten was being used to develop the cult of the living king. At Memphis Amenhotep became the living embodiment of Ptah, worshipped at the temple of Nebmaatre[Amenhotep III]-United-with-Ptah.

Outside Egypt's borders, away from the influence of the Amen priesthood, the situation was simplified. Ill-educated foreigners could not be expected to understand the complexities of state theology; they needed a simple god. At Soleb in Nubia Amenhotep built a new temple for Amen-Re; at nearby Sedeinga Tiy, too, was given a temple dedicated to a local version of the goddess Hathor. These twin temples were not just built for the royal couple, they were actually dedicated to them, and at Soleb we can see the curious sight of the king offering to his own divine image. At the furthest point of their empire, Amenhotep and Tiy were worshipped as gods. Amenhotep had become Nebmaatre Lord of Nubia.

Even a living god must die. In 1353BC Amenhotep was called to join his ancestors. His had been a glorious thirty-eight-year reign; few of his people could remember any other king. Egypt mourned, stunned and bereft by her loss. As the royal undertakers started their melancholy task, messengers sped out from Thebes. From Nubia to Mitanni there was consternation, and perhaps a hint of calculation. Amenhotep's death left a power void which would be difficult to fill. Meanwhile all wrote to address the proper condolences to the widowed Tiy. Tushratta of Mitanni, true to form, combined his condolences with a request for a delivery of golden statues promised by the dead king:

> To Tiy, Mistress of Egypt... You are the one that knows that I always showed love to Nimmureya [Amenhotep III] your husband, and that your husband always showed love to me... You know better than any other the things that we said to each other... I had asked your husband for statues of solid gold... but your son has sent gold-plated

wooden statues. As gold is as plentiful as dirt in your son's country, why has my request so distressed your son that he has not sent them to me? . . .

*Amarna Letter 26*

Amenhotep was buried in the tomb abandoned by his father; tomb WV 22 in the remote Western Valley, an offshoot of the Valley of the Kings. This was one of the largest of the New Kingdom tombs and we must assume, given his wealth and his longevity, that Amenhotep's was the most magnificent burial of any Egyptian king; a burial which would have made the splendours of Tutankhamen's tomb seem insignificant. However, Amenhotep's tomb was completely emptied in antiquity. Soon afterwards his badly damaged mummy was rescued, rewrapped and stored for safety in the tomb of Amenhotep II. Today a mummy attributed to Amenhotep III is housed in Cairo Museum. Unwrapped in 1905, it is the body of an obese man suffering from painful, possibly fatal, toothache.

# CHAPTER 8

# The God:
# 'The Hidden One' of Thebes

You are Amen, Lord of the silent, who pays heed to the voice of the poor. When I call to you in my distress you come to rescue me.

*Stela recovered from Deir el-Medina*

Amen, and his priesthood, have become ever-present background figures in our account of the rise of the New Kingdom empire. In theory, of course, Amen takes full responsibility for Egypt's astonishing success. As the dominant Egyptian god, he alone empowers the pharaohs and assures their victory. At a more practical level, he is fast emerging as Egypt's second greatest landowner. By the reign of Amenhotep III only the king is richer than Amen, only the king has more influence. In times of war, kings had been happy to pay for Amen's support. Now, as Egypt enjoyed unbroken peace and prosperity, the later 18th Dynasty pharaohs are starting to worry that too much wealth, and too much potential power, is concentrated in a single, independent cult.

Who was the shadowy Amen? Like all the sophisticated New Kingdom deities he had evolved from the ancient totems worshipped in the independent villages and towns of the prehistoric, pre-unification age. Then each god had his or her own well-defined territory, within which he or she was the supreme supernatural power. These local gods devised their own rituals, and developed their own legends to explain life's mysteries. Served by local priesthoods, they endorsed and were endorsed by the local rulers. Beyond their territorial boundaries, however, the gods – and the priests who served them – recognised that their authority would be limited and that others would have more effectual powers. This situation was accepted and understood by all, and the regional gods and their separate priesthoods lived side by side in apparent harmony.

Monotheism had little appeal in a country accustomed to a multiplicity of deities. As Egypt united under a single king there was no attempt to impose either a single national god or a consolidated state priesthood upon the people. Instead, pharaoh became the acknowledged head of a wide variety of cults, and the individual deities continued to be worshipped in their own specific ways in their own local temples by their own specialised priesthoods. The overlapping – and to modern eyes curiously contradictory – myths and legends continued to be respected; the Egyptians did not demand consistency of their theology. Therefore, to label any one god as, for example, the god of creation is an impossible over-simplification because Egypt recognised several equally valid creation myths and, indeed, each god was capable of filling several roles.

To modern eyes, Egypt's gods are a curiously mixed bunch. Some, such as Isis and Mut, appear fully human, but many regularly take an animal form. A fully animal appearance, however, restricts the activities of the god. When Hathor appears as a cow, for example, she can suckle the king but has difficulty shaking a sacred rattle. Therefore we find the

animal-associated gods appearing as hybrids: Sobek the crocodile, Anubis the jackal and Horus the falcon each have their
animal heads perched unconvincingly on top of the human
bodies which will allow them to sit on thrones, carry imple-
ments and receive offerings. Thoth, scribe of the gods, could
be an ibis or a baboon, but when required to write in his scroll
was best represented as an ibis-headed man with functioning
arms. Amen himself could be a ram or a goose – hence the
prevalence of ram-headed sphinxes at Thebes – but he usually
took the form of a man dressed in a simple short kilt and
wearing a distinctive headdress topped with two tall feathers.
Occasionally a god's appearance would modify with age; so the
Aten who started life as a falcon is today best known as a
faceless, multi-armed sun-disk. Whatever their appearance, the
gods displayed distinctly human behaviour. Just like their
creators, they were emotional, capable of love, hate and
jealousy. They ate, drank, slept and, being gender specific,
enjoyed a rich and varied sex life.

Not all gods were created equal. Already there were divisions
apparent in heaven. While many gods retained their restricted
local role, a few were becoming dominant, their authority
recognised up and down the Nile. As the kings supported, and
acquired the support of, these more influential gods the pantheon developed an 'A list' of state deities (Re, Ptah, Osiris, Isis
and Hathor, to name just a few) and a 'B list' of less influential
beings revered in their own local area, respected as oracles, but
of little national importance. The state gods were rich and
powerful, the local gods far less so. However, status was
dependent upon royal patronage, and gods could move freely
between the two classes.

The earthly kings had a controlling interest in the heavenly hierarchy; they determined who was 'king of the gods' at any given time. Throughout the Old Kingdom the northern sun god Re had been dominant. However, thanks to enthusiastic Middle Kingdom royal support, the southern warrior god Montu eventually eclipsed Re, becoming the principal god of the 11th Dynasty before fading back into obscurity. Montu was followed by Amen, a relatively insignificant local god who, promoted first of all by the Theban 12th Dynasty, and then by the 17th and 18th, quickly assumed super-god status. When combined with Re, to form the compound deity Amen-Re, Amen was truly king. Yet he too was to be temporarily eclipsed by a B list god who enjoyed a meteoric rise, followed by an equally swift fall, due to the patronage of Amenhotep IV.

To these high-ranking deities must be added the 'C list'; the more accessible demi-gods and supernatural beings (ghosts and spirits) who played a major role in popular religion, but who were not themselves the object of major state cults or indeed state funding. Bes, the dwarf god of fertility and a universal protector, and Taweret, the pregnant hippopotamus goddess of childbirth who was believed to bring babies to the childless, are perhaps the most important of these lesser deities. Although superficially connected with obviously female rituals, Bes and Taweret had universal appeal and we should not underestimate their influence; they were to be among the few gods to survive unscathed during the desecrations of the Amarna age. Amenhotep III, a king fully entitled to converse with the greatest of the gods, chose to sleep in a bedroom decorated with a Bes frieze. His wife, the otherwise elegant Queen Tiy, was happy to be portrayed with the cumbersome body-shape of Taweret, which suggested that she too might be associated with divine fertility and motherhood.

Expressed in this simple way, the divisions between the various classes of gods and goddesses seems logical and clear-cut. In fact, as we might expect when dealing with a subject as imprecise and fluid as personal belief, this is an entirely artificial modern classification imposed on a disorganised, overlapping and constantly shifting system.

A 'typical' New Kingdom Theban man, if we could ever meet such a statistical phenomenon, would recognise the supreme authority of Amen of Karnak and would celebrate his many festivals with the dedicated eating and drinking which such occasions demanded. Although Amen was prepared to listen to pleas from the common people, and even had a part of his temple set aside for private petitions, our Theban is more likely to have addressed his personal devotions to his more accessible local gods: the deified Amenhotep I and his mother the deified Queen Ahmose Nefertari. Like any good son he would take his duties to his dead ancestors seriously, making regular visits to the family tomb to offer the food and drink necessary to ensure the survival of the deceased in the Afterlife.

His wife, more concerned with domestic matters, would place great reliance on the protection of Bes, Taweret and Meskenet during childbirth, and would revere the family- and harvest-orientated snake goddesses Renenutet and Meretseger. She would use a variety of amulets and spells – 'superstition' rather than official theology – to protect her children from accident and disease. Both husband and wife would be happy to defer to the judgement of the local oracle – Amenhotep I, who as combined king and god made an excellent judge – when faced with an otherwise insoluble problem.

Belief, or superstition, had become an integral, inescapable part of Egyptian daily life. The temples, obelisks and colossal statues which dominated the New Kingdom cities provided obvious signs of state piety, but as we have already seen, even the most innocent of items might carry a subtle hidden message. Colours, cats, fish, mirrors, even lucky days; all brought their own religious baggage. The obvious abundance of gods and demi-gods, amulets, charms, rituals and superstitions, impressed visitors to Egypt. Herodotus, as a Greek, was no stranger to complex pantheons, yet he was struck by the intricate piety of the Egyptians:

> They are religious to excess, beyond any other nation in the world... They wear freshly laundered linen clothing. They practise circumcision for the sake of cleanliness, considering it preferable to be clean than comely. Their priests shave the whole body every other day so that no lice or other impure thing might adhere to them when they are engaged in the service of the gods.
>
> *Herodotus*, Histories II: 37

Throughout the Old and Middle Kingdoms the state cults and their various priesthoods had coexisted with little sign of friction. However, as the unprecedented prosperity of the Egyptian empire allowed successive pharaohs to make increasingly generous offerings, one god developed disproportionate power. Amen the arriviste, 'The Hidden One' of Thebes, was a secretive god who represented the abstract concept of 'hiddenness'. Literally hidden from prying eyes, he dwelt unseen in the darkest recesses of the Karnak temple, and even when he left his home to process through the streets or visit his fellow gods Amen remained concealed within the sanctuary of his boat shrine. Only the king and the highest-ranking priests would ever gaze upon the god's face.

> Incense was burned for Amen in the inner sanctuary... for this is where he... had given the sword of victory to... Kamose the mighty, who conquered the south and overran the north, who seized the land by force...
>
> *2nd Kamose Stela*

Amen was an elemental god associated with the air. He was not a complete yokel; as a god associated with the creation myth of Hermopolis Magna he had a venerable pedigree and was included among the four divine couples (the ogdoad) who generate life in this particular tale. However, as a late-starter in the A list pantheon, Amen never developed the elaborate mythologies of his fellow deities. It seems that all the good stories had already been given out, and there is no legend of Amen to compare with the inspiring story of Isis and Osiris, or the epic tale of Horus and Seth. This means that Amen, lacking the human characteristics which make Osiris and co. so entertaining, survives today as a bland, even boring individual. All we can say of his private life is that he had a wife, the goddess Mut, and a son, the moon god Khonsu.

Bland Amen may have been; poor he certainly was not. Increasing status went hand-in-hand with increasing wealth as successive pharaohs sought to prove their piety with increasingly generous donations. Fortunately, his representatives were well able to deal with their embarrassment of riches.

Egypt's priests were not drawn to their god by vocation. Recruited from the ranks of the educated male elite, they were men who had chosen (or who had been chosen by the king) to

145

work for a particular god as a sensible alternative to working for the secular state. Both bureaucrat and priest were, at the end of the day, deputies of the king, and both worked hard to ensure that Egypt functioned as she should. There was in fact a fine line between priests and non-priests. Anyone, regardless of training and even gender, became a temporary priest when making an offering and so our 'typical New Kingdom Theban', who makes regular offerings to his dead parents, is himself a part-time priest. Many officials held a mixture of sacred and secular posts – either contemporaneously or successively – throughout their working lives. While some were content to spend their days serving one god, others moved from cult to cult seeking professional advancement with each change. Some had priesthood thrust upon them, inheriting their religious duties from their fathers and grandfathers.

Priests were required to perform the daily rituals which would satisfy their god, and ensure the maintenance of *maat*. They did not have to prepare sermons, hear confession or interface with the sick and the poor. But equally time-consuming was their work as the god's agent. The priests of Amen were administrators and accountants rather than ministers and theologians. Not only did they preside over the largest and most impressive religious complex the world had ever seen, they worked alongside the lay temple employees – scribes and administrators – controlling vast tracts of land, and a series of economically important industries, spread throughout Egypt and Nubia.

With a wide portfolio of income-generating assets including fields (many rented to tenant farmers), labourers, herds (also leased out), ships and mines, Amen was able to support an ever-expanding payroll of priests, lay-workers and temple servants.

He thus became the dominant economic force in the south while pharaoh – so often absent in Memphis – became a somewhat peripheral figure to his people. The thousands of temple employees, not just priests but farmers, miners and sailors, surely felt a primary allegiance to the temple who owned their livelihood rather than to the distant king. With Amen paying a hefty tax on his profits, the king saw little reason to worry. Amen's efficient management was relieving him of a great deal of work.

Every day the god was presented with generous offerings; thousands of loaves and hundreds of jars of beer were supplemented by assorted delicacies including meat, cakes and wine. The offerings were ceremonially presented to the god and then redistributed among his staff, with the higher-ranking priests taking the first share of the goodies. Any non-perishable surpluses could be stored in the huge warehouses kept safe within the thick temple walls. Although officially the property of the god, these surpluses could, in times of national emergency, be commandeered to pay the palace's bills; thus they provided a secure yet easily accessible reserve for the king. The late Ramesside kings had reason to be grateful for this surplus when, in a time of serious economic decline, they were forced to pacify striking Theban necropolis workmen with funds taken from the temple stores.

The institution of God's Wife of Amen, the priestly title invented for Ahmose Nefertari by Ahmose and since conferred on successive ladies of the immediate royal family, allowed the palace some, but not enough, control over the cult and its assets. Amenhotep II, Tuthmosis IV and Amenhotep III – Thebans by descent but not by permanent residence – each attempted to extend this control by appointing their own

followers, northerners rather than southerners, as High Priest
– or First Prophet – of Amen. Eventually, beyond the end of
the New Kingdom, Ahmose's dream was to become reality
with the God's Wife of Amen developing more power than the
High Priest. For the moment, however, the God's Wife could
be of little help in thwarting Amen's growing influence.

Amenhotep III was right to be concerned. Less than three
centuries after his death the New Kingdom would falter to a
halt with Egypt ignominiously split in two. The north would
be ruled by pharaohs, the south by an independent dynasty of
High Priests of Amen. The dying Amenhotep had left his son,
also named Amenhotep, to deal with the situation. Encourag-
ingly, Amenhotep IV was already showing an interest in
religious matters.

# CHAPTER 9

# Akhenaten:
# The Heretic Pharaoh

When day breaks and you have arisen from the horizon to shine as the Aten of the daytime, you dispel darkness. When you cast your rays the Two Lands are festive. The people wake up and rise to their feet because you have lifted them up. They wash themselves and get dressed, their arms raised in praise at your rising. The whole land goes about its work. The herds are happy in their pasture. Trees and plants grow green. Birds take off from their nests, their wings praising your soul...

*The Great Hymn to the Aten*

Amenhotep III – the golden pharaoh whose reign had outlasted an entire generation – was dead. Stunned, the ancient world took comfort in the fact that Amenhotep IV, son of Amenhotep III and Queen Tiy, would continue his father's legacy.

The new Amenhotep was very much an unknown quantity. As a younger son he had not been trained to rule; it was his elder brother Tuthmosis, Crown Prince, Overseer of the Priests of Upper and Lower Egypt, High Priest of Ptah in Memphis and *Sem*-Priest of Ptah, who had been groomed to wear the double crown. Tuthmosis was clearly interested in the traditional northern animal-worshipping cults. Tuthmosis, however, was dead and buried, and the untried Amenhotep, a devotee of the solar cults, was to rule in his stead.

For a brief period it seemed nothing much would change. The royal court remained based at the Theban Malkata palace and building work continued in and around the Karnak Temple of Amen. Here, like any dutiful son, Amenhotep completed his father's unfinished works. Amenhotep IV is not known to have fought for his country, yet now – in deference to established New Kingdom tradition – the Third Pylon was decorated with a scene showing the new king as pharaoh triumphant smiting a bunch of unsavoury foreigners. The southern pylon bore a series of traditional offering scenes including Amenhotep offering to Re-Herakhte '... he who rejoices in the horizon in his name "Sunlight-that-is-in-the-Disk" '. In Nubia Amenhotep finished his father's Soleb temple, embellishing it with scenes of himself worshipping his deified father.

King Tushratta of Mitanni had addressed his condolences (and his request for gold statues) to Queen Tiy, assuming that she was to continue her influential role at the Egyptian court. He had, however, misjudged the situation. Tiy had less control over her son than he had supposed; there was a new queen in her place. The new pharaoh was less concerned with diplomatic etiquette than his father – it is hard to imagine the proud Amenhotep III attempting to pass off gold-plated statues as the real thing – and was not inclined to be generous with his brother king. Amenhotep IV, not one to be bound by conventional courtesies, simply ignored all letters from Mitanni and eventually Tushratta stopped writing.

Now something strange was happening on Egypt's temple

walls. While Amen-Re, king of the gods, assumed a curiously muted presence, the ancient sun god Re-Herakhte, and the deified sun's disk, or Aten, were very much in evidence. Clearly, these sun gods were very important to the new king. From seeds sown in the reign of his father, an idea was growing in Amenhotep's mind, driving him in a direction that no pharaoh had travelled before. His interest in solar worship via the Aten – a complex god, evolved from the ancient sun gods, who represented the light of the sun rather than the sun itself – was already apparent.

During Year 2 came the announcement that a *heb-sed* or jubilee was to be celebrated at Thebes on the third anniversary of Amenhotep's accession. This was very unusual; jubilees were expected after thirty years of rule, not three. What was Amenhotep celebrating? Was it his thirtieth birthday, his late father's posthumous fourth jubilee, or the recognition of a new state god? Perhaps, following the precedent set by his father, Amenhotep intended to use the jubilee as a means of revealing some important development in his own royal divinity? The people probably did not care overmuch; jubilees were enjoyed whatever their official pretext and everyone looked forward to days of feasting, drinking and merrymaking. Over on the west bank, at Deir el-Medina, a headache resulting from over-enthusiastic participation in state celebrations was considered a valid excuse for absence from work.

Egypt's builders took up their tools. Memphis, Heliopolis and Nubia received new sun-temples; temples open to the sun's rays rather than the gloomy enclosed edifice favoured by Amen. But attention remained firmly focused on Thebes. To the east of the extensive Amen complex Amenhotep built his own impressive series of temples orientated towards the east, the land of the rising sun, and dedicated to the worship of the Aten. Here he was to reinterpret the traditional *heb-sed* rituals, excluding many of the great state gods, Amen included, from his festivities. In a clear insult to the old order the shrines which would normally have housed the traditional deities now contained depictions of the king beneath the Aten's disk.

Amen's priests did not like this new development. What had once seemed a minor religious foible – the king's personal devotion to a relatively obscure cult – was gathering a frightening momentum. It was now obvious that Amenhotep was prepared to discard casually almost two thousand years of polytheistic religious tolerance, along with all the certainties that had caused Egypt and her kings to flourish. By the end of Year 5 the Aten was undeniably Egypt's dominant god. Offerings which had once been presented to Amen were now being diverted to the Aten so that the new cult grew rich as Amen grew poor. Soon many of the old temples were closed, while their treasuries and assets, confiscated and officially presented to the Aten, were being administered by government officials rather than local priests. Thus pharaoh, High Priest of the Aten, kept a firm control over the finances of the rapidly expanding cult.

Amenhotep, with seemingly effortless efficiency, had radically simplified Egypt's pantheon, replacing the many deities with one principal god. Some of the old solar gods were allowed to remain, but they played a much reduced role in official religious life. The state gods had always been remote from the people; now they paid the penalty for their aloofness. No one was prepared to fight for their survival and we have no record of anyone daring to oppose the temple closures. Indeed, we are left with a suspicion that many of the old priests simply changed their allegiance to more acceptable solar cults and got on with their work. Wisely, Amenhotep did not attempt to interfere overmuch with the more popular superstitions and rituals which comforted the mass of the population, and many of the demi-gods, including the ubiquitous Bes and Taweret, survived the coup. For most Egyptians the change of state god therefore became little more than a technicality. Only the priests, and those closely associated with the king, were forced to rethink their approach. Now the king, rejecting his given name Amen-hotep, or 'Amen is Satisfied', adopted a name that reflected his personal creed. Henceforth he was to be known as Akhenaten 'Living Spirit of the Aten'.

The new god felt uncomfortable living in Thebes. Thebes was, after all, the acknowledged home of Amen and his family, and everywhere seemed tainted with centuries-old reminders of the forbidden cult. The new Aten temples, although splendid, were essentially inferior annexes to the closed but still magnificent Amen temple complex. Over on the west bank stood the royal mortuary temples, each dedicated to a form of Amen and each serving as a silent witness to the old religion. Akhenaten understood this. He undertook to build his god a new capital, a splendid city on unconsecrated virgin soil, where the Aten could reign supreme.

New Kingdom Egypt did not have an endless supply of untouched building sites; the best spots had already been taken. However, Middle Egypt provided what to Akhenaten seemed the ideal location. Here, in a vast natural bay of cliffs, the king founded Akhetaten or 'Horizon of the Aten', a city today widely known by its modern name, Amarna or Tel el-Amarna. By extension the site has given its name to the period of Akhenaten's rule; the Amarna Period.

Then they prostrated themselves before His Majesty and grovelled in the dust in front of him. And His Majesty said to them, 'The Aten wanted Akhetaten to be built for him as an everlasting monument to his name. It was my father, the Aten himself, who pointed out the site for Akhetaten; none of my advisers suggested it, none of the inhabitants of the whole land suggested it... Remember before His Majesty found it, it did not belong to any king or queen, it did not belong to any official or commoner to exploit it for profit...'

*Amarna Boundary Stela*

To Akhenaten it seemed that he had found the very site of creation. For when the sun set behind the arc of the mountains the natural shaping of the Amarna cliffs suggested the hiero-glyph for 'horizon' on a cosmic scale. It was as if the divine sun disk itself had chosen the site.

There was to be no turning back. Akhenaten intended to live, die and be buried in his new city, and woe betide anyone who disagreed. On vast boundary stelae, limestone billboards cut into the cliffs around his new city, Akhenaten proclaimed his irrevocable determination:

This is how it will be. My queen will never say to me, 'Look, there is a better site for Akhetaten somewhere else.' If she does, I will pay no attention to her. None of my advisers or favoured courtiers... and none of the inhabit-ants of this whole land will say, 'Look, there is a better place for Akhetaten somewhere else'...

The speed with which the king accomplished his dream is truly impressive. Using mud-brick and specially designed small stone blocks known today as *talatat* blocks, the Amarna workmen managed to convert bleak desert into a fully functioning city in a mere four years. The new city was to be provided with an instant population. Akhenaten, anticipating all future needs, transferred his family, his harem and his courtiers from Thebes and many of his scribes, accountants and bureaucrats from Memphis, although the northern vizier was allowed to retain his traditional offices. Priests, soldiers, officials, labourers and servants, all were forced to abandon their homes and family tombs and travel with their families to Middle Egypt. An estimated 20,000 people were to move to the new desert site. Here they would live to serve the king and his god.

Akhenaten, always self-obsessed, had made little provision for his followers. Only the palaces, temples and tree-lined processional ways had been formally planned by the royal architects; the rest of the city was to be completed by its intended citizens. The wealthy courtiers were forced to send their own representatives to reserve and subsequently build on the best sites; later the less privileged would arrive and build their own more humble houses around the estates of the elite. Now, as Akhenaten prepared to leave Thebes, his people loaded their possessions into a flotilla of boats and set off for a new life.

Many must have been dismayed by their forced relocation. The dusty, dry conditions hardly seemed an ideal setting for a bustling metropolis and Amarna life had several drawbacks; leaving aside the theological complications, there was a shortage of water, and the agricultural land was inconveniently situated on the opposite bank of the Nile. Amarna was a backwater; no one would live there through choice. Ironically, these very drawbacks were to save Amarna for Egyptology. When the site was abandoned following the death of its founder, no one else was tempted to build there and, although many of the stone buildings were dismantled so that their blocks could be reused, the city remained essentially untouched.

Amarna quickly developed into an isolated city, her people very much cut off from the more normal Egyptian world outside Akhetaten's borders. Theirs was a protected, cushioned environment which somehow lacked the gritty realism of life in Memphis or Thebes. The king, who might have been expected to worry about the dangers of isolation, seemed unperturbed. Akhenaten had rejected the traditional, peripatetic style of kingship and cared little that he grew increasingly remote to his people.

As a permanent city, Amarna was provided with everything that a king and his god could possibly need. There were impressive mud-brick palaces, magnificent stone temples, housing for rich and poor, offices, factories, storage facilities, roads, processional ways, wells, gardens, a port and, of course, a socially stratified burial ground. While the ordinary Amarna residents would be interred in humble pit graves, a section of the cliff face was reserved for the rock-cut tombs which the king would use to reward his elite. The exclusive 'Royal Wadi', the Amarna equivalent of the Valley of the Kings, was dedicated to the royal burials. The Boundary Stelae make this arrangement clear:

My tomb will be built in the mountain to the east of Akhetaten, and I will be buried in it, after I have celebrated the millions of jubilees allocated to me by my father, the Aten. My chief queen, Nefertiti, will be buried here too, after millions of years. If I die millions of years from now in some other town, north, south, east or west of here, my body should be brought back and buried at Akhetaten. Similarly, if my chief queen, Nefertiti, dies millions of years from now in some other town north, south, east or west of here, her body shall be brought back and buried in Akhetaten ...

Tombs shall be built in the eastern cliff of Akhetaten for the High Priests, the God's Fathers and the temple staff of the Aten, and they shall be buried there. Tombs shall also be made in the eastern cliffs of Akhetaten for nobles and commoners alike and they should be buried there ...

Akhenaten had always been concerned about his own security. Even at Thebes he had surrounded himself with armed troops. Now Amarna rejoiced in an exceptionally high military presence, with *medjay* (police) and both foreign and Egyptian troops stationed within the city. His own home was exceptionally well protected, and the royal family never ventured outside without a bodyguard. Given that he was a pharaoh intent on destroying centuries of tradition, this is perhaps understandable. More sinister is the attention paid to guarding the people. The tracks worn by the soldiers who patrolled the eastern cliffs and desert around the city are still clearly visible today. Whether these soldiers were employed to keep strangers out of Amarna, or to keep the citizens in, is less clear. Elsewhere we find uncomfortable evidence that the people of Amarna may not have enjoyed the relaxed lifestyle which Akhenaten's propaganda would suggest. Commoners had always been respectful to their king; now even elderly dignitaries were compelled to approach Akhenaten bent double.

Akhenaten was married, and already a father, before his

accession. His consort, Queen Nefertiti, is today – three thousand years after her death – famed throughout the world for her haunting beauty. She was, however, far more than a beautiful face.

Nefertiti's existence had been revealed to scholars in 1822, when Champollion's decipherment of hieroglyphics had finally allowed the reading of the tantalising texts which littered Egypt's ancient monuments. However, the Amarna age remained a dark, intricate mystery and Amarna itself lay unexplored beneath a blanket of sand. Nefertiti was therefore classified as an unexceptional consort and more or less dismissed, and it was Tiy, Akhenaten's forceful mother, who was celebrated as the feminine influence behind her son's unconventional reign.

In 1891 Flinders Petrie became the first to conduct a scientific excavation at Amarna. In 1902 Norman de Garis Davies arrived to compile a detailed epigraphic record of the dirty, damaged and bat-infested tombs of the nobles. Then, in 1907, a team of archaeologists from the German Oriental Society arrived to excavate the city. Under the direction of Ludwig Borchardt, they conducted a preliminary survey and then started to dig. In 1912 they made a spectacular discovery. Borchardt himself tells the tale (*The Excavations of the German Oriental Society at Tell el-Amarna* 3: 30-1):

On December 6th, 1912, just before the lunch break, I was called by an urgent note from Prof. Ranke, who was supervising the excavations, to House P47.2. Just inside the door to room 19 ... I came across the broken remains of a life-sized coloured bust of Amenhotep IV, which had just been uncovered. Near by, slightly further into room 19 ... more artistic masterpieces were unearthed ... Then, a little in front of the east wall ... a flesh coloured neck appeared ... 'Life-sized coloured bust of the queen' was duly announced, the pickaxes were set aside and work was carefully continued by hand. The next minutes confirmed our initial identification – above the neck was the lower part of the bust and below it the back of the royal headdress came into view ...

Borchardt and his team had been excavating in the Southern Suburb; a residential district known to have included several palace and temple workshops. House P47.2 proved to be the remains of the combined home and studio of the celebrated master-sculptor Tuthmosis. Tuthmosis, a royal favourite, had held a position of highest honour at Amarna. But he had been forced to abandon his studio when, soon after the death of Akhenaten, the court relocated to Thebes. Like any sensible craftsman, he had taken with him the tools and materials of his trade, leaving behind a jumble of unwanted, valueless items including a collection of unfinished statues and model heads. Images of dead royals were of very little use to anyone. A rejected limestone bust of the late queen, Nefertiti, was left sitting on a shelf but eventually, as the shelf collapsed, fell forward into a heap of rubble. It was this piece which Borchardt had now brought to light.

Stunned by his find, that evening the archaeologist wrote just one line in his diary: 'Description is useless, see for yourself.' Today this remarkable piece is displayed in Berlin Museum.

Nefertiti's delicate bust is carved from limestone which has been coated with a layer of moulded plaster and painted with a sure realism. The queen has been given a delicate pinky-brown skin, red-brown lips and well-groomed black eyebrows. She wears her unique flat-topped blue crown and, as there is no hair showing, we can assume that she has a shaven head. Around her truncated shoulders there is a wonderful, intricate beaded collar whose vibrant tones match the colourful streamers which decorate her crown. Nefertiti has suffered remarkably little damage, although her ears and the top edge of her crown have been slightly chipped. However, while her right eye is intact, inlaid with rock crystal, ringed with black kohl and with a black pupil, her left eye is missing from its socket. Borchardt launched an immediate search but was unable to find the missing eye and, as the socket shows no trace of glue, it is generally accepted that this was missing when the head was abandoned.

Like any true romantic heroine, Nefertiti is a woman of mysterious origins who remains tantalisingly silent about her parentage. As she never claims to be a king's daughter we know, however, that she was not a member of the immediate royal family. It seems that Akhenaten, like his father before him, had rejected an incestuous union and married a commoner. Who was she?

Her name, 'A Beautiful Woman Has Come' hints at an exotic origin but comes nowhere near to proving one; many Egyptian girls were named 'beautiful' by their proud mothers. Suggestions that Nefertiti may have been a Nubian, Syrian or Mitannian princess are entertaining but fail through a fundamental lack of evidence. As we have an Egyptian lady, Tey wife of Ay, who claims to have been Nefertiti's wet-nurse, and a second Egyptian lady, Mutnodjmet, who claims to be her sister, we are probably safe in accepting that Nefertiti was a member of Egypt's elite. Indeed, as there is strong circumstantial evidence to suggest that the courtier Ay, husband of the wet-nurse Tey, was a brother of Queen Tiy and the Second-Prophet of Amen, Anen, we might speculate that Tiy had engineered her young son into marrying a suitable girl from her own family.

The marriage of Akhenaten and Nefertiti was consistently – almost embarrassingly, by traditional, restrained Egyptian standards – promoted as a genuine royal love match. The royal couple appear virtually inseparable from their first days together. In unprecedented displays of public intimacy they touch, hold hands and even kiss, their closeness emphasised by the flimsy, transparent garments which leave few of the queen's charms to the imagination. In one memorable scene, carved on the wall of an Amarna tomb, the besotted king turns to kiss the queen and share the *Ankh* of life with her while driving the royal chariot, apparently oblivious to the fact that his eldest daughter, Meritaten, is determinedly beating the horse with a stick.

> May old age be granted to the Great Queen Neferneferuaten-Nefertiti... for she is in the charge of the pharaoh, and may old age be granted to her children, Princess Meritaten and Princess Meketaten, for they are under the authority of their mother the queen...
>
> *Amarna Boundary Stela*

Together, king and queen play again and again with their growing family. Nefertiti was to bear her husband six daughters within the first ten years of marriage, the elder three (Meritaten, 'Beloved of the Aten'; Meketaten, 'Protected by the Aten'; Ankhesenpaaten, 'Living through the Aten') being born at Thebes and the younger three (Neferneferuaten-the-Younger, 'Exquisite Beauty of the Sun-Disk'; Neferneferure, 'Exquisite Beauty of Re'; Setepenre, 'Chosen of Re') at Amarna. Amid

161

such scenes of domestic bliss, it comes as something of a
shock to remember that Akhenaten was not averse to availing
himself of the charms of his many other wives, housed in
the royal harem which had been conveniently relocated to
Amarna.

From the beginning Nefertiti assumed a strong role in her
husband's reign; a role that was to grow increasingly prominent
as the reign progressed. It is difficult for us to determine the
extent of her political power; we simply do not have enough
evidence to assess whether or not she was allowed a hand in the
running of the country and she has little input into the Amarna
correspondence. However, carved blocks recovered from Karnak
and Hermopolis – the fragmented remains of scenes carved
during the Amarna age – confirm that Nefertiti was a full
participant in religious rituals. Nefertiti never attempts to
eclipse the king; she is always a dutiful, passive helpmeet, the
living embodiment of the goddess Maat who stands behind her
husband as he distributes gold to his followers, or ritually
slaughters the enemies who threaten his land. But, away from
her husband, Nefertiti, too, is able to wield a mace to execute a
(female) enemy.

Even more amazing is the realisation that, in a specialised
sun temple at Thebes, Nefertiti had been allowed to make
offerings to the Aten. The Hwt-Benben, or 'Mansion of the
*Benben*-Stone' was, as its name suggests, a temple dedicated to
solar worship before the *benben*-stone. At Heliopolis the
original *benben* had been a pyramid-shaped stone associated
with the cult of Re. At Thebes, Akhenaten's *benben* was the
Karnak obelisk erected by Tuthmosis IV. The Karnak cult of
the *benben* was an exclusively female cult and not even the king
was allowed to participate in its rituals. Hwt-Benben was

dismantled at the end of the 18th Dynasty, when many of its blocks were used as filling in the Second Pylon. However, the reconstructed pillars of the colonnade show multiple scenes of Nefertiti, assisted by her eldest daughter Meritaten, offering to the Aten. In separate scenes we see mother and daughter shaking their sistra (sacred rattles) as they are blessed by the Aten's rays.

The religious revolution caused a few headaches among Egypt's artists and masons. The ancient myths and legends were gone and the traditional temple and tomb scenes, scenes which invariably depicted the old gods and their rituals, had perforce to be abandoned. Now there was essentially one sole god, a god who lacked decorative potential. Amarna's walls, however, were not to be left blank. Where there had once been gods and goddesses there would now be scenes of Akhenaten, his wife and family offering to the Aten.

The Aten, a small, faceless, disembodied sun disk equipped with long rays and a multitude of miniature hands, could not play the traditional dominant god's role in these scenes. He could not, for example, sit on a throne to receive offerings and instead was compelled to hover in the sky above the royal family. Essentially he became a passive observer while the royal family took a more active role in proceedings. Akhenaten now became the most prominent standing figure in any religious scene; all eyes were firmly focused on the king. At the same time, in order to develop a pleasing, triangular symmetry, Nefertiti was allowed to abandon her traditional place behind or beside her husband, and on private stelae we now find the queen standing or sitting opposite the king.

The highest-ranking courtiers were expected to display a conspicuous loyalty to their monarch, and many of the more luxurious Amarna houses have yielded stelae carved with intimate scenes of the royal family. We see, for example, a relaxed Akhenaten and Nefertiti seated on stools, playing with their daughters under the protection of the Aten's rays. These are not mere pictures; they are domestic shrines whose apparent informality would have conveyed a clear message to their owners. The divine triad or trio of Amen, his goddess wife Mut and their son Khonsu has gone for ever. In their place we now have a major triad composed of the Aten, the king and the queen (a triad which those well-versed in theology could compare to that formed by the ancient creator god Atum and his twin children Shu and Tefnut), and a lesser triad of king, queen and children. Akhenaten's courtiers are now expected to worship the Aten via their pharaoh; in many cases, it would seem, they were actually persuaded to worship pharaoh himself.

So complete was the dominance of the royal family in art that even in the elite Amarna tombs, private places where we would normally expect to find images of the tomb owner and his wife enjoying the amenities of the Afterlife, we now see Akhenaten, Nefertiti and their children going about their daily tasks. The tomb owner may be present, but he has become a peripheral character in the royal saga. This is a sad development for those raised to welcome death as an escape to the certainty of eternal life. Osiris and his magical kingdom may not have been entirely condemned – Akhenaten still allowed much of the old funerary equipment including anthropoid coffins, *shabti* figures and even mummification itself – but their role has been severely curtailed. Now only the king can look forward with any degree of certainty to an existence beyond the grave. His loyal subjects seem doomed to spend eternity as restless ghosts, haunting the sun temple by day and sleeping by night.

Egyptian art, for all its beauty, had for over a thousand years maintained a conservative, highly formalised style. The king was a stereotypical hero; the queen was a slender, elegant being; the royal children were curiously absent from scenes of family life. Even nature was regimented so that birds flew in straight lines, flowers grew in neat rows and the Nile fish swam in well-disciplined ranks. Towards the end of Amenhotep III's reign a relaxing of this rigidity began to be evident, with the newly plump king himself appearing in a variety of relaxed poses. Now this process was accelerated. The first to change was Akhenaten himself.

It had always been considered a matter of great importance that Egypt's king should be seen as a flawless, handsome male with an athletic, muscular body. This was *maat*; a tradition so strong that Hatshepsut had been prepared to transform herself into the stereotypical pharaoh in order to conform to expectation. Akhenaten, however, was not afraid of change; he and his father had developed their own artistic style. Where Amenhotep III had proceeded with caution, Akhenaten leapt in with both feet. By the end of Year 5 he had developed a decidedly effeminate body with underdeveloped shoulders, arms and lower legs but wide hips, thunder thighs, obvious breasts, a narrow waist and a bloated stomach. His long face, with its narrow eyes, pendulous jaw, hollow cheeks and thick lips was equally striking. And yet, in assuming his androgynous appearance, Akhenaten had acquired a curious, disturbing sensuality.

Was this merely artistic convention, or was the king a sick man determined to reveal himself 'warts and all' for posterity? As Akhenaten's mummy has never been identified, all attempts to diagnose his 'illness' have through necessity been based on a study of his two- and three-dimensional portraits. Given that Egyptian art was never intended to convey a simple story, this situation is far from ideal. Nevertheless, two possible diseases have been suggested; Frohlich's syndrome, a group of symptoms caused by damage to the pituitary gland which may cause a female-type distribution of fat over the breasts, hips and thighs; and Marfan's syndrome, a genetic abnormality that leads to lengthening of the skull. There is, however, one major problem in attributing any feminising disease to Akhenaten. We know that his wife Nefertiti gave birth to at least six live babies.

The royal sculptor, Bak, tells us that he was merely 'the pupil whom His Majesty taught'. This may be diplomatic modesty, but seems likely to be the literal truth. Akhenaten was certainly confident enough to have developed his own artistic style; Bak was bound to follow his master's instructions however curious they may have seemed. It is telling that, following the move to Amarna and the replacement of Bak by Tuthmosis, the king's extreme appearance was modified although never corrected to its pre-Amarna normality.

You create the foetus in women, semen in men. You keep the child alive in the womb of its mother, you sooth it and stop its tears. You nurse it even in the womb and give it the breath to sustain all that you have made. When he comes down from the womb to breathe, on the day of his birth, you open his mouth utterly and provide everything he needs. When the chick is still in the egg, chirping inside the shell, you let it breathe inside it and sustain it. You have fixed its gestation period, and the time to break out

166

from the egg. It comes out of the egg to chirp at the appointed time and can walk on its legs as soon as it comes out.

*Great Hymn to the Aten*

Pharaoh's new image mingles male and female attributes in a way that would have appealed to a devotee of a sole, sexless creator god. A single broken statue recovered from Thebes even shows the king naked (itself highly unusual, as nakedness was considered undignified in a king) and obviously lacking male genitalia. Rather than leap to the immediate assumption that the statue is a truthful portrait, and that Akhenaten was in some way deformed, we should remember that ancient Egypt was no stranger to the concept of the hermaphrodite creator god. Indeed, we even have an image of Mut, the impeccably feminine wife of Amen, which shows her with an extra two animal heads plus a prominent phallus. Here we would appear to have an experimental piece, carved for a temple, which shows the king in the role of sexless creator. As we have only one such piece, we may perhaps deduce that the experiment was considered to be something of a failure – too avant garde even for Akhenaten.

Whatever its origins, the new style was soon extended to Egypt's elite and we now find the Amarna courtiers, from Nefertiti downwards, developing flabby stomachs, wide thighs, breasts and relaxed poses. The change to Nefertiti is particularly striking, given that she is today fêted as one of the world's greatest beauties. Although she starts married life in Thebes as an entirely normal woman, her appearance soon reflects that of her husband, so that the two become virtually impossible to differentiate. Not only does Nefertiti look like the new-style

Akhenaten, she copies his posture and to a limited extent his clothing. As 'mirroring' was a well-established artistic convention used to suggest a link between the king and the gods, we may guess that Nefertiti is deliberately reflecting the king so that she becomes associated with his power and divinity. At Amarna Nefertiti starts to lose some of her angularity and her face becomes slightly rounder while her body is more feminine. Finally she evolves into the conventional (to western eyes) beauty of the Berlin bust.

The Aten was a highly visible yet curiously remote god. Each day he could be seen shining in the sky, impartially dispensing his light to king and commoner alike. But, although they could see and feel his warmth, the ordinary people could not worship the Aten. In Amarna art, only the royal family were embraced by the Aten's rays. Akhenaten had no intention of weakening the position of the monarchy by losing control over his god. Indeed, he intended to use the Aten to reinforce his own divinity. He therefore retained the old tradition of restricting access to his god, proclaiming that the Aten could only be worshipped by his appointed priest in his own appointed temple. Here, in courtyards open to the sun, Akhenaten and his deputies made regular offerings. For a disembodied being the Aten required a surprising amount of sustenance, and his Great Temple has so far yielded an impressive 920 mud-brick offering tables.

In the temples of Amarna a new type of hymn could be heard, devised some said by the king himself. Akhenaten's vision of the Aten as the creator of all life, the Great Hymn to the Aten, was inscribed on the wall of Ay's Amarna tomb. Its message, rejoicing in a single god and the natural world which he has created was, five hundred years later, to find an echo in the biblical Psalm 104. The Aten would appear to be not only the god of Egypt, but the god of foreigners, too:

> You have also done so many things that are hidden from sight. You are the only god – there is no one apart from you. Because you were alone, you created the earth to please you; people, cattle and flocks, everything which walks on land, or takes off and flies using wings; the foreign lands of Syria and Nubia as well as Egypt. You gave everyone a position and supplied what they needed. Everyone has his food and each has an allotted lifetime. The languages they speak are different and so are their characters. Even their skins are different for you have marked out foreigners ...

The God of the Jews is, however, a very different entity to the Aten. The Aten was not a god for all men; he was the exclusive property of the royal family. Nor was Akhenaten promoting monotheism. His Aten was merely the principal god of many, including Re, Maat, Bes and, of course, the semi-divine Akhenaten himself.

Despite the major upheavals involved in establishing the new city, twelve peaceful years had passed, and all seemed well. Now there was to be a major celebration, an international pageant. Messengers were sent far and wide; everyone of note was to be invited to Amarna. As distinguished ambassadors arrived bearing gifts, and as his mother came out of semi-retirement to join her family, Akhenaten could be confident that Egypt was still an international power. Envoys from Africa brought gold, ivory, leopards and monkeys. From Punt came incense, musk and sandalwood. Syrians brought chariots decorated with gold, an antelope, a lion and an oryx; Libyans brought ostrich eggs; Minoans paraded through Egypt's new capital with rows of extravagantly decorated amphorae.

All of the known world was there. And so was Nefertiti, sitting beside her husband and her children at the height of her political and religious power. Then, suddenly, Nefertiti disappeared, possibly fallen victim to the plague which was at that time sweeping the east. She was not the only one to vanish from Amarna: Tiy, Meketaten, Neferneferuaten, Neferneferure and Setepenre all disappeared at roughly the same time. Akhenaten remains silent over the collapse of his world, but it seems likely that the visitors who had showered the king with gifts had also brought the illness which was to bring about the end of the Amarna idyll.

The loss of his beloved Nefertiti – whatever its cause – hardened Akhenaten's resolve. After twelve years of relative tolerance he started to turn his power to increasingly destructive ends. Once he had been content simply to replace the old gods with the new. Now Akhenaten began actively to pursue the old deities. The remaining traditional temples were closed, their assets confiscated and their festivals banned. An attempt was made to delete all references to the old gods, but this proved an impossible task and eventually the attack was focused on Amen and his family. From the most distant temples in Nubia to the tops of the highest Karnak obelisks, the name and image of Amen were hacked out. Amen did survive the attack, but only because many of those charged with his destruction were haphazard in their work, possibly because they could not actually read the hieroglyphs that they were supposed to erase.

Time seemed to stand still at Amarna, but in the outside world things had moved on and almost a decade of highly centralised rule was starting to take its toll. So far we have concentrated very much on Akhenaten's religious and artistic reforms, but hand in hand with these had gone important changes to the national economy. By closing the temples, Akhenaten had assumed total responsibility for Egypt's land management. However, his ministers could not hope to replace the networks of experienced temple administrators who had for centuries regulated much of the land and its workforce. For as long as his reserves lasted, Akhenaten need not face the fact that Egypt was slowly going bankrupt. Now it seems that the economy was starting to flounder through neglect. We have few contemporary documents from outside Amarna but Akhenaten's successors, kings who, of course, had their own political agendas, have left monumental inscriptions suggesting that corruption and inefficiency among unsupervised local officials were rife.

Akhenaten enjoyed a well-established contempt for foreigners. He was happy enough to invite them to Amarna, particularly if they were going to bring him presents, but it was well known that visitors would be expected to stand for hours, bareheaded, beneath Egypt's burning sun while pharaoh inspected them from the comforting shade of a parasol. Akhenaten, not a natural diplomat, had long since lost contact with Tushratta. He did not seem to care that the kingdom of Mitanni, once Egypt's oldest ally, had collapsed, even though this left a vacuum for other, power-hungry nations to fill. The Hittites and the Assyrians, traditional enemies of Egypt, were now strong enough to pose an immediate threat to the empire. Indeed Egypt and Hatti now shared a common border while the Hittite sphere of influence extended over most of Egypt's eastern territories. Egypt not only lost prestige, she lost tribute and access to the Levantine ports which allowed her to import precious wood.

Akhenaten's loyal vassals found themselves without any real protection, and many made the sensible decision to change allegiance. The Amarna letters make Akhenaten's neglect obvious. Urgent, pleading letters were rushed to the king:

> The king my lord should be informed that the king of Hatti has seized all countries that were the vassals of Mitanni...
> In the time of Tuthmosis III anyone threatening Tunip would have been plundered by the king. Now Tunip weeps: In Canaan some locals beat my merchants and stole their money... Canaan is your country and its kings are your slaves – in your country I was robbed...

Akhenaten was no pacifist; he had been happy to send troops to Nubia to quash a Year 12 rebellion. However, he was curiously unmoved by the pleas of his imperial subjects. Perhaps assuming that his empire would last for ever, certainly secure in his own isolation, he turned his eye from the empire to focus on the sun. While the city of Akhetaten basked in the desert heat of the sun's disk, the hard-won New Kingdom empire stood on the brink of destruction.

Then, in his 17th regnal year, Akhenaten died. He had always intended to be buried in the multi-chambered Amarna royal tomb which already housed his second-born daughter Meket-aten, and even though the tomb was unfinished at his death, we have no reason to assume that this plan was not carried out. In spite of the new religion, the old funerary rituals, including mummification, were to be performed. The masons had seventy days to prepare for the funeral. Luckily, the pink granite sarcophagus engraved with images of Nefertiti, its grey granite lid and the alabaster canopic chest were already complete.

When the Amarna royal tomb was officially discovered in the late nineteenth century, it had already been stripped by the local villagers who had speedily sold its contents on the black market. As early as 1882 Amarna jewellery was being offered to tourists; the Reverend W. J. Loftie was shown several pieces including a signet ring engraved with Nefertiti's cartouche; this eventually made its way into the collection of the Royal Museum of Scotland, Edinburgh. Another clergyman, A. H. Sayce, writing from Luxor on 26 February 1890 (*The Academy* 933: 195), provides us with the sorry details:

> The tomb and mummy of Amenophis IV, the 'Heretic King' of Egyptian history, have been found at Tel el-Amarna... The tomb has proved a second pit of Der el-Bahari to the antiquity dealers of Ekhmim, by whom it has been worked. Now that it has been despoiled of the precious objects it once contained, they have conde-scended to inform us of its exact position... The mummy of the king has, unfortunately, been torn to pieces... The beautiful objects of ivory and alabaster which lately have been on the market of 'antikas', the bronze rings and enamelled porcelain [faience] which bear the cartouches of Amenophis IV and the solar disk... have all come from the desecrated sepulchre.

The 'newly discovered' tomb had been fitted with gates but then largely ignored by the French authorities who were at that time responsible for guarding Amarna. It was not to be recorded and published for over a century. This is very unfortunate as the engraved tomb walls, although attacked during the post-Amarna New Kingdom, were in 1890 substantially intact. They have since been subjected to both natural deterioration and deliberate vandalism.

The archaeologists who finally got to examine the tomb found no trace of the king's body. His once splendid sarcophagus had been smashed to pieces and his grave goods were gone. Sayce may be correct in his assumption that the body had been torn to pieces by local robbers. However, there was always a hope that Akhenaten's successors had, as Amarna was abandoned, taken the king from the Royal Wadi and reburied him in or near the Valley of the Kings. For a long time experts thought that an anonymous but obviously royal male mummy recovered from tomb KV 55 must be Akhenaten. However, recent anatomical and dental investigation has shown the KV 55 body to be that of a man who died in his early twenties. Too young to be Akhenaten, and closely related (on the grounds of blood type and skull shape) to Tutankhamen, this burial would appear to be the remains of Akhenaten's ephemeral elder son, Smenkhkare.

During Year 15 of her father's reign Princess Meritaten had married her half-brother Smenkhkare, son of Akhenaten and a favoured lady of the harem, Kiya. Their marriage had signalled the start of Smenkhkare's brief co-regency with his father, and legitimised Smenkhkare's position as heir to his father's throne. Unfortunately, Smenkhkare died soon after – perhaps even slightly before – his father. As Smenkhkare and Meritaten were childless, the throne passed to Tutankhaten, hitherto insignificant younger brother of Smenkhkare. Tutankhaten took as his queen his half-sister, Ankhesenpaaten, third-born daughter of Akhenaten and Nefertiti.

Egypt's new king, just nine years old, was to reign for less than a decade. He should have been only a footnote in Egypt's long history. However, a fortunate combination of circumstances – the loss of his tomb beneath the debris of later construction, and the perseverance of archaeologist Howard Carter – ensured that he was to become Egypt's most famous king.

CHAPTER 10

# The Producers:
# Egypt's Unsung Heroes

The god Osiris, son of the earth god Geb and the sky goddess Nut, had brought agriculture to Egypt. As king of the living, Osiris taught his subjects to grow crops and husband cattle while his gentle sister-wife Isis showed their wives how to make bread, beer and clothing. Egypt prospered under their rule and only one person was unhappy. Seth, the evil brother of Isis and Osiris, plotted to kill the king and seize the throne for himself. This he did in a particularly devious way. Osiris was murdered and his body dismembered and scattered throughout the world. The loyal Isis was able to restore and resurrect her husband but he now became king of the Afterlife while his son, Horus, took his place as ruler of the living. Thus the burial and rebirth of Osiris came to symbolise the agricultural cycle. In tribute to their dead god his people would include Osiris beds – god-shaped seed trays – in their elite tombs.

They [the Egyptians] obtain the fruits of the field with less trouble than any other people in the world, since they have no need to break up the ground with a plough, nor to use the hoe, nor to do any of the work which all other peoples find necessary if they are to get a crop. The river rises by itself, irrigates the fields and then sinks back again. Then each man sows his field and lets pigs into it to trample the seed. All he then has to do is to wait until the harvest.

*Herodotus,* Histories II: 14

For three thousand years – from the beginning of the dynastic age until its very end – Egypt's upper classes dreamed of an idyllic life away from the stresses and smells of the city. A spacious, well-staffed country bungalow, set in its own verdant garden complete with pool and firmly separated from the uncomfortable realities of the countryside by a thick mudbrick wall, was every rich man's dream. It was a dream that extended beyond death. The Afterlife – the Field of Reeds – was determinedly rural. It had fields, animals and a replica River Nile. Here the elite, dressed in their finest white garments and ornamented by glittering jewels, expected to perform simple yet satisfying agricultural tasks under the warming rays of the eternal sun. Leisure hours would be spent hunting in the marshes, fishing on the placid river, or simply watching others toil in the fields.

At Amarna, Akhenaten had come close to fulfilling this dream for a favoured few. Egypt's new capital may have been uncompromisingly sited in the barren desert, but Akhenaten was not prepared to let a shortage of soil and water thwart his plans for a garden city. The more luxurious of the Amarna villas were up-to-date mansions equipped with all modern conveniences including stone-lined bathrooms and lavatories, yet their occupants had only to step outside, into their formal gardens, to imagine themselves transported to the simplicity of the countryside. Trees, shrubs, flowers and artificial pools provided a relaxing environment for jaded officials to sit, reflect and drink wine. Garden shrines made a suitable setting to worship the royal family, while outside the compound wall, trees shaded the processional ways.

This love of all things rural was reflected in the interior decoration of the Amarna houses. Akhenaten's own official office, the Great Palace, is today largely destroyed. However, discovered amid its crumbled remains was a beautiful gypsum pavement painted blue to represent a pond stocked with lazy fish. Around this pond was painted a glorious assortment of animals, birds and plants. The pavement was rescued by Flinders Petrie, who hit upon an ingenious but time-consuming method of preserving it by painting it with a coating of weak tapioca solution applied by the tip of one finger, and was put on public display. Unfortunately, in 1912, it was deliberately vandalised by a disgruntled employee of the antiquities service. Today the restored remains are housed in Cairo Museum.

Better preserved is the North Palace, a complex used by Princess Meritaten, Akhenaten's eldest and most favoured daughter. Here the rooms were centred around a large pool. As well as the expected private rooms, bathroom and servants'quarters there was a garden courtyard and an open-air court with altars for sun worship. More surprising – and so far unexplained – is the beautifully decorated menagerie which includes animal pens and aviaries. Nature was again a predominant decorative theme, and the spectacular walls of the 'Green Room' were painted with a papyrus thicket full of wonderful wild birds.

At the other end of the scale, in the walled workmen's village associated with the Amarna cemeteries, space was at a premium. Families were provided with purpose-built terraced housing measuring a mere 5m x 10m (16 ft × 32 ft), and the only way to expand was upwards. Gardens, and indeed bathrooms, were an impossible dream. Undeterred, the enterprising families tended allotments in the desert outside the village wall. Although every drop of water and every grain of soil had to be imported from the main city, it proved possible to raise pigs and grow vegetables under these difficult conditions. Here, in the tranquillity of the artificial countryside, the workmen built their private chapels and worshipped in peace.

> Speaking in general terms, every kind of agricultural labour among other peoples involves them in great expense and toil, and only among the Egyptians is the harvest gathered in with an insignificant outlay of time and money.
>
> *Diodorus Siculus*, Histories, I:36

The elite, of course, took a highly sanitised view of the countryside. They were observers, not participants in the annual agricultural cycle and they seldom got their spotless garments dirty. Those forced to live the life knew that, while life in the enclosed towns and cities may have been crowded, smelly and uncomfortable, rural life, too, had definite drawbacks. Middle Kingdom teachers, attempting to convince their young pupils to become scribes rather than farmers, had outlined the uncomfortable realities of hard agricultural labour. Although they were intentionally exaggerating, their account has a ring of well-observed truth:

> The gardener carries a yoke which makes his shoulders bend with age; it causes a nasty swelling on his neck, which

180

festers. He spends the morning watering his leeks and the evening tending his herbs, having already toiled in the orchard at noon. He works himself into an early grave.

The peasant cries all the time; his voice is like a raven's croak. His fingers swell and stink to excess. He is exhausted from standing in the mire; his clothes are in rags and tatters . . .

*Satire of the Trades*

Everyone was, however, agreed on one thing. Egypt owed her economic success to her strong agricultural base and the labours of her peasant farmers. Egypt's fertility, the envy of her less fortunate neighbours, was in turn the direct result of the dependable, predictable behaviour of her river. Herodotus summed up the situation in seven often-quoted words: 'Egypt is the gift of the Nile.' Without the Nile there would have been no pyramids, no stone temples and no New Kingdom empire.

Herodotus was accustomed to the expensive, time-consuming state-controlled irrigation systems required to water Greece. The idea that an entire country could be dependent on a river which repeatedly flooded in the summer (not the winter!) seemed bizarre and he could find no explanation for the phenomenon. However, he was quick to appreciate its worth.

Concerning the nature of the river, I could get no information from either the priests or anyone else. I was anxious to learn why the Nile begins to rise at the summer solstice, continues to do so for one hundred days, and then falls again so that it remains low throughout the winter until the summer solstice comes round again.

Nobody in Egypt could explain this...
                                    *Herodotus,* Histories II: 19

Egypt's agricultural calendar had a simple rhythm. Every year from July to October, following heavy rainfall and melting snows in the distant Ethiopian highlands, the Nile would swell and burst her banks. Soon Egypt's fields from Aswan to Memphis were covered with the red-brown silt-laden waters while her cities, towns and farming communities, built on raised ground and protected by dikes, had become temporary islands linked by raised paths. The cemeteries, safe in the desert sands, remained dry. For weeks water seeped into the parched soil, filling the canals and irrigation basins which would provide an additional source of water for the coming year. Meanwhile the peasants, temporarily unemployed, could be summoned by *corvée* to work on state projects.

By late October the waters had started to retreat, revealing moist fields newly covered with a thick layer of highly fertile mineral-rich soil and a layer of fresh fish abandoned by the Nile. The farmers gathered the fish, sowed their crops and waited. In late spring they would gather a wonderful harvest. The land would then have time to dry out under the hot, sterilising sun which effectively eliminated agricultural pests and diseases, before the river level rose and the whole cycle began again.

Hapi, the god who personified the Nile inundation, was a cheerful, plump being celebrated throughout Egypt for his bounty. Unfortunately Hapi, and his river, did not always behave as they should. Regular, consistent Nile levels were regarded as a sign of *maat*; Amenhotep III had been blessed with a series of optimal Nile levels which made a huge contribution to his economic boom. Too low a flood was dangerous as it would prevent the water from covering all the land and, with the irrigation basins left dry, would lead to a shortage of food. Worse was the havoc wrought by too high a flood; not only would the harvest be delayed, the network of fields and canals might be destroyed and there was a real danger that mud-brick houses, too, would be lost.

The Egyptians, always prudent, placed a great emphasis on storing up surpluses against times of need. The warehouses attached to the temples and palaces would ideally be maintained at maximum capacity. They were capable of holding a vast amount of grain; the British archaeologist Barry Kemp has calculated that the granaries attached to the Ramesseum, the mortuary temple of Ramesses II, could have held some 16,522,000 litres of cereal!

And in the seven plenteous years the earth brought forth by handfuls. And he gathered up all the food of the seven years, which were in the land of Egypt, and laid up the food in the cities; the food of the field, which was round about every city, laid he up in the same. And Joseph gathered corn as the sand of the sea, very much, until he left numbering, for it was without number...

And the seven years of plenteousness, that was in the land of Egypt, were ended. And the seven years of dearth began to come, according as Joseph had said: and the dearth was in all lands; but in the land of Egypt there was bread. And when all the land of Egypt was famished, the people cried to Pharaoh for bread... And the famine was all over the face of the earth: and Joseph opened all the storehouses... And all countries came into Egypt to

Joseph to buy corn; because the famine was so sore in all lands.

*Genesis 41: 46–57*

The Nile brought other important benefits to Egypt. As the fertile land was restricted to a thin strip on either side of the river, and as the communities were strung out along the Nile in a more or less straight line, the Nile made the perfect highway. There was no need to develop an expensive network of roads; boats sailed northwards aided by the current, and southwards propelled by the breeze. The transport of huge blocks of stone, which would have been so difficult by wheeled vehicle, thus became relatively easy; canals could be cut to connect Egypt's quarries and building sites to the Nile, allowing barges to transport their heavy loads virtually 'door to door'. Thus it became possible for the pharaohs to construct their impressive monuments.

The Nile, of course, was an important source of water not only for the human population who used it for drinking, cooking, washing and as a sewer, but for the plants, fish, waterfowl and wild game which were harvested by the Egyptians. Fish was an important element of the peasant diet; caught in traps, or by net, it could be dried and salted or smoked to provide a valuable reserve against lean times. Papyrus, which grew on the river banks, was harvested to make Egyptian 'paper'.

Let me tell you about the fisherman. He has the worst job of all. He works on the river, surrounded by crocodiles; he is always complaining...

*Satire of the Trades*

184

The Nile, however, could bring dangers. Some – such as accidental drowning – were obvious. The hippopotami who basked in the waters were not too dangerous, but if cornered on land, where they were forced to graze, they could prove lethal as they thundered their way back to the safety of the river. Slightly more subtle was the threat posed by the crocodiles who lurked on the banks of the Nile until the building of the Aswan Dam. The crocodile was seen as a mysterious animal often used to symbolise fate. Those who died by crocodile, a death which all too often left no body for burial, were accorded their own particular mortuary rituals.

A less obvious danger was posed by the invisible diseases and parasites carried by the Nile waters. As the Nile was both a source of drinking water and a drain, the Egyptians must have suffered more than their fair share of stomach upsets. Diarrhoea, in the absence of modern medicines, could prove fatal. Malaria, too, was an ever-present incurable menace, as the stagnant waters of the canals and irrigation basins provided a fertile breeding ground for mosquitoes.

Anyone who came into contact with stagnant water risked contracting a parasitic disease. Bilharzia (schistosomiasis) infestation was particularly prevalent, and could cause serious medical complications; in extreme cases it might even lead to the development of cancer. The first sign of infestation was usually blood in the urine and a feeling of lethargy and sickness. Today we know that bilharzia worms lay their eggs in the human host. These make their way to the bladder or the intestine and then escape via urine or faeces. The eggs hatch in water, allowing their larvae to burrow into a temporary host: the water snail. Having left the snail, the parasite re-enters the water and then tunnels into a human, usually via the feet. Moving to the liver or the bladder, it mates and produces eggs; the whole complex cycle then begins again. The Egyptians had no way of understanding this and saw no reason to avoid still water. For many, including farmers, fishermen, laundrymen and the housewives who collected water from the river-bank, wet feet were an unavoidable part of daily life.

Bilharzia, although perhaps the most widespread, was by no means the only parasitic infestation. Guinea worms have been found in several mummies; these could potentially grow to an astonishing 1m (3 ft) and longer within the human leg. Strongyloides infection was another common problem. This worm penetrates the skin of the feet or hands to reach the blood vessels and then travels around the host, visiting first the heart and then the lungs, the windpipe and the throat. The worm, duly swallowed by the unfortunate host, then reaches the intestine, causing bloody diarrhoea. Strongyloides eggs are eventually excreted and re-deposited on the muddy river-bank where they await their next victim.

The Nile could not be blamed for all of Egypt's ills. Modern mummy studies are starting to reveal that the majority of the population – rich and poor alike – consistently suffered from a variety of debilitating complaints. Arthritis, tapeworms, lung disease caused by sand and smoke inhalation, even prolonged and painful toothache brought about by the unavoidable inclusion of sand in the diet; all combined to make life miserable for peasant and elite alike.

Egypt's farmers made up the bulk of the population, yet their lives are largely lost to us. Often poor and almost invariably illiterate, they have had little direct impact on the surviving written record although they do occasionally feature as characters in tales told by others. They appear, too, as minor roles in the tomb scenes painted by their superiors; while the principal characters – the tomb owner, tomb owner's wife and children – invariably have the bland, stereotyped appearance of all Egypt's upper classes, the peasants in the background are often painted with a degree of realism which brings life to the scene. Here we can see real people – old, ugly and deformed – going about their work.

The *Tale of the Eloquent Peasant* is an amusing story written during the Middle Kingdom. It tells of Khun-Anup, a prosperous farmer, who has set off on a journey to take surplus produce to market. In the absence of any form of money, Khun-Anup hopes to exchange his produce for the surpluses of others. Unfortunately, he is forced to pass by the estate of a greedy man named Djehutinakht, who, having caught sight of Khun-Anup's heavily laden donkeys, decides to steal the peasant's goods. Laying a sheet across the narrow road, he bars the way. As Khun-Anup argues against this unreasonable restriction, one of his donkeys leans into a field and eats a wisp of Djehutinakht's barley. Djehutinakht immediately demands compensation for his 'loss' and seizes the donkeys and their loads. Fortunately Khun-Anup is a man who knows his legal rights. He takes Djehutinakht to court and, after a legal battle distinguished by the plaintiff's long-winded speech-making, receives full compensation for his ordeal. The greedy Djehutinakht is punished with the confiscation of his own goods.

The Eloquent Peasant was by no means a typical farm-worker. He was one of Egypt's growing band of independent farmers who rented their fields from one of the major land-owners (the palace, the temples and the large estates). Others inherited the right to farm a given patch of land, or maintain a small herd of temple cattle. Pharaoh routinely gave small estates as a reward to his loyal followers, and we have already seen the faithful soldier Ahmose son of Ibana receive a gift of 'many fields': a pension which would have supported him through his old age. Khun-Anup and Ahmose would have been entitled to keep their surpluses, but would have been expected to pay taxes and, in the case of Khun-Anup, rent.

The majority of those who worked the land were considerably more humble. Effectively serfs employed by the major estate owners, they were tied to land which they did not own and, denied any form of education or training, forced to work under the supervision of a supervisor or bailiff who reported to higher authorities. The surpluses which they grew would be taxed and then passed to the landowners, with the peasants receiving a basic payment in kind for their hard work.

The tied peasants lived in conditions far worse than those offered by the well-organised Amarna workmen's village. Egypt's hamlets grew organically, with new mud-brick rooms and houses being added on to existing structures as and when needed. Narrow, twisted alleys linked together the cramped, dark and unavoidably dirty houses where extended families often shared their accommodation with their livestock. Inside there was little furniture; indeed, the peasants owned little of value and had nothing to pass on to their children. Outside there would be a source of water, and a communal rubbish dump.

The tax collectors, civil servants employed by the vizier's office, were seen as the scourge of the gentlemen farmers. The state was entitled to a percentage of all crops, and few primary producers were exempt from this burden; during the New Kingdom the god Amen was Egypt's highest taxpayer. Each year the hated tax inspectors would arrive to measure the fields and assess the growing crops. Payment would fall due at harvest time, and there was no mercy for those unable or unwilling to meet the demand. Armed with sticks, and escorted by bailiffs, Egypt's tax collectors meant business:

> Now the tax collector lands on the river bank. He surveys the harvest. He is attended by bailiffs armed with staffs and Nubians with clubs. They say to the farmer 'Give us grain!' but he replies 'There is none.' The farmer is beaten savagely. He is tied up and thrown into the well where he is ducked head first. His wife is tied up in his presence and his children are bound in fetters. His neighbours abandon them and run away. When the ordeal is over, there is no grain...
>
> *Papyrus Lansing*

Farming was hard physical labour conducted with simple but highly effective tools which remained fundamentally unchanged throughout the dynastic age. The work was, as we would expect, highly seasonal, with the busiest time of year being the few weeks following the retreat of the waters when the soil was still soft enough to manipulate. This was the best time to clean and repair the dikes and drainage canals which would have become clogged with silt during the flood. It was, of course, the only time to sow the seeds.

Using the hoe and the ox-drawn (occasionally man-drawn) plough, the fields were prepared for the sower. The principal crops were cereal (emmer wheat or barley which formed the basis of the Egyptian diet) and flax (used to make linen garments and rope), although vines were an important Delta crop. Whatever the crop, the seed was scattered by hand, and a flock of sheep or goats was encouraged to run across the field to trample the seed into the ground.

As the crops grew they would need weeding, while bird- and animal-scaring was a job reserved for children. However, there was seldom a need for extra water. Only the fields on the very edge of the cultivation, and the gardens which surrounded the larger houses, were artificially watered. For centuries the only way to take water to the fields and gardens was to transport it from the river or canal in large pots carried by donkeys. Water carrying took up an inordinate amount of time in ancient Egypt, with whole communities, most notably the Theban workmen's village of Deir el-Medina, relying on the water carriers for every life-giving drop. In the New Kingdom came the invention of the *shadoof*, a simple counterpoise mechanism for raising water from the canal to the soil. For small-scale watering this was a great advance; soon all the best gardens were equipped with a *shadoof*. It was not, however, suited to large-scale irrigation and the farmers had to wait until the Graeco-Roman period for the invention of the water wheel, or *saqqiah*.

Harvest was another busy time. Entire families took to the fields as the sickle-wielding grain cutters were followed by the gleaners, the women and children who gathered up the ears of corn. The ears were taken in baskets to the threshing floor where the grain was separated from the enclosing husks; this was done either by beating the ears with pitchforks or trampling them with animals. Winnowing – tossing the mingled grains and chaff high in the air – would allow the wind to sort the crop. As the feather-light chaff blew away, the heavier grain would fall to the ground and could be scooped into a storage sack. The straw, left in place in the fields, would be collected later and used as fuel, animal feed, and in the manufacture of mud-bricks.

Flax had a variable harvest-time; young, green stalks were gathered to make fine linen threads while the older, riper stalks produced coarse threads which were turned into rope and the cord used for basketry and matting. The oldest crops of all were allowed to mature and produce seeds which would be used both for linseed oil production and to provide the seeds for the next year's planting. The strong flax stalks were pulled whole from the ground; the plant would first be trimmed of its root and then combed to strip the seeds. Later the stalks would be soaked or retted (to rot the unwanted woody parts and separate them from the valuable fibres) and recombed, ready for the rope and thread makers.

Cattle make frequent appearances in elite tomb scenes although, in the Nile Valley proper, they were probably relatively few and far between. In the north, the green fields of the Delta made suitable grazing for the herds of cattle owned by the palace and the temples. Beef was a luxury food rarely available to the peasants who were employed to tend the herds; it had high prestige, but contributed little to the Egyptian economy which was firmly based on arable agriculture. Many Egyptians, however, town dwellers as well as country folk, kept their own animals. Sheep, goats, pigs and ducks could be raised on the scraps left over from family meals and made a valuable addition to the somewhat restricted diet.

# CHAPTER 11

# Tutankhamen and Horemheb:

# The Restorers

The dusty floor itself maintained eerie footprints of the last people to breathe that very air, 3,500 years earlier. As you note the signs of recent life around you – the half-filled bowls of mortar for the door, the blackened lamp, the finger-marks on the freshly painted surfaces, the farewell garland dropped on the threshold – you feel as if it might have been put there yesterday. Time is annihilated by such intimate details as these, and you feel an intruder...

*Diary of Howard Carter*

By the turn of the twentieth century AD it seemed that all of the New Kingdom royal tombs must have been discovered. Long-since stripped of their precious contents, filled with a mass of smashed artifacts and torn mummy-wrappings mixed with sand, mud, limestone chips and rubble, and bearing the evidence of many centuries of vandalism, the open tombs were a depressing sight.

Archaeologists still journeyed to the Valley of the Kings, but they were starting to lose heart. The west bank was slowly but surely turning into a giant amusement park populated by ever increasing flocks of tourists who liked nothing more than to visit the desecrated temples and tombs. Here they would picnic amid the picturesque ruins, and give a sophisticated shudder before the horrific 'mummy pits' filled with decomposing Late Period bodies by the enterprising local guards. A daring few would even buy antiquities on the black market; countless mummies and mummy parts – some genuine, some fake – were purchased as pleasingly gruesome holiday souvenirs and made their way westwards to end up, unwanted, in the collections of local museums. The once-sleepy town of Luxor had become a popular holiday resort; wintering in Egypt was the height of fashion.

Most of the New Kingdom royal mummies had by now been recovered from their protective caches and were safely housed in Cairo Museum. One king, however, was still missing. Tutankhamen's body had never been identified and his tomb had never been located. There had been some excitement in 1907, when Theodore Davies had discovered a collection of discarded embalming material bearing the king's name, but this had fizzled away when there was no sign of a nearby tomb. Davies, so often linked to Tutankhamen, seemed destined to find his tomb. Previously, in 1905–6, his team had uncovered a faience cup engraved with the king's name; in 1909 Davies was to find a small tomb which yielded fragments of gold foil stamped with Tutankhamen's cartouche. Davies believed that this undistinguished chamber represented the desecrated tomb of Tutankhamen; in fact he had uncovered the sorry remains of the burial equipment of King Ay. Glumly, he published his thoughts in *The Tombs of Harmhabi and Touatankhamanou* (1912, London: 3): 'I fear that the Valley of the Tombs is now exhausted.'

Most experts agreed with Davies that the Valley must now be

empty of undiscovered tombs. Howard Carter begged to differ. Always a man of strong opinion – a man who had resigned from a previous employment over a matter of principle – he deliberately set out to look for Tutankhamen. He would comb the Valley floor inch by inch if he had to. Fortunately, Carter had found a wealthy patron who was prepared to bankroll his search.

Lord Carnarvon, in frail health following a serious car crash, was dutifully following his doctor's advice and taking full advantage of the mild Egyptian climate which was believed to be so much better for him than the damp British winter. Like many other visitors before and since, he arrived in Cairo with little interest in ancient history but soon found himself bitten by the Egyptology bug. He started to collect antiquities, developing a fine private collection, most of which was to be sold after his death to the Metropolitan Museum, New York, and he longed to excavate. As an excavator he would be entitled to a percentage of the finds; more importantly, he would share in the excitement of discovery.

In the early twentieth century most archaeological missions were financed by private sponsorship. Carnarvon had the wealth to pursue his hobby but he lacked professional expertise. In 1908 he teamed up with the experienced but decidedly unwealthy archaeologist Howard Carter and the pair excavated with a modest degree of success in the Nile Delta and in the private tombs of Thebes before gaining permission to dig in the Valley of the Kings. Their stated aim was to discover a royal tomb, but this was easier said than done. By 1921 the patient Carnarvon was losing faith (and a great deal of money) in the joint project; he felt that a spectacular find was now unlikely, and it had been agreed the 1922–3 season was to be their last.

The story of the discovery of Tutankhamen's tomb – lost for many centuries beneath a pile of rubble from the excavation of a later, higher tomb (Ramesses VI; KV 9) – is one that has been told and retold. Theodore Davies had in fact been within six feet of his goal when he stopped digging in the Valley in 1914. The more methodical Carter had more luck. On 4 November 1922 a workman uncovered the first of a flight of sixteen stone steps leading down to a sealed doorway. Although Carter was on site, his partner was still in England. Excitedly, Carter rushed to the telegraph office:

At last have made a wonderful discovery in Valley; a magnificent tomb with seals intact; re-covered same for your arrival; congratulations.

On receipt of the message Carnarvon departed post-haste for Egypt accompanied by his daughter, Lady Evelyn Herbert. Only when he had reached the Valley almost three weeks later did Carter recommence digging.

The name stamped on the door was clear for all to read: Tutankhamen. Unfortunately, it was also clear that the door had been opened and resealed at least twice. Carter and Carnarvon braced themselves for disappointment. Would this be yet another ransacked tomb? They could only hope as their workmen carefully dismantled the doorway and cleared the corridor beyond of its filling of limestone chips. By 26 November the pair once again stood before a sealed door. Carter made a small hole, tested the air for purity, and then pushed his candle inside:

At first I could see nothing, the hot air escaping from the chamber causing the candle flames to flicker, but presently,

as my eyes grew accustomed to the light, details of the
room within emerged slowly from the mist, strange animals, statues and gold – everywhere the glint of gold.
      *Howard Carter:* The Tomb of Tut.ankh.Amen I: 95-6

This was merely an antechamber; a storeroom casually crammed
with all the goods that Tutankhamen might need in his Afterlife.
The astonished Carter could see golden couches, statues and a
mass of smaller objects; caskets, vases, chairs, chariot parts and
what would later prove to be boxes of food (joints of meat,
bread, legumes and spices). There were even poignant bouquets
of funeral flowers. Beyond lay an annexe, a smaller chamber also
filled with wonderful things, while to the right the burial
chamber – the last resting place of the king – lay concealed
behind a partition wall guarded by two imposing life-sized
statues of the king. It was obvious that the ancient thieves had
burrowed their way through the wall into the burial chamber;
equally obvious that the tomb had been restored and resealed in
antiquity. Was Tutankhamen still lying in his sarcophagus,
hidden behind the fragile wall?

Howard Carter was highly disciplined, but he was also
human. The team needed to know what they were dealing with.
Carnarvon in particular was interested in recouping some of his
expenses by selling his story to the press and that story would
be all the more lucrative if Tutankhamen was indeed resting in
his coffin. Privately Carter and Carnarvon reopened the hole
made by the ancient robbers and, accompanied by Lady Evelyn,
crawled through. They found themselves in a chamber dominated by a huge gilded shrine. Beyond, a third store room, 'the
treasury', held the promise of even more golden wonders.
Elated, they returned to the antechamber and re-covered the

robbers' hole. It seemed that the tomb must be substantially complete.

Meanwhile, the antechamber had to be cleared. Carter had been trained in archaeological techniques by the master himself, Flinders Petrie. Despite the almost overwhelming temptation to rush the work and head for the burial chamber, he knew that the tomb and its precious contents were unique. They had to be properly recorded for posterity. The empty tomb of Seti II was opened up to serve as a laboratory and store; other tombs were already serving as a dark-room and the expedition dining room. It was to take seven weeks of painstaking labour – labelling, planning, photography, drawing and conservation – for the ante-chamber to be cleared. Eventually, on 17 February 1923, the official opening of the burial chamber took place with the King of Egypt and the British High Commissioner as invited guests. The ceremony passed off splendidly, the stone partition was demol-ished, and nobody noticed the tell-tale hole low down in the wall.

I shall expect [the sarcophagus] to be of alabaster... I expect it will be filled with flowers and will contain the royal regalia. In the sarcophagus I shall first expect to find the ordinary wooden coffin. Inside there will probably be a second coffin of thin wood, lined with finely chased silver. Inside this, again, there will be a coffin of thin wood, richly gilt. Then we shall find the mummy...
*Lord Carnarvon speculates in* The Times, *18 December 1922*

The burial chamber was almost completely filled by the vast gilded wooden shrine inlaid with blue faience. Drawing back the bolts, Carter swung open the doors to reveal a wooden frame holding a delicate linen pall spangled with golden daisies.

Beyond this came three further gilded shrines, their unbroken seals proving that the burial was indeed intact. The innermost, unbolted, shrine housed an immense yellow quartzite sarcophagus, its lid still in place, but to open the sarcophagus it was first necessary to dismantle and remove the delicate enclosing shrines.

By February 1924 the burial chamber was finally clear, and a block and tackle were brought in to lift the massive, cracked sarcophagus lid. A shrouded, garlanded, larger-than-life figure emerged into the arc-light. Beneath two fragile linen sheets a substantial gilded and inlaid anthropoid coffin rested on a carved bier. Here was Tutankhamen in the form of Osiris, patiently awaiting his fate.

At this crucial moment diplomatic squabbles interrupted the work, and the sarcophagus lid was left suspended over the burial as the Egyptian authorities and the British archaeologists argued over rights to the tomb and its contents. By 13 October 1925, with everything resolved, Carter was back in the tomb and the first coffin lid was raised to reveal a second gleaming coffin. Beneath this came a third coffin, this time of solid gold one inch thick. The separation of the heavy but fragile coffins was to be a difficult, time-consuming task but finally, the young king's mummy was revealed to the world:

> Before us, occupying the whole of the interior of the golden coffin, was an impressive, neat and carefully made mummy, over which had been poured anointing unguents... In contradiction to the general dark and sombre effect, due to these unguents, was a brilliant, one might say magnificent, burnished gold mask or similitude of the king, covering his head and shoulders, which, like

the feet, had been intentionally avoided when using the unguents.

*Howard Carter:* The Tomb of Tut.ankh.Amen II: 82-3

The spectacular mask, engraved on the reverse with a spell from the *Book of the Dead,* was just one of Tutankhamen's accessories. His wrappings concealed over 150 items, including collars, bracelets, rings, a heart scarab, an iron dagger and a delicate beaded cap.

Tutankhamen's preserved organs – his lungs, liver, intestines and stomach – had been given an equally elaborate burial. The four miniature golden coffins had been wrapped in linen and then stored in separate cylindrical compartments carved into the top of an intricate calcite chest. The compartments were plugged by four human-headed stoppers, and the whole chest was covered by a curved lid. The chest had been shrouded by a linen pall, and then placed in a gilded shrine bearing the carved figures of the goddesses Isis, Nephthys, Neith and Selkis. These goddesses, their arms comfortingly outstretched, would protect Tutankhamen on his journey to the Afterlife.

Howard Carter was to dedicate the rest of his life to emptying and recording the tomb. The more spectacular arti-facts – the gold death mask, the shrines, beds, furniture, chariots and much, much more – are currently displayed in Cairo Museum where they serve as a tribute to Carter's persistent vision. But what of the king himself? Today Tutankhamen's body rests in solitary splendour in the Valley of the Kings. Sealed below a covering of armour-plated glass, he is for the time being protected and untouchable. We know, from past examinations, that he died a relatively young man, and that he was closely related to the body discovered in tomb KV 55, the

200

body now attributed to Smenkhkare.

However, Tutankhamen's burial is in one way disappointingly mute. There is a surprising shortage of written material within the tomb, and even the painted walls of the burial chamber are bare of informative text. The burial tells us nothing of the king's parentage, nothing of his immediate predecessor, and nothing of the sudden ending of the Amarna idyll. To reconstruct events following the death of Akhenaten, we are forced to rely once again on a miscellany of archaeological detective work.

Some three thousand years earlier, plans were afoot to abandon Amarna. Akhenaten's new city had only ever appealed to those who wished to spend their days in the desert worshipping the sun. True devotees of the new religion had always been few and far between; Akhenaten's courtiers had been inspired by political necessity rather than belief. Now, with Akhenaten dead, the keystone of Atenism was gone and no one wanted to carry on. Those who had formerly expressed their public devotion to the Aten were quickly and happily reconverted back to the old ways. The bulk of the population, who had remained largely untouched by the religious experiment, carried on much as they had before.

As the Aten experienced a rapid decline in popularity his city became an impractical and expensive irrelevance. After three or four years at Amarna, Tutankhaten and Ankhesenpaaten declared a permanent move. Thebes would once again take her place as Egypt's religious capital, while the bureaucracy would return to Memphis. Unwanted, the diplomatic archive would be left to rot at Amarna. There was no compulsory or mass exodus; the Amarna elite, accustomed to royal whims, merely boarded up their houses and waited to see what would happen next. Meanwhile the royal sculptor Tuthmosis packed up his belongings, and work gradually ground to a halt in the tombs of the courtiers.

Today these tombs remain half-finished; elaborate reliefs emerge from basic drawings, and walls and pillars stand half-trapped in the living rock. It is as if the workmen have just stepped out for a moment. There was still a significant population at Amarna, but as it became clear that the court would not be returning, numbers dwindled until eventually the town was deserted. Amarna, at the best estimate, had lasted a scant thirty years. In contrast, the workman's village was reoccupied and even expanded during Tutankhamen's reign, before being abandoned during the reign of Horemheb.

As they abandoned Amarna, the royal couple altered their names to remove all reference to the Aten, becoming Tutankhamen (Living image of Amen) and Ankhesen-amen (Living through Amen). This, the exact reversal of Akhenaten's name-change less than twenty years earlier, signalled the official end of the Aten's dominance. Now the old temples were quietly reopened and as the Aten was stripped of its assets the old priesthoods were re-established with regular royal offerings. Superficially, it was as if Akhenaten's lapse had never been. The remaining 18th Dynasty monarchs would, however, find it difficult to shake off the inherited taint of heresy. Egypt might deny her history but she could not go backwards, she had to move on. Art, literature and architecture would henceforth show unmistakable Amarna influences.

Meanwhile, Tutankhamen intended to make good use of what had gone before. The Amarna Period was to provide the new pharaoh with a convenient scapegoat. Everything that was now wrong with Egypt – her inefficiency, her corruption, her lack of funds and her dwindling empire – could be laid at

Akhenaten's door. Everything good could be attributed to Tutankhamen, the restorer.

Tutankhamen, raised at Amarna with no knowledge of the old cults, quickly developed a well-judged devotion to Amen. At Karnak he even erected a large stela, known today as the 'Restoration Stela', which unequivocally proclaimed his loyalty to the traditional gods:

> Year I, 4th month of the inundation, day 19 in the reign of... the king of Upper and Lower Egypt... and the son of Re Tutankhamen... He restored what was ruined, creating everlasting monuments. Truth [*maat*] is back in her proper place, for he put an end to wrongdoing throughout Egypt...
>
> When His Majesty's reign began, from the southern border to the northern marshes, the temples of the gods and goddesses were in ruins. Their shrines had crumbled into piles of rubbish choked with weeds. Their sanctuaries might never have existed, their chapels were little more than footpaths. The land was in chaos because the gods had abandoned it. Whenever the army was sent to Syria to extend Egypt's territory, it always failed. If someone called on a god in prayer, they got no response. In just the same way, if someone petitioned a goddess, they got no answer...
>
> Sometime later His Majesty inherited his father's throne... The whole of Egypt was under his control and every land submitted to his authority.

This is a less than subtle message in the grand old style: it carries a clear echo of Hatshepsut's (false) triumphal claim to have reinstated *maat* by expelling the hated Hyksos. Akhenaten had instituted a *maat*-less regime, and Egypt had suffered accordingly. Now Tutankhamen was to reverse this wrong, restoring the ancient gods and so re-establishing *maat* throughout the land. He was to become a traditional New Kingdom pharaoh, the upholder of all that Egypt held dear. He would build at Karnak, restore the neglected monuments of his ancestors, and even take up archery so that he might become a sporting hero in the mould of Amenhotep II. Meanwhile Egypt's sorely neglected international position was to be strengthened, either by diplomacy or, where talking failed, by General Horemheb's revitalised army.

Now Tutankhamen's image was added to the Karnak statuary, while a new avenue of ram-headed sphinxes allowed Amen to travel in style to the home of his wife, Mut. The human-headed Amen started to appear with Tutankhamen's face; his son, the moon-god Khonsu, too, was blessed with the features of the young king. Thus the link between Tutankhamen and his gods was made as clear as the link had been between Akhenaten and his.

Tutankhamen, not yet fifteen years old and not raised to be king, was showing an astonishing political maturity. Who was guiding his steps? Who was pointing him towards the old religions and beliefs? Under normal circumstances we would expect to find a forceful mother or perhaps a royal stepmother standing behind an immature king, but both Kiya and Nefertiti had died at Amarna. There was only one survivor of the nuclear royal family. The queen, fully royal by birth, must have worked with her husband-brother; indeed, we find Ankhesenamen playing a prominent role both throughout Tutankhamen's reign and beyond it. But Ankhesenamen, perhaps slightly older than her husband, was still relatively young. The king, needing a more experienced adviser, turned to Ay for help.

Ay, the distinguished courtier last seen at Amarna, was well placed to advise the young king. He was an experienced politician who had already proved his loyalty serving alongside Amenhotep III, Akhenaten and Smenkhkare. Although himself of non-royal birth, Ay had several intimate links with the royal family; he was most probably the brother of Queen Tiy, and the father of Queen Nefertiti, and this made him both grandfather to Ankhesenamen and great uncle to the king. God's Father Ay was promoted to the post of vizier; pharaoh's second in command. Now the army, in the person of General Horemheb, lent their support to the new regime.

The decision to move the court had left Tutankhamen with one major headache. What was to be done with the Amarna royal tombs; not only the principal royal tomb but also the lesser royal burials which had been cut into the exclusive royal wadi or royal burial ground? The dozen years at Amarna had not been good to the royal family; the royal graveyard included the burials of his father Akhenaten, his mother Kiya, his stepmother Nefertiti, his brother Smenkhkare, his half-sister/sister-in-law Meketaten (and possibly also Meritaten, Neferneferuaten, Neferure and Setepenre, who have all by now vanished) and maybe his grandmother Queen Tiy. Experience showed that an abandoned graveyard – no matter how well guarded – had little chance of avoiding the attention of the thieves who preyed on Egypt's dead. If Tutankhamen cared at all for his relations, he would need to have them reburied, and quickly. Even if he did not care about the deceased, it was imperative that he empty the tombs and recycle their contents before someone else did.

As far as we know, only one body was rescued from Amarna for reburial at Thebes. Had the others already been destroyed by thieves? Were they reburied elsewhere (and if so do they remain to be discovered)? Or did Tutankhamen not care overmuch about the reburial of his immediate family?

The one known rescued and reinterred body is that of Smenkhkare, full brother and predecessor to Tutankhamen. It is perhaps not being too fanciful to imagine that Tutankhamen would indeed have felt the greatest loyalty and love for his brother. As the sons of a lesser wife, Smenkhkare and Tutankhamen would probably have been raised together, and might not have had a great deal of contact with their higher-born relations. Tutankhamen in particular, as the younger son, may have been kept away from court. The two were linked not only by blood but by kingship; as the living king Tutankhamen automatically became the Horus to Smenkhkare's Osiris. We may therefore imagine the young king instructing his men to search out his brother and give him a dignified, but not excessive, burial at Thebes.

The evidence recovered from the Theban tomb KV 55 – a jumbled secondary burial which included a mixture of artifacts apparently taken from several Amarna tombs (sacred bricks bearing Akhenaten's name; a folded-up shrine dedicated to Queen Tiy; canopic jars which once belonged to Kiya; an anonymous body identified as Smenkhkare) – shows that Tutankhamen provided his brother with a parody of a royal burial, using discarded and essentially worthless objects retrieved from Amarna. Was this because the Amarna tombs had already been emptied by thieves, or can we speculate that Tutankhamen reserved the most precious of the Amarna grave goods for his own burial? This would go a long way towards explaining how an impoverished monarch, reigning after years of royal neglect, could accumulate so many riches. Several items from his tomb show clear evidence of cartouches originally engraved with Smenkhkare's names and it may be that Smenkhkare's burial at least was untouched before Tutankhamen's men arrived.

The other royal bodies may well have been stripped of their valuables (if any remained) and left to their fate. As his reign progressed, Tutankhamen increasingly preferred to gloss over his connection with his heretic father, associating himself instead with his well-loved grandfather Amenhotep III, even occasionally claiming to be his son. Unfortunately, official memory was not so short. Akhenaten, Nefertiti, Smenkhkare, Tutankhamen and Tutankhamen's successor Ay were all to be omitted from the official king lists, which neatly erased all evidence of the Amarna Period by jumping straight from Amenhotep III to Horemheb.

Tutankhamen was young, but he was very aware that he was the last of his line. The queen had already given birth to two still-born daughters; their tiny bodies were carefully mummified and then saved so that they might be buried within their father's tomb. Time appeared to be on Tutankhamen's side, and there was no obvious reason why he should not yet father a living son, but the public adoption of a successor seemed a prudent measure. Egypt felt secure when the succession was known. Ay, although elderly, was the obvious choice and so Ay now became 'eldest king's son', heir to the throne. He must have been well over sixty years of age. No one seriously expected Ay to outlive the teenage Tutankhamen, but that is exactly what happened. After nine years of rule, Tutankhamen died in January 1323BC.

Sudden deaths were all too common in ancient Egypt; fatal accidents and inexplicable, incurable diseases were accepted as an inevitable fact of life and, as Smenkhkare's untimely death showed, the royal family were not immune to such disasters. Tutankhamen's body is in a bad condition, and is currently unavailable for medical examination, but the evidence of damage to the chest suggests – while by no means proving – that he may have died as the result of an impact, possibly sustained during a chariot or boating accident. More contentious is the suggestion that the king may have been assassinated: killed by a deliberate blow to the head. While x-ray analysis does reveal an area of slight thickening at the base of the skull where Tutankhamen's head joins his neck, the interpretation of this thickening is inconclusive. It may be evidence of a haemorrhage; equally, it may simply be that Tutankhamen had a slightly dense skull.

For over fifteen years the Valley of the Kings had been abandoned in favour of the Amarna royal wadi. Now the Deir el-Medina workmen were slowly getting back into their stride, but Tutankhamen's regal tomb was nowhere near finished. Ay was forced to inter Tutankhamen in KV 62, a modest private tomb (possibly Ay's own) hastily adapted to accommodate a king and as many of his belongings as could be squashed into the limited space. By burying the dead pharaoh, Ay himself became king. Having outlived almost all his family, Ay was now officially 'God's father Ay, Divine ruler of Thebes, beloved of Amen', and his elderly wife, the former wet-nurse Tey, was queen of Egypt. It was now Ay's turn to adopt a successor. He looked outside his own family, choosing General Horemheb who brought with him the support of the Egyptian army. When, after a mere four years of rule, Horemheb replaced Ay, the Amarna Age was well and truly over.

Ankhesenamen, as a relatively young dowager queen without a son, was bereft of an obvious political or religious role. We

THE RAMESSEUM, MORTUARY TEMPLE OF RAMESSES II
(STEVEN SNAPE)

THE PROCESSIONAL ROUTE LEADING TO LUXOR TEMPLE
(STEVEN SNAPE)

THE GODS OF THE NILE AT ABYDOS
(STEVEN SNAPE)

A STATUE OF AMENHOTEP III RE-CARVED TO REPRESENT RAMESSES II
(STEVEN SNAPE)

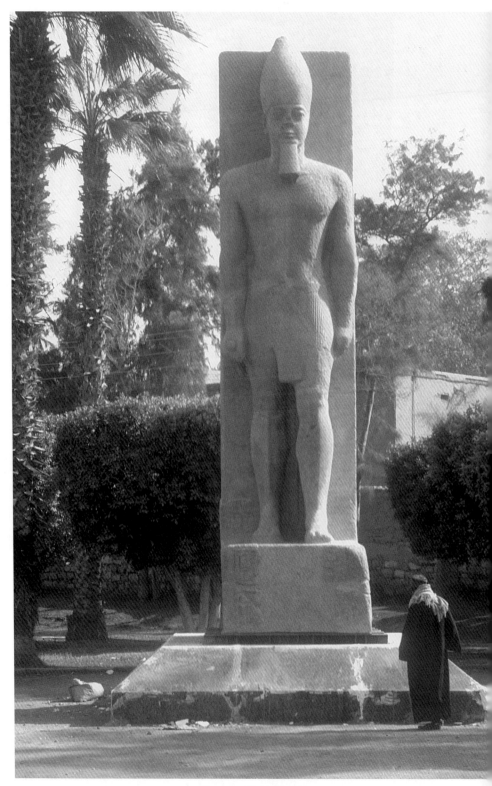

RAMESSES II AT MEMPHIS
(STEVEN SNAPE)

AN OBELISK OF RAMESSES II ORIGINALLY FROM PI-RAMESSE, NOW AT TANIS
(STEVEN SNAPE)

THE VALLEY OF THE KINGS
(STEVEN SNAPE)

THE MEDINET HABU PYLON
(ALEX LAY/LION TELEVISION)

MEDINET HABU, MORTUARY TEMPLE OF RAMESSES III
(STEVEN SNAPE)

LIBYAN ENEMIES OF EGYPT

(STEVEN SNAPE)

COUNTING THE PENISES CUT FROM THE DEFEATED LIBYANS

(STEVEN SNAPE)

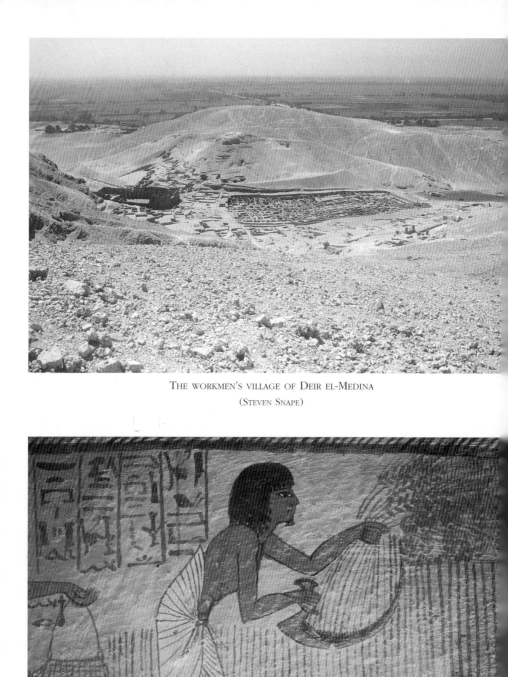

THE WORKMEN'S VILLAGE OF DEIR EL-MEDINA
(STEVEN SNAPE)

DEPICTION OF A TOMB WORKER ON THE WALL OF HIS TOMB IN DEIR EL-MEDINA
(ALEX LAY/LION TELEVISION)

may have expected her to retreat to the seclusion of the royal harem and live out her remaining years in peace. Instead, we find her writing to Suppiluliumas, king of the Hittites, pleading for a husband who can rule Egypt. To say that this is an unusual development is a major understatement. Egyptian queens were certainly not expected to marry foreigners – let alone enemy foreigners – while the idea that the Horus Throne might pass to a Hittite in this way was unthinkable. Ankhesenamen, as a royal princess, would have known this. What exactly had the queen written?

> My husband has died and I do not have a son. But, they say, you have many sons. If you would give me one of your sons he would become my husband. I shall never pick out a servant of mine and make him my husband.

Unfortunately, the cuneiform copy of this letter which has survived is undated and the queen's name, given as Dahamunzu (a phonetic version of *ta hemet nesu* or 'King's Wife') is not recognisable. We can work out that it was written by Ankhesenamen – there is no other possible author as there was no other widowed sonless queen at this time – but we do not know the desperate circumstances which provoked it. Is Ankhesenamen writing immediately after the death of Tutankhamen, and therefore attempting to thwart the ascent of her venerable grandfather, Ay? Or is she writing soon after Ay's death? In this case, it would be Horemheb who is perceived as the danger. Is the letter genuine, or could it be a trick designed to allow the Egyptians to capture a valuable Hittite hostage? This is the last that we see of Ankhesenamen; she now disappears like her many sisters before her.

Suppiluliumas was, as we might expect, tempted but extremely suspicious. The two nations were not on good terms and they were increasingly competing for the same territories. Indeed, at the time of Tutankhamen's death the Egyptian army was busy sparring, unsuccessfully, with the Hittites in Syria. Why should Egypt welcome an enemy king? The Egyptian attitude towards foreigners had become legendary; for century after century the pharaohs had despised all non-Egyptians, proclaiming their policy of hatred on the outer temple walls for all to see. Even Akhenaten, a non-conformist in so many ways, had shown the traditional Egyptian contempt for foreigners.

Eventually greed overcame caution. Egypt, even in her weakened state, was a great prize, a prize too tempting to be missed. It was surely worth risking the life of one son for the chance to win so much. First the Hittite ambassador was instructed to make extensive enquiries, then Prince Zannanza was dispatched to marry the anonymous queen. No one can have been too surprised when the unfortunate bridegroom failed to arrive for his wedding. Had he been ambushed and killed (by troops loyal to Ay, to Horemheb, or to Egypt)? Had he simply fallen victim to the plague which was still ravaging the Near East? His father chose to believe the worst, and relations between Egypt and the Hittites immediately plunged to an all-time low. Horemheb's reign was to include several inconclusive anti-Hittite Syrian campaigns.

Egypt's new pharaoh, General Horemheb, was an experienced politician with a strong military background who had sensibly kept a low profile during Akhenaten's reign but who had served with distinction under both Tutankhamen and Ay. Already he had acquired numerous titles, and he had started to build himself a magnificent tomb in the Memphite cemetery. Horemheb is a man of obscure origins but his second wife, and consort, is a lady whom we last met at Amarna. Queen Mutnodjmet is the sister of Nefertiti and therefore the last known surviving member of the Amarna elite. Like her sister before her, Mutnodjmet proved to be a strong queen. She died in her late forties during Year 14 or 15 of her husband's rule, and was buried at Memphis. Included in her grave was the skeleton of a baby, suggesting that Mutnodjmet had died trying to provide her husband with an heir.

Horemheb followed Tutankhamen's lead and developed into a traditional New Kingdom pharaoh; a proven warrior and a prolific builder who would restore *maat* to chaos. However, although his wife became God's Wife of Amen, Horemheb did not share Tutankhamen's loyalty to the Theban cults. His own local god was his namesake, the falcon-headed Horus of Hutnesu, and we find this version of Horus playing an important role in the tale of Horemheb's coronation. It is Horus of Hutnesu who crowns Horemheb in the presence of Amen. Rather than focus his offerings on one priesthood, Horemheb allowed all of Egypt's traditional gods a share in the royal bounty. At Gebel Silsila he now built a rock-cut chapel dedicated to no fewer than seven deities; Sobek, Amen, Mut, Khonsu, Taweret, Thoth and the deified Horemheb.

No lover of the Aten, Horemheb systematically dismantled and reused many of Akhenaten's Karnak sun temples, accelerating a process which had started tentatively during Tutankhamen's reign and which was to continue into the reign of Ramesses II when much of Amarna would be demolished and its stone blocks reused. Horemheb must have known many of the Amarna elite; his own wife was Akhenaten's sister-in-law while his late patron, Ay, had been a prominent member of Akhenaten's court. It would therefore be wrong to assume that Horemheb's destruction was motivated by hate rather than political expediency. Only Neferti-ti's Theban *benben* temple shows evidence of anything other than an impersonal cleansing. Here the reconstructed blocks retrieved from Horemheb's pylon show evidence of deliberate mutilation with the Aten's rays viciously slashed across the fingers.

Horemheb chose Memphis, rather than Thebes, as Egypt's principal city. From here he was well placed to instigate a much-needed reform of the civil service and the judiciary. Egypt's bureaucracy, once the envy of the ancient world, had grown lazy and corrupt, her legal system had become a farce; the treasury was now starting to suffer. Horemheb took his role as upholder of justice (*maat*) seriously. He had determined to 'protect the whole land ... repelling wrongdoing and destroying falsehood'. The legal system was to be strengthened by the establishment of a network of local courts and judges; even the harem was to be regulated. Justice was once again to be available to all. A decree was published outlining a detailed programme of reforms. The penalties for those who disobeyed the king's law were severe:

> If there is a man who wants to pay his taxes ... and there is anyone who interferes and takes away his craft the law shall be applied against him in the form of the cutting off of his nose, and he will be sent to Sile ...

The new laws, while seemingly designed to offer protection against official corruption, were really intended to guard state and temple assets. Horemheb, a true politician, was able to appear as the champion of the people while acting to protect his own interests.

At the same time the army, equally demoralised, was

reorganised into two separate divisions, north and south, each under its own commander. The newly energised troops were then put to work in Nubia and Syria.

Horemheb had no living son. Like Ay before him, he looked to the army for his heir, choosing an ex-officer named Paramessu, or Ramesses, son of the Commander of Troops Seti. Ramesses, a near-contemporary of Horemheb, had proved his abilities through many years of loyal service. Blessed with a living son and grandson, he also had the potential to found a dynasty.

Horemheb had long since abandoned his Memphite tomb. As a true king of Egypt, he intended to be buried in pharaonic style alongside his equals. The royal workmen took up their tools and started work on KV 57; the first full-sized royal tomb to be built in the Valley of the Kings since the time of Amenhotep III. The tomb was to be endowed with long corridors, multiple flights of steps, columned halls and a protective well or pit; its walls were to be decorated with the innovative sunken relief. Even a twenty-year reign, however, was not long enough to see it completed. When Paramessu buried Horemheb, transforming himself into Ramesses I in the process, the tomb was full of limestone chips left by the masons who had suddenly abandoned their work.

The tomb was rediscovered by a team of British archaeologists working under the patronage of Theodore Davies in 1908. It still housed its mountains of limestone chips, and the incomplete painted reliefs still shone bright on the walls, but Horemheb's splendid engraved sarcophagus stood empty and the shattered, discarded remains of his precious grave goods now littered the tomb. Various human remains were recovered from the burial chamber and corridors and, as Horemheb's body has not been identified in either of the royal caches, it may be that these represent the remains of the king and his immediate family.

Horemheb had sought to distance himself from the heresies and inefficiencies of the Amarna age. In twenty years he had done much to restore Egypt to her former glories. Ultimately, however, it was impossible to shake off the Amarna connection. Although Horemheb had more in common with his successor than his predecessor, Manetho classified Horemheb (or Oros), as the last king of the 18th Dynasty. Ramesses I, protégé of Horemheb, was destined to be celebrated as the founder of the 19th Dynasty.

# Pi-Ramesse, 1213BC:
# The 19th Dynasty

King of Kings I am, Ozymandias. If anyone would know
how great I am and where I lie let him surpass my works.

*Diodorus Siculus, 60BC,* Histories *I. 47*

I met a traveller from an antique land
Who said: Two vast and trunkless legs of stone
Stand in the desert. Near them, on the sand,
Half sunk, a shattered visage lies, whose frown,
And wrinkled lip, and sneer of cold command
Tell that its sculptor well those passions read
Which yet survive, stamped on these lifeless things,
The hand that mocked them, and the heart that fed:
And on the pedestal these words appear:
'My name is Ozymandias, king of kings:
Look on my works, ye mighty, and despair!'
Nothing besides remains. Round the decay
Of that colossal wreck, boundless and bare
The lone and level sands stretch far away.

*Percy Bysshe Shelley,* Ozymandias

R amesses II, 'The Great', was nearing death. As he looked
back over his long life, he felt immense satisfaction.
Sixty-six years of peaceful rule – of good Nile floods,
bountiful harvests and international stability – had allowed him
to achieve more than any other pharaoh. Throughout the civilised
world he was a living legend. To many of his subjects, he was
already a god.

Today, over 3,000 years on, the name of Ramesses [Ozyman-
dias to classical scholars] still epitomises the grandeur of Egypt
and her empire. His reign is recognised as a time of military
success and unrivalled control. It is his image we see when we
think of a pharaoh, his buildings we visit when we travel to
Egypt.

Ramesses was undoubtedly a master of propaganda. If we
strip away the rhetoric and hyperbole, and turn a blind eye to
the colossal statuary which still dominates the Nile Valley, what
is left? Ramesses' lengthy reign – perhaps too long? – heralded
the beginning of the end of the New Kingdom. Slowly but
surely his successors lost their grip and, less than 150 years after
Ramesses' passing, Egypt was once again a divided land. The
glorious days of Ahmose, Tuthmosis, Amenhotep and, of
course, Ramesses, were nothing but a distant memory.

How could this happen?

# CHAPTER 12

# Ramesses II:
# The Divine Pharaoh

His Majesty was confident, an unstoppable fighting force.
Everything near him was ablaze with fire – all the foreign
lands were blasted by his scorching breath. He charged
straight into the doomed Hittite forces and the foreign
hordes who were with them. His Majesty was like Seth the
almighty, like Sekhmet at the moment of thunder. He
slaughtered all the troops of the doomed Hittite, his
noblemen and his brothers, along with the chiefs of all the
countries which had supported him. His infantry and
chariotry fell on their faces, one on top of the other. His
majesty struck them down and killed them where they
stood.

*Kadesh Battle inscription of Ramesses II*

Ramesses I knew that he was destined to found a
dynasty. With a healthy son and a grandson to succeed
him, his line would surely rule Egypt for many years.
Now, as Egypt's army prepared for battle, the new pharaoh
determined to make his presence felt. A swift, successful raid on
Canaan sent a clear warning message to the Levantine states.
The Ramesside era had begun!

217

The Ramesside kings blew a breath of northern fresh air into the stultified Egyptian court. If Horemheb had felt little personal devotion to Amen, the new kings felt even less. They revered their own local gods and their family names, chosen for alternate generations, betrayed their devotion to both Re of Heliopolis (Ramesses: Born of Re) and Seth of Avaris (Seti: Man of Seth). Seth, sworn enemy of Osiris and Horus, was at first sight a curious choice of patron. At many levels he represented disorder and rebellion, the very opposite of *maat*. Nevertheless, Seth was seen as a vital, even essential member of the pantheon. He perhaps represented a misguided form of *maat*, the naughtiness which allowed the other gods to demonstrate their goodness, rather than the dreaded chaos. Certainly New Kingdom Egyptians, including the new royal family, were happy to take his name.

Although their statues show the Ramesside kings to be classically handsome, totally conventional warriors in the accepted pre-and post-Amarna royal mode, their appearance may have inextricably linked them to Seth. Today the mummy of Ramesses II has a scanty covering of white head hair masked by a yellow-red staining. However, analysis of his hair roots has confirmed that the king once sported a vibrant crop of red hair. Red hair tends to run in families; perhaps all the Ramesside kings had auburn tresses? This would have been something of a mixed blessing. As the overwhelming majority of Egyptians had brown or black hair, the red-head would certainly stand out in a crowd. But red was an ambiguous, ambivalent colour. It was the colour of the desert, the inhospitable 'Red Land' which served as Egypt's cemetery. It was also the colour of Seth.

The elderly Ramesses I was full of ambitious plans. First, though, it was crucial that work start on the excavation of a regal tomb in the Valley of the Kings. As the Deir el-Medina labourers picked up their tools, the Karnak architects were busy submitting designs to convert an open court built by Horemheb into a spectacular columned hall – a hypostyle hall – dedicated to Amen. Time was not, however, on the new king's side. When Ramesses died a mere sixteen months into his reign, he was buried in an incomplete tomb (KV 16). His son and co-regent, Seti, took over his Karnak project.

Seti I had determined to restore Egypt's lost empire. Straight away he embarked on a campaign to suppress the bedouin who were threatening Egypt's precarious control over the Sinai land-bridge. Over the next few years he was able to reinforce Egypt's control over her eastern territories, advancing inland as far as Damascus and securing the crucial Levantine ports which would once again allow Egypt to import much-needed wood. These were relatively small, local triumphs, but they had a high propaganda value. They reinforced Seti's right to rule as a restorer of *maat*, and they warned his enemies – the Hittite empire – that there might be worse to come.

Suddenly Seti was forced to look to his western border. Once again the peace and prosperity of the Delta were attracting unwanted attention. The despised Libyans were emerging from the desert, taking full advantage of Seti's preoccupation with eastern affairs. The army was recalled from Syria, and the teenaged Prince Ramesses was allowed to experience his first glorious battle in defence of the Delta.

As Seti campaigned in the east and west, the south remained essentially peaceful. A minor rebellion in Year 8 met with such a swift and brutal response that it was to be five years before the Lower Nubians plucked up the courage to challenge their northern neighbours. Again, the response was quick and decisive. The sight of the mighty Egyptian army, led by Prince Ramesses, caused the nervous rebels to drop their arms and flee.

Seti returned in confidence to Syria, where he captured first Amurru and then Kadesh. However, Egypt's new pharaoh was a realist. Small-scale local battles fought against small-scale local armies were all very well, but he knew that he was never going to be able to defeat the massed Hittite army. Reluctantly, he agreed to negotiate a truce which would apportion the eastern territories between the two superpowers in an equitable manner. Kadesh and Amurru were to revert to Hittite control while Egypt was permitted to retain her hold on the all-important Levantine sea ports.

Thanks to Horemheb's internal and Seti's external restorations, Egypt was making a rapid recovery from the economic depression which had followed the Amarna Age. Foreign tribute and domestic taxes were filling the treasury, the temple estates were once again flourishing and, after a royal tour of inspection, the mines and quarries were operating with unprecedented efficiency. Now Seti could use his wealth to finance his ambitious building projects. Both the temple of Re at Heliopolis and the temple of Ptah at Memphis attracted royal funding, while the Luxor temple received a new pylon and a forecourt decorated with colossal statues and obelisks. At Karnak the hypostyle hall designed by Ramesses I was renamed 'Glorious is Seti in the Domain of Amen' and decorated with elegant raised relief. Inside there were controlled scenes of temple ritual; outside scenes of bloody battle featuring the heroic Seti.

Seti understood the importance of making the succession clear. Prince Ramesses had already been declared First King's Son, or Crown Prince. Now he was to become an official co-regent, junior partner to his father. This momentous occasion was later recorded on the wall of Seti's Abydos temple by the grateful (and self-justifying) Ramesses:

Then my father appeared to his subjects while I was still a baby cradled in his arms and spoke about me as follows: 'Crown him as king and let me see his success while I am still alive ...' This is what he decreed for me when he was still alive ... He provided me with personal attendants and with female companions who were the great beauties of the palace. He selected women for me ... harem women and female companions.

Work had already started on the construction of Seti's mortuary temple and his Valley tomb (KV 17), the longest, deepest and most beautiful of the royal tombs. But Seti did not consider one mortuary temple and one tomb to be enough. At the ancient necropolis of Abydos, the traditional burial place of Osiris, Seti endowed a small cenotaph temple for his father and a huge cenotaph temple for himself, complete with subterranean dummy tomb. Here, in the seven temple sanctuaries, were worshipped Osiris, his wife Isis, his son Horus, Amen-Re, Re-Herakhte, Ptah and the deified king Seti. Later Ramesses was to confirm his family links to Abydos by building his own, smaller temple.

When Seti died in June 1279BC, few of his ambitious projects were complete. Ramesses, arriving in Thebes for the funeral, took the opportunity to review, and take over, his father's unfinished works. Thus started a lifelong habit of renovating and usurping other kings' monuments and statues. Time was on Ramesses' side. By the end of his long reign there

221

would be scarcely a monument in the Nile Valley which did not bear his deep-carved cartouche.

Seti's east bank temples were fair game. Now the Luxor pylon and its associated statuary officially belonged to Ramesses, and were decorated with scenes of his triumphs. At Karnak the complete but only partially decorated hypostyle hall was to be renamed 'Glorious is Ramesses II in the Domain of Amen'. Seti's masons habitually used raised relief (the images standing proud of the walls), a time-consuming technique but one that added a characteristic elegance to their work. Now the workmen adopted the faster but far less delicate sunken relief (images carved into the walls) which was to be employed in the decoration of almost all Ramesses' monuments. Ramesses, as an incorrigible usurper, probably recognised the true advantage of deep-sunken relief; it would be almost impossible for his successors to erase his carvings and superimpose their own names on his works.

Over on the west bank, Seti's mortuary temple obviously had to retain its link with the dead king. Now, however, it bore a message, carved high above the portico for all the world to see: Ramesses had both 'renewed' and 'erected' the monument for his father. Thus he turned his filial duty to his own advantage; the conspicuous renewal of an ancient (or not so ancient) monument would earn him credit as a true pharaoh, upholder of *maat*.

In October Ramesses left Thebes for Abydos. Here Seti's cenotaph temple was still incomplete, and the whole complex had an unfortunate air of neglect. Ramesses did not like what he saw, and recorded his disgust:

Since their lord passed away and flew to heaven, no son maintained his father's monuments in the necropolis. Even the facade and the back of the temple of Seti were still under construction when he passed away. Its monuments were unfinished, no columns had been stood on their pedestals, its divine image had toppled over ... The supply of offerings had been cut off, and the temple staff had stopped working. The temple fields were in chaos, as their boundaries were no longer being fixed ...

The workmen were summoned, and soon Seti's temple was complete.

Building, however, was an older king's hobby. As a young man Ramesses was impatient to pick up his father's abandoned foreign policy. He intended to challenge the Hittites and their allies, and effectively conquer the world.

First he needed to make sure that his own land was protected. Already Ramesses had established a chain of forts running along the edge of the Delta; this would avoid the inconvenience of a Libyan invasion while his troops were occupied elsewhere. The southern border was less of a problem. Nubia seemed settled and, if not exactly happy, at least resigned to Egyptian rule. Only once, during Year 21, would Ramesses need to send his army southwards. With Egypt secure, Ramesses was free to look eastwards, towards the city-state of Kadesh.

Ramesses regarded the battle of Kadesh – by no means a great triumph – as the highlight of his reign. Like Tuthmosis III, he travelled with military scribes who were kept busy recording daily events on the campaign trail. Back home, their accounts were consolidated into a glorious battle epic. Ramesses made sure that this story was recorded in stone many, many times. It appeared before his people as prose, epic poetry and in relief, and accounts of the 'victory' are still preserved on temple walls throughout Egypt and Nubia. All proclaim Ramesses' greatness on a massive scale. Combined, they allow us to reconstruct the details of his campaign in unprecedented detail. The excerpts quoted below are all taken from Ramesses' own inscriptions.

Ramesses started his 'Campaign of Victory' in Year 4. Marching northwards along the Levantine coast, he turned inland towards the Hittite vassal city-state of Amurru. Benteshina, Prince of Amurru, was overwhelmed by the arrival of the mighty Egyptian army on his doorstep. Wisely, he experienced a sudden change of loyalty, and Amurru quickly became a garrison for Egypt's elite soldiers. Ramesses returned home with the bulk of the army. In Hatti, King Muwatallis, grandson of the great Hittite ruler Suppiluliumas, was not amused by the defection of his henchman. Egypt would not be allowed to steal his territory. Summoning an immense army, the Hittites headed for Kadesh:

Then His Majesty reached the town of Kadesh. The doomed Hittite wretch was already there, and had assembled all the foreign lands as far as the edges of the sea. The whole of the Hittite empire had come, along with the land of Naharin ... Nowhere had been left out; every land, however distant, had been brought there. And their leaders were there alongside him, each at the head of their army and chariotry. [They formed] a countless host, which seemed to have no end. The mountains and the valleys were covered by them – they were like a swarm of locusts. There was no silver left in his country now; he had used it all up, paying all those foreign countries to side with him in the war ...

Ramesses remained undaunted. The Hittites and their numerous allies made a formidable enemy, but he was the living embodiment of Montu, ancient god of war. In his own mind, he simply could not lose. In the spring of Year 5 he formed an army of some 20,000 men subdivided into four divisions each named after a protective god: Amen, Re (or Pre), Ptah and Seth (or Sutekh). The convoy took a month to make its way along the coastal road through Canaan and south Syria and, passing through the Bekaa Valley, to approach Kadesh from the south. Meanwhile the elite force had left Amurru for Kadesh.

Eventually the Egyptians reached the bank of the Orontes, just ten miles to the south of Kadesh. Here they were lucky enough to capture two enemy soldiers, deserters from the Hittite army. The deserters were happy to talk, and gave Ramesses welcome news. The Hittites, paralysed with fear of the Egyptians, were still 120 miles away:

> Then two Shasu bedouin turned up and said to His Majesty: 'We have been sent... by our brothers, who are tribal chiefs allied with the doomed Hittite, to tell you that we are prepared to desert the ruler of the Hittites and switch our allegiance to Pharaoh...' Then His Majesty asked of them, 'Where are these brothers of yours, who sent you to suggest this course of action to me?' And they told His Majesty, 'They are in the same place as the vile ruler of the Hittites. [And he] is currently in the region of Aleppo, north of Tunip. Since he heard that Pharaoh was on his way north, he has been too scared... to come any further south...'

The tense Ramesses relaxed his guard. With the enemy so far

distant, it seemed a good idea to head straight for Kadesh. He could take the city early the next morning, before the Hittites arrived. He gave orders accordingly. The army split into its four divisions and started to cross the river. Amen division, and Ramesses, went first, followed shortly by Re, while Ptah and Seth waited on the far bank. Soon Amen division had struck camp to the north-west of Kadesh and, while his remaining three divisions made their leisurely way towards the camp, Ramesses was able to enjoy a precious few moments of peace in his tent.

Spies! Ramesses was jolted out of his complacency. Two more 'deserters' were captured and dragged in for questioning. Given that the Hittite army was supposed to be over 100 miles away, why were there so many deserters lurking on the banks of the Orontes? The soldiers were given a severe beating, and Ramesses' growing suspicions were confirmed:

Then one of His Majesty's own spies arrived, bringing two of the doomed Hittite's scouts, and he dragged them into the king's presence. And His Majesty asked them, 'Who are you?' And they answered, 'We work for the ruler of the Hittites. He sent us to find out your position.' And then His Majesty asked, 'And where is he, the doomed Hittite? I have heard that he is near Aleppo.' And they told His Majesty, 'The vile ruler of the Hittites and the many foreign lands he brought as his allies ... have already advanced ... Their infantry and chariotry have been organised and issued with weapons. There are more of them than there is sand on the seashore. Right now, they are waiting, in formation and ready for battle, just behind Old Kadesh ...'

It was a disaster. The inexperienced Ramesses had fallen for the simplest of tricks. The 'deserters' had been enemy agents, sent to spy on the Egyptian camp. Muwatallis and his troops were not 120 miles to the north; they had already reached the eastern side of Kadesh and were waiting over the next hill. With the Egyptian army spread out on either side of the Orontes, the enemy were poised to attack.

Frantically, Ramesses sent orders for his divisions to move up to his position. It was too late. There was barely time to usher the royal family to a position of safety; Ramesses liked the idea of his family watching his triumph, but was less keen on the idea of them being captured and held hostage. Suddenly the Hittites launched a fierce chariot attack on the isolated Re division. The Egyptian soldiers, taken completely by surprise, fled northwards, leading the Hittites straight to Ramesses' camp.

Amen division forgot all their training, took one look at the advancing chariots, and ran away. Re division had already fled. Ptah and Seth were still crossing the river. Ramesses found himself abandoned, surrounded by Hittites.

While His Majesty was sitting and talking to his officers, the doomed Hittite wretch was advancing with his army, his chariotry and his numerous foreign allies. They forded the river, south of Kadesh, and then smashed into His Majesty's army while it was still marching when it least expected [an attack]. Faced with this, His Majesty's army and chariotry lost all hope of going north and joining His Majesty. And the doomed Hittite troops were able to surround His Majesty's bodyguard who were protecting him. When His Majesty noticed this, he leapt up to rage

227

against them like his father Montu. He grabbed his
weapons and strapped on his armour, like Seth in his
moment of power. After harnessing his mighty warhorse,
'Victory in Thebes', he set off at a gallop, completely
alone . . .

Only the great warrior-god Amen could save him now.
Ramesses prayed, reminding his god of the favours which he
had done for him:

Have I not built you an enormous number of monuments?
Your temples are filled with captives I have taken and I
have even built you a new temple to last for millions of
years. I have bequeathed all my possessions to you. I have
organised the whole world to supply you with offerings. I
have had tens of thousands of oxen sacrificed to you and
offered you sweet-smelling plants . . .

Suddenly, at the most vital moment of battle, the story leaps
into the realm of legend. We shall never know exactly what
happened next, because Ramesses spins a tale that turns defeat
into victory and transforms him from a naive and gullible
commander into a godlike warrior king. Ramesses would have
us believe that he charged the entire Hittite army single-handed,
while his men fled around him, ignoring his rallying cries. Taken
at face value, the written accounts describe the superhuman
victory of one pharaoh and his gods (*maat*) over the chaotic
foreign multitude.

What really happened? Ramesses had been extremely lucky.
Overconfident, Muwatallis had not committed his full infantry
to the ambush of Re division and the mass of the Hittite army

still waited on the far bank of the Orontes. Technology was on the Egyptians' side; they had the lighter, swifter and stronger vehicles which were better suited to the forested environment. While the timely arrival of the Amurru-based elite troops came as a complete shock to the Hittite charioteers, the arrival of Ptah division was the final straw that broke the enemy. By the time that Seth division arrived, the Hittites had swum back across the river (with many drowning) and the excitement was all over.

The two greatest armies that Syria had ever seen were now poised on opposite banks of the Orontes; both had already suffered heavy losses, both were reluctant to commit themselves to open battle. It is not clear what happened the next day. In his own inscriptions Ramesses tells us that the cowardly Hittites pleaded for peace. Of course, he would say that. The Hittites, in their own accounts, claim that they themselves were the victors, the Egyptians the cowards who sought peace. Both sides agree that a truce was negotiated although no formal treaty was signed. Both kings returned home in triumph.

Ramesses' 'victory' was a public relations sham. He may have convinced his people that he was a hero, but Muwatallis knew differently. As Ramesses marched back towards Egypt, the Hittites were reaffirming their control over Kadesh and Amurru. They then pushed further south through the Bekaa Valley to secure the Egyptian territory of Upi. Soon Egypt's sphere of influence was once again restricted to Canaan and Ramesses was forced to embark on a series of campaigns in order to reassert his authority on vassals less than impressed by the Kadesh escapade.

Fortunately for Ramesses, the Hittites were not in a position to press home their advantage. They were preoccupied with domestic problems. The unexpected death of Muwatallis led to a succession crisis which was only resolved when Hattusilis, brother of the late king, staged a successful coup. King Hattusilis was an experienced diplomat who realised that both Egypt and Hatti were threatened by an as yet untried force: the Assyrians. Rather than fight, it made sense that they should unite and conserve their energies. In Year 21 (sixteen years after their Kadesh confrontation) a treaty was negotiated, witnessed by the massed gods of the two lands. The two nations pledged to respect each other's territories and to defend each other against enemy attack:

> As regards these terms, written on the silver tablet, which apply to the land of Hatti and Egypt – whoever fails to uphold them, a thousand gods from Egypt and a thousand gods from the land of Hatti will act together to destroy his household, his land and his vassals. But whoever upholds these terms which are written on this silver tablet, whether they are Egyptian or Hittite, will come to no harm. A thousand gods from Egypt and a thousand gods from the land of Hatti will act together to keep them healthy and alive, along with their household, their country and their vassals.

As diplomacy replaced enmity, the two courts exchanged letters and presents. Then, in Year 34 Hattusilis offered Ramesses the ultimate gift: his daughter, who came with the added bonus of a magnificent dowry. Ramesses accepted with alacrity, and after lengthy negotiations the young princess set off on an 800-mile journey to the magical new city of Pi-Ramesses. Her arrival was recorded on a royal stela:

Then the Hittite princess was ushered into the presence of His Majesty after travelling all the way to Egypt, her massive dowry trailing behind her as far as the eye could see ... And his Majesty realised that she was a first-class beauty ... like a goddess. It was an amazing event, a true marvel – no one could remember anything like it, there were no stories about anything similar, and it was not recorded in the inscriptions of earlier kings ... And His Majesty thought she was beautiful and he loved her more than anyone else ...

The newly named Maathorneferure (the One who sees Horus, the Visible Splendour of Re) bore Ramesses a daughter but then vanished; we must presume that she died young. Some ten years after the first marriage Hattusilis agreed to send Ramesses a second daughter plus a second enormous dowry. This anonymous Hittite bride vanished into the royal harem and is never seen again.

Ramesses had given Egypt a splendid new city. Pi-Ramesse (the Estate of Ramesses-Great-of-Victories), lay close to the Ramesside family home, beside the old Hyksos capital of Avaris. Here he had built a near-island; Pi-Ramesse was surrounded by water which offered not only a defence, but a valuable source of drinking water, sanitation and transport. Beyond the water, the fertile Delta fields offered all the amenities that the Hyksos had appreciated at Avaris; an unfailing supply of crops, fowl, fish and game, and links with the eastern empire. The visitor Pabasa, writing to the scribe Amenemopet, was clearly very impressed by such abundance:

This letter is to reassure my master and to let him know

that I have reached Pi-Ramesse. It seems like an amazing place, a beautiful area unlike any other, a perfect replica of Thebes, built by Re himself. The palace is an ideal place to live. Its fields are full of all sorts of beautiful things – every day [they supply] food and sustenance. Its pools are alive with fish and its lakes are covered in ducks. Its gardens are lush with vegetation... Its granaries are overflowing with barley and emmer, piled so high it reaches the sky... Its ships moor and set sail constantly, delivering food and supplies every day. Everyone who lives there is happy, and no one ever says, 'If only...!' The lowliest person there is treated just the same as the most important...

All that now remains visible above the ground is broken statuary; much of Pi-Ramesse was reused in the building of the new city of Tanis, and her few remaining treasures are buried beneath the moist Delta soil. But in its heyday, the city was an awesome sight, 'radiant with halls of lapis-lazuli'. The thick mud-brick walls of the palace complex were embellished with limestone columns and brightly coloured tiles so that the building sparkled and glittered enticingly in the sunlight. Pi-Ramesse was a garden city, planted with ornamental gardens, vineyards and orchards. There was even a zoo; lion, giraffe and elephant bones have been discovered in the palace grounds. Most splendid of all were the stone temples and the 'Halls of Jubilee', the venue for the celebration of the king's *heb-sed* ceremony which was fronted by a granite gateway and three pairs of obelisks.

Pi-Ramesse was also a working capital. As at Amarna, the royal residence was complemented by offices, storehouses, workshops and, of course, the housing of the more humble citizens. There was a large industrial complex, including a bronze foundry, and an army camp complete with chariot garrison and stables. Here, too, foreigners arrived to do business. Its architecture reflected the city's international nature with Minoan- and Palestinian-style housing appearing among the typical Egyptian homes.

The state gods remained hidden in their Pi-Ramesse temples; only the king could fully appreciate their presence. But, as if to compensate, there were colossal images of Ramesses everywhere. These were not simply tributes to the city's founder. Each figure was designed to become the focus of a cult with its own hereditary priesthood. Ramesses was providing his people with an accessible focus for their religious feelings. These statues were not confined to Pi-Ramesse; Memphis, too, was dominated by giant versions of Ramesses.

Who was building the splendid new city? The Bible would have us believe that 'Ramesses' was built by Hebrew slaves forced to work for pharaoh under the most oppressive of conditions:

There arose up a new king over Egypt, which knew not Joseph, and he said unto his people, 'Behold! The people of the children of Israel are more and mightier than we are ...' Therefore they did set over them taskmasters to afflict them with their burdens. And they built for the Pharaoh treasure cities, Pithom and Raamses [Pi-Ramesse] ... And the Egyptians made the children of Israel to serve with rigour. And they made their lives bitter with hard bondage, in mortar and in brick, and in all manner of service in the field ...

*Exodus 1: 8–14*

233

Ramesside Egypt included a significant minority of foreigners and Egyptians of part-foreign descent: economic migrants, prisoners-of-war, slaves bought on the international slave-market, even royal brides and their extensive retinues. The Delta certainly had its settled Semitic-Egyptian communities and, although we have no Egyptian record of the mass enslavement of these peoples, we do know that they were liable to be summoned to work under the *corvée* system of forced labour.

The Bible goes on to record the story of Moses and the freeing of the Israelites. With God's help, Moses was able to dispose of the entire Egyptian army:

> And Moses stretched out his hand over the sea; and the Lord caused the sea to go back by a strong east wind all that night, and made the sea dry land, and all the waters were divided. And the children of Israel went into the midst of the sea upon the dry ground: and the waters were a wall unto them on their right hand, and on their left. And the Egyptians pursued, and went in after them to the midst of the sea, even all Pharaoh's horses, his chariots and his horsemen ... And Moses stretched forth his hand over the sea, and the sea returned to his strength ... and the waters returned and covered the chariots and the horsemen, and all the hosts of Pharaoh that came into the sea after them; there remained not so much as one of them.
>
> *Exodus 14: 21-28*

The evil pharaoh goes unnamed, although the given name of his city, 'Ramesses', provides us with a hefty clue to his identity. If it was a real event (rather than an inspiring Hebrew legend), and if forced foreign labour really did help to build Pi-Ramesse, the Exodus must have occurred either during Ramesses' reign or the subsequent reign of his son, Merenptah. Construction of Pi-Ramesse enjoyed one major phase during the first part of Ramesses' reign, but then continued at a reduced pace for decades. However, what was to the Hebrews a major, defining moment, was to the Egyptians an event of little consequence; we have no Ramesside record of any mass departure, or indeed of any plagues. It is true that Prince Amenhirwenemef, Ramesses' first-born son, died young, but this was a routine tragedy not necessarily attributable to the last and most drastic of the seven plagues of Egypt:

> And it came to pass that at midnight the Lord smote all the firstborn in the land of Egypt, from the firstborn of Pharaoh that sat on his throne unto the firstborn of the captive that was in the dungeon; and all the firstborn of cattle. And Pharaoh rose up in the night, he, and all his servants, and all the Egyptians; and there was a great cry in Egypt; for there was not a house where there was not one dead.
>
> *Exodus 12: 29-30*

Ramesses had learned from Akhenaten's mistakes. He loved his new city, but he was not prepared to abandon the peripatetic lifestyle of the 18th Dynasty kings. He was determined to make himself known to his people, and to understand his country's abundant resources. Now he had decided to investigate the Nubian gold mines. The eastern deserts were rich in gold, but a shortage of water was making the mines impossible to work. Seti had attempted to establish a well in the Wadi Allaki, but had failed to find water. Ramesses, aware of his father's failure, summoned his advisers:

'Call my courtiers so that I can discuss this desert with them. I am determined to find a solution'... And they said to the king, 'You are like Re in everything you do – what you want always happens... If you were to tell water to come out of solid rock, it would come flooding out straight after you spoke... But this is what the Viceroy of Nubia said about the land of Akuyati... This water problem has existed since the beginning of time – people have always died of thirst there. All of your predecessors have wanted to dig a well there, but none of them has succeeded. Even King Seti tried, and had a well dug there during his reign that was 120 cubits deep. But it was abandoned half-built because there was no water in it'...

Heartened by this advisers' faith in his abilities, Ramesses ordered his men to start digging. Sure enough, water was found a mere 12 cubits beneath the sand and rock; Ramesses would not have preserved this tale had he failed in his dowsing. The new well was predictably named 'The Well, Ramesses II Achieves Amazing Feats'. By redigging wells, and making sure that there were relay stations between the various wells, Ramesses ensured that the donkey trains could go from the Nile Valley out into the eastern desert to collect the mined gold. Thus the vital flow of gold could be maintained.

Ramesses was determined to make the best of his empire's resources. Copper, as well as gold, was needed. The mines of Atkia, in the south of modern-day Israel, lay out on the edge of the wilderness of Zinn, between Sinai and the Negev Desert.

This was a harsh, waterless region. Those chosen to work at the mines considered themselves extremely unlucky. Egyptians did not like to live far from the River Nile; for them the desert, the Red Land, was a dangerous and difficult place in which to live.

The organisation of long-term mining operations in such a difficult environment was a triumph of administration over a hostile environment. Hundreds of lives would be lost to produce Egypt's copper weapons and tools. But for Ramesses, the rewards of these expeditions more than outweighed the human cost.

Under his successors, Timna would become one of the most profitable copper mines in the ancient world:

I sent my representatives to the massive copper mines which were in this region of Atkia. Because there were too many of them to go by boat, some of them had to travel overland by donkey. Ever since kings have existed, nothing like this has been heard of. The mines proved to be full of copper, and it was loaded into their boats in vast quantities. Under their watchful eye, it was then shipped to Egypt. It arrived safely and was unloaded and heaped up below the royal window of appearance. There were thousands of copper bricks, all the colour of third rate gold. And I made everyone admit it was an amazing feat.

*Papyrus Harris (dated to the 20th Dynasty reign of Ramesses III)*

All along the Nile Ramesses was filling the Valley with monuments to his own glory. On the west bank of Thebes his sandstone mortuary temple, today known as the Ramesseum, was already a fully functional temple of Amen. After Ramesses' death it would become a temple dedicated to the late king combined with Amen. Meanwhile the temple precincts included a royal palace complete with audience chamber and throne room, where Ramesses and his court could stay while visiting the west bank monuments.

The Ramesseum included a small chapel dedicated to Ramesses' mother, Tuya. Here Ramesses inscribed the story of his divine birth; a story which he had, of course, copied from Hatshepsut and Amenhotep III. Once again a queen of Egypt sits unchaperoned facing Amen. Once again '... his scent was that of the land of the gods and his perfume was that of Punt...' Ramesses was perhaps not as confident in his kingship as we might suppose. Technically, he was less royal than both Hatshepsut and Amenhotep III, having been born a commoner. Now Ramesses was not only the son of Seti, he was the son of Amen himself. Thus he confirms his right to be king, while leading us gently to the acceptance that he himself might be semi- or even fully divine.

In Nubia, hints at divinity were gradually crystallised. Here, like Amenhotep III before him, Ramesses moved slowly but surely from mortal king to god. Ramesses was to build at least seven Nubian temples. His earliest, at Beit el-Wali, was firmly dedicated to Amen-Re. At Wadi es-Sebua, one of the last temples to be built, the mortal Ramesses is shown worshipping his own divine self.

In AD1816 the ex-circus strongman Giovanni Battista Belzoni arrived at the massive Nubian dunes of Meha and Ibshek, intent on stripping off their sand. He had heard that there were monuments underneath and already he could see the tops of colossal statues – statues apparently made by giants – sticking out of the sand. By Friday 1 August 1817 enough progress had been made to allow him to crawl inside a long-lost temple. Here he wrote his name on the wall. Belzoni was the first visitor to the Great Temple of Abu Simbel for more than a thousand years.

Ramesses had carved twin temples into the Abu Simbel cliffs. The Great Temple belonged to Ramesses himself. The frontage makes this obvious; two colossal statues of the king sit on either side of the central doorway. Originally brightly painted, these four colossi would have been visible for miles, an awesome sight for any traveller on the Nile. The statues dwarf the solitary figure of the god who stands high above the doorway. *Re*-Harakhte, accompanied by the goddess *Maat* and the hieroglyphic sign for *User* is in fact a visual pun; 'User-Maat-Re' (*Maat* is the strength of Re) was one of Ramesses' chosen royal names.

Within the living rock of the temple the shrine, the deepest, darkest, holiest part, still holds four seated gods; Ptah of Memphis, Amen-Re of Thebes, Re-Herakhte of Heliopolis and, of course, Ramesses of Pi-Ramesse. Just twice each year, in February and October, the rising sun would pierce the dark of the temple and light up the four imposing figures.

The neighbouring Small Temple was officially dedicated to a local form of Hathor, but effectively belonged to the Queen Consort Nefertari. Two colossal Nefertaris appear on the facade, outnumbered by four colossal Ramesses and, just in case anyone is in any doubt about who has paid for the temple, the facade explains, 'Ramesses II has made a temple, excavated in the mountain, of eternal workmanship... for the Chief Queen Nefertari Beloved of Mut... for whom the sun shines'. This temple is the Ramesside equivalent of Queen Tiy's Sedeinga temple; a part of the king's Great Temple complex rather than a temple in its own right. Its sanctuary holds the carved image of

Hathor as a cow protecting Ramesses.

The most exciting part of Abu Simbel's history was yet to come.

In 1954 the decision to build the Aswan High Dam threatened many of Nubia's monuments with submersion. Some could be dismantled and moved with relative ease, but the Abu Simbel complex was huge, and cut into the cliff face. Eventually, after much academic debate, the decision was taken to move the monuments upwards, clear of the water. At a cost of $36,000,000, a vast sum in the 1960s, this was done.

Queen Nefertari did not live to see the completion of her temple. Having acquired an impressive portfolio of monuments, and having presented her husband with eleven children, she had died and was now interred in her beautifully painted tomb in Ta Set Neferu or 'The Place of Beauty'.

The Place of Beauty, a dry valley in the south-western part of the Theban necropolis, is today known as the Valley of the Queens. This valley was to become the principal burial ground of the Ramesside royal wives and children. Unfortunately, like the neighbouring Valley of the Kings, it proved insecure and was thoroughly looted in the turbulent late New Kingdom. The only Ramesside human remains recovered from the Valley – part of a leg – come from the tomb of Nefertari. This is unexpected. Comparison with the Valley of the Kings suggests that we should have found numerous small traces of the desecrated mummies (bandages and bones) littering the tombs, the sad evidence of the hasty stripping of the deceased which occurred within the dark security of the burial chambers. This offers Egyptologists a glimmer of hope. Were the queens and the royal children rescued in antiquity? Is there another royal cache awaiting discovery?

Nefertari's tomb (QV 66) was discovered in 1904 by an Italian archaeological mission directed by Ernesto Schiaparelli. It was empty, and in plan unremarkable. However, its brilliant painted scenes made it a monument of great beauty. Poor quality limestone had stopped the workmen from carving directly into the rock; instead they had covered the tomb walls with a thick layer of plaster which could be carved and then painted. When discovered, the walls were highly fragile, with naturally forming salt crystals pushing fragments of painted plaster off the walls. The Nefertari conservation project, a joint enterprise conducted between the Egyptian Antiquities Organisation and The Getty Conservation Institute, has been able to rescue the tomb, restoring many of the paintings to their original state.

Nefertari was not, of course, Ramesses' only wife. We know that at the time of his co-regency, Seti had presented the delighted young prince with a harem full of beautiful women. Now, faced with an urgent need for a consort, Ramesses promoted one of his lesser queens. Judging from the ages of their children, Ramesses must have married Iset-Nofret and Nefertari at approximately the same time; while Nefertari gave birth to Ramesses' first-born son, Amenhirwenemef, Iset-Nofret bore his second son, Ramesses, and his first daughter, Bintanath. Iset-Nofret eventually bore Ramesses at least four children including Merenptah, Ramesses' eventual successor, and Bintanath, Ramesses' future wife. Like Nefertari before her, Egypt's new queen was an enigma of unknown origin.

Iset-Nofret, too, died, and the elderly Ramesses, in need of a consort, started to use his daughters to replace his dead wives. Amenhotep III had married his daughters Sitamen, Henut-Taneb, Isis and Nebetah; now Ramesses was to marry Bintanath, Meritamen, Nebettawi and Hentmire. Bintanath, his favourite daughter, is known to have borne her father at least one child, a daughter.

Ramesses was so proud of his children that he featured them on the walls of his temples. Here we may count an impressive forty-five or forty-six sons and forty to fifty-five daughters – far too many to be the children of the immediate royal family (Ramesses plus Nefertari, Iset Nofret, the two Hittite Princesses and the royal daughters). Ramesses must be acknowledging all the children born in the harem. It must have seemed to him that his fertility was a good thing. The dynasty would surely flourish after his death. Unfortunately, this was not to be the case. Although the succession of Prince Merenptah (thirteenth son) went unchallenged, the vast number of royal and semi-royal children, grandchildren and great grandchildren were to cause endless family squabbles. Ramesses, with his longevity and his many children, had effectively sown the seeds of his own dynastic destruction.

Ramesses outlived many of the princes and princesses. So many dead children meant so many sad royal funerals; but where are the royal tombs? If the more important Ramesside women were buried in the Valley of the Queens, where were their brothers buried? In 1989, the rediscovery of tomb KV 5 provided a spectacular and unexpected answer. KV 5 had been explored during the eighteenth century, and was included on some of the earliest maps of the necropolis, but had since disappeared, lost beneath tons of debris dumped during Howard Carter's higher-level excavations. When it was realised that a road-widening scheme might destroy KV 5, the Theban Mapping Project, a team led by American Egyptologist Kent Weeks, set out to rescue the lost tomb using old maps and geophysical survey techniques.

The tomb, when rediscovered, was filled by a mass of compacted rubble. Clearance progressed slowly, but gradually the astonishing nature of the tomb was revealed. First came anterooms and an extensive sixteen-pillared hall. Then a long corridor beyond the hall. Doorways opened off the corridor, ten on each side, while the lowest two doorways led to more corridors with further side-chambers. The tomb was effectively a catacomb, designed to house the remains of the royal sons.

The elderly Ramesses – now far older than any of his people – was badly in need of renewal. He was suffering with severe arthritis of the hip, arteriosclerosis in his lower limbs, and badly decayed teeth and gums. His back was curved and if he walked at all, it was with the aid of a stick. His repeated *heb sed* festivities, celebrated in years 30, 33/34, 36/37, 40, 42/3, 45/46, 48/49, 51/52, 54/5, 57/8, 60/61, 63/64 and 66/67, were becoming almost annual events. Those closest to the king must have realised that he was ailing. But the ordinary people of Egypt did not have this personal insight. They were well aware that Ramesses had now survived Nefertari by over forty years. Perhaps he really had become a god, and would live for ever. Then, in August 1213BC, in his sixty-seventh regnal year, the king died. The shock must have been enormous. An era was at an end.

# CHAPTER 13

......................................

# The Villager:
# Servant in the Place of Truth

Year 29, 2nd month of winter, day 20. On this date the gang passed the five checkpoints of the royal necropolis, chanting, 'We are starving — it's now the 18th day of the month [and we still have not been paid]. And they sat down in protest behind the temple of Tuthmosis III. Then the necropolis scribe, the two chief workmen, the two deputies and the two district officials turned up. The workmen shouted, 'Let's go in.' But the officials swore powerful oaths, and said, 'Come on then! We have got royal authority on our side.' They stayed there for the day and spent the night in the royal necropolis.

*Turin Strike Papyrus*

Throughout the New Kingdom the welfare of the royal tomb workers was considered a matter of utmost importance. For the tomb workers knew the deepest, hidden secrets of their kings.

The New Kingdom had seen a drastic reduction in the workforce needed to build a royal tomb. It had taken tens of thousands of temporary labourers to raise a pyramid. We cannot be certain of the exact numbers, but it has been estimated by

245

archaeologists working in conjunction with construction experts that the Great Pyramid of Giza must have been built by a workforce of 20,000–25,000 labourers working in shifts for as many as twenty years. So many workers posed a logistical nightmare. They had to be fed, watered, clothed and provided with sanitation and health-care; their work had to be coordinated not only on the building site but with the mining and transport operations which extended the length of the Nile and throughout the Delta; they had to be guarded, and the royal burials had to be guarded from them. With such a large workforce there was no hope of keeping the pyramid geography secret. Too many people knew exactly where the pharaoh lay deep within his tomb.

In the early New Kingdom, as we have already seen, the royal burial shaft had been split from the mortuary temple. Many convincing theological reasons can be put forward to explain the abandonment of the pyramid complex, but it seems that practical considerations may have played a part in the change. Rock-cut tombs were bound to be more secure. Their simple entrances could be hidden from view, so that only the priests and the workers would know of their existence. They could be worked – indeed, due to the constricted space they had to be worked – by small, specialised gangs. Fewer workers obviously equalled increased tomb security.

The west bank village of Deir el-Medina was established to accommodate the workmen employed in the Valleys of the Kings and Queens. Unlike the haphazard, untidy mud-brick villages and hamlets which dotted the Egyptian countryside (but like the purpose-built workmen's village at Amarna), Deir el-Medina was planned down to the last detail by government officials. It emerged a tight-packed camp of small, dark, stone-built terraced houses confined by a forbidding mud-brick wall. Here, under the sacred mountain that overlooked Thebes and Karnak, lodged the respected 'Servants in the Place of Truth'. Here, too, lived their wives, children, dependants, servants, pets and livestock. Deir el-Medina was occupied for almost five centuries, with only a minor interruption while the workmen spent two decades at Amarna building for Akhenaten.

The tradition of employing temporary workers, workers summoned for the public good under the *corvée* system, was deeply ingrained in the Egyptian bureaucracy. This is how the pyramids had been built, and it is how the first Valley tombs were cut. Initially Deir el-Medina served as a temporary camp for a fluid band of itinerant labourers. However, the old tradition was gradually fading; already the old system of military call-up had been scrapped in favour of a professional standing army. The highly efficient Horemheb had recognised the advantages of a dedicated necropolis workforce; not only could the work be better controlled, there would be a reduced security risk. Now Deir el-Medina was used to isolate a permanent population of approximately 120 families, making a total village population of maybe 1,200 people.

Life in the workmen's village could never be entirely normal. Too much separated Deir el-Medina from the typical Egyptian village. The geography, for a start, was very different. While most Egyptian villages lay close to the river on the edge of the cultivated land, Deir el-Medina was built away from other villages, out in the desert. This allowed easy access to the royal tombs, but made almost every other aspect of daily life very difficult. Space within the village was limited. More importantly, everything – food, clothing, raw materials and, of course, water –

had to be imported. With some ingenuity it proved possible to raise animals (ducks, pigs, even sheep) in the cramped houses, and to grow crops in garden plots outside the village wall, but the villagers were essentially reliant on the government agents who supplied their rations.

The thick mud-brick wall, its gateways guarded by necropolis officials, meant that there could be no casual comings and goings. Everyone and everything who entered or left the village was inspected and those carrying goods might be asked to account for their property. The risk of theft was an ongoing concern; not only theft from the precious burials, but theft from the government-owned equipment stores. The 'Guardians of the Tomb' were honest men appointed to guard the valuable copper tools, paint and lamps used in the tombs; they counted them out at the beginning of each shift, and counted them back in at the end.

While there were higher- and lower-ranking workmen, with the overseers, scribes and government agents naturally occupying the highest social positions, the composition of the village was skewed towards the skilled and the educated. It was a remarkably static, close-knit community. The Deir el-Medina fathers trained their sons to fill vacancies in the work gangs and, as generations of Deir el-Medina daughters married Deir el-Medina sons, everyone was interrelated, everyone knew everyone else's business. This was a village without peasants; the desert made farming impossible. Instead, as hand-picked specialists, the villagers had valuable skills which they could put to good use. Not only did they provide themselves with elaborate tombs, they sold their labours to the city dwellers across the river, offering a tempting range of funerary artifacts. Already well-paid for their royal services, the workmen grew even more wealthy.

Although they were not confined to the village, the workmen and their families were effectively isolated both by geography and by the nature of their work, which lent them an enviable air of mystery. This was no coincidence; the necropolis officials reasoned that the fewer people who knew the secrets of the royal Valleys, the better. It is therefore ironic that we know more of the lives of these isolated people than we do of any other new Kingdom villagers. The unfriendly desert location has helped to preserve the village secrets. Building land is rare in modern Egypt but, thanks to the shortage of water, no one was tempted to build on top of Deir el-Medina. While other domestic dynastic sites have disappeared beneath modern housing and ploughed fields, Deir el-Medina exists today as a well-defined archaeological site.

Normally in New Kingdom Egypt only the most important matters were written down. Few could read and write and anyway papyrus was extremely expensive. At Deir el-Medina, however, the educated workforce were exceptionally literate; even the women could read. Papyrus was still prohibitively dear, but this did not matter. The local stone flaked into smooth chips which could be picked up anywhere, written on and then discarded. The people of Deir el-Medina were free to record the most mundane and transient details of life; not only official records but scribbled letters, shopping lists and even laundry chits. When, at the end of the 20th dynasty, Deir el-Medina was abandoned, the villagers left behind copious written records dealing with all aspects of their lives.

The Deir-el-Medina residents never intended their private messages to be read. This gives them an air of spontaneity and accuracy which is missing from the monumental pronouncements – so very obviously intended to be read –

carved by their masters. The Deir el-Medina records speak not for the pharaohs, but for the 'ordinary', voiceless Egyptian people. For example, they introduce us to Kenhirkhepeshef, the adopted son of the scribe Ramose. Ramose had been a pillar of the community but Kenhirkhepeshef, also a scribe, was a nasty character suspected of sharp business practices. His habit of diverting workmen away from the tombs to work on his own projects did little to endear him to his subordinates.

The painter Prehotep writes to his boss, the necropolis scribe Kenhirkhepeshef:

Why are you treating me so badly? I'm no better than a donkey in your eyes. When there is work to be done, you fetch a donkey. When it is feeding time, you fetch an ox. But when there is beer, you never invite me. You only ask for me when there is work to be done. If – god forbid – I was the type that couldn't hold their drink, then you would be right not to invite me ... But I'm just someone who is a bit short of beer in his own house. By writing to you, I'm only trying to fill my stomach.

Eventually one of his exploited underlings lodged a complaint against him. Kenhirkhepeshef received a ticking off from the vizier but his official reputation remained unsullied. He continued to work on the tombs and eventually, thanks to his unofficial businesses, became extremely wealthy. His riches made him attractive and, at the ripe old age of seventy, he married a young bride, Naunakhte. Naunakhte had probably not expected her husband to live to the age of eighty-six, far beyond the average life expectancy, but she stuck to her part of the bargain. After his death she remarried and bore several children, most of whom she disinherited:

> Year 3 of the reign of Ramesses II, the 4th month of Inundation, Day 5... On this date, the female citizen Naunakhte formally made her will before the court... This is what she said: As you know, I am a full citizen of the land of Pharaoh. I raised these eight children, and helped them to set up homes, with all the things which are normally given to people in their position. As you can see, I am getting old now. And believe me, they are making no effort to provide for my needs at all. Those of them who have given me a helping hand will get some of my property, but those of them who have given me nothing will get none of my property...

Of course, like any other small village Deir el-Medina was a hotbed of gossip. Some of the scandals that are recorded still ring true today. Paneb was one of the biggest scandal makers. He had actually been caught desecrating the tomb of Seti II:

> And when the burial of all the kings was made I reported the fact that Paneb had stolen some of the grave goods of King Seti Merenptah... he stole the upholstery of his chariot... He stole incense from the necropolis gods and shared it with his cronies. He stole Pharaoh's oil and wine as well. He even went as far as sitting on the sarcophagus... Yet he still swore an oath saying, 'I have never disturbed so much as a pebble anywhere in the neighbourhood of the Place of the Pharaohs.' Those were his very words.

Paneb did not stop at stealing. The document quoted above (*Papyrus Salt 124*), a draft copy of a letter of complaint written to the vizier, makes reference to his sexual offences. These, in a tight-knit community, were guaranteed to generate bad feeling:

> I accuse him of stripping Iyemwaw, throwing her down on top of the wall and [violated? raping?] her...
> Paneb slept with the villager Tuy, when she was married to the workman Kenna, with the villager Hunro when she was living with Pendua, and again with the villager Hunro when she was with Hesysenebef. His own son said this. And after he had slept with Hunro he slept with her daughter, Webkhet. What's more his son, Apahte, slept with Webkhet too...

We do not know what happened when the vizier received this letter; Paneb simply disappears from the written record and we read of his bad deeds no more. He would almost certainly have been called to account for his actions before the court of the vizier, at Thebes. Official investigations into necropolis affairs were taken very seriously, and while rape and seduction would have been matters of little official interest, those found guilty of stealing from the royal tombs faced banishment, mutilation or death by impaling on a pointed post.

In times of affluence, when the all-important rations were paid on time and Valley security was high, serious crimes were few and far between. Instead the local Deir el-Medina open-air court, the *kenbet*, was kept busy dealing with a seemingly endless series of petty thefts, contractual disputes and arguments over property and wills. The families of Deir el-Medina, inescapably bound together in conditions which allowed little or no privacy, spent a great deal of their time squabbling. Those who wished to accuse a fellow villager of a particular offence would make an official statement, naming the perpetrator, before the court. The defendant would then have the right of reply and the court might summon other witnesses. The judgement of the *kenbet* was both simple and final — A is right, B is wrong — and the court had the power to fine the loser. Unfortunately, it lacked the ability to enforce its own judgements. When the police chief Mentmose was found guilty of obtaining a pot of fat by deception, he took a remarkable eighteen years to pay off his debt.

The literate 'Servants in the Place of Truth' knew themselves to be a cut above Egypt's other workmen. Their top-secret mission ensured that they were both respected and well-paid. Life, for an artisan, could not get any better. They could even, if they wished, hold the necropolis authorities to ransom. Any slight delay in the payment of rations was met with a threat to down tools. Any serious delay, and it was well understood that the workmen might turn to the tombs themselves.

Nevertheless, no amount of respect could disguise the fact that their work differed little from the daily drudgery of the despised mine or quarry workers. The cutting of a tomb was hot, dirty and dangerous manual work conducted under difficult conditions. The work followed a long-established plan. First would come the religious ceremonies; a ritual implement would be used to make a symbolic initial cut. Then, the easy part over, the labourers, divided into two gangs to work the left- and right-hand sides of the tomb, would start to dig downwards through the rock. Immediately behind the labourers and their basket-men came the skilled men, the plasterers, draughtsmen, sculptors and painters who would finish the higher levels while the labourers excavated the lower chambers. This was not ideal; the basket-men were constantly brushing past the wet paint with their loads of dirty chippings, but it did mean that, should the king die unexpectedly, there was a reasonable chance that he could be accommodated in the upper part of his otherwise unfinished tomb.

Records show that absenteeism was rife; almost any excuse was considered valid, and so we find workmen absenting themselves to brew beer, because a daughter was having a period, or even to mummify a dead friend. Those who did turn up to work spent the eight-day working week living in temporary camps close to the tombs. They would return to the village for a two-day weekend. This meant that, back in the village, the wives of the gang-members were left to their own devices. They cared for their children, cooked, cleaned, and even found the time to run small businesses bartering surpluses on the open market. For some, like the notorious Paneb, the absence of the menfolk proved too tempting. Rumours of sexual dalliance were rife.

While adultery was not illegal, the blatant flaunting of an extra-marital affair was considered anti-social. In Chapter Four we have already considered the case of Nesamenemope, the married man from Deir el-Medina who had a far from secret affair which provoked a near riot. This tale of male infidelity is balanced by the case of an unfortunate, unnamed workman. The workman was engaged to be married, but had caught his future wife consorting with the play-boy Mery-Sekhmet. Curiously, for his fiancée's behaviour was unfortunate but by no means criminal, the workman reported the matter to the magistrates. Even more curiously, the magistrates ordered that the wronged man be punished with 100 blows. It was left to one of the foremen to fight for justice. Mery-Sekhmet was made to swear an oath that he would leave the girl alone. In spite of this pledge the affair continued and the girl fell pregnant! Although it was obviously far too late, Mery-Sekhmet appeared again before the magistrates where he again swore to keep his distance. Frustratingly, the tale breaks off at this point and we are left to wonder what happened next.

# CHAPTER 14

······································

# Ramesses III:
# The Traditional Pharaoh

I have made other countries afraid to remember Egypt. At
the mere mention of my name, they are immediately
scorched. Since my reign began . . . I have not allowed any
foreign land to look at the borders of Egypt with greedy
eyes . . . On the contrary, it is I who have seized their lands
and added their territory to my own. Their rulers and
people are in awe of me . . . so, Egypt, let the sound of
your rejoicing reach the heights of heaven, now that I am
ruler of the Two Lands . . .

*'Sea Peoples' inscription of Ramesses III*

To the Egyptian people the change of ruler seemed
seamless. Merenptah – pharaoh in all but name during
Ramesses' last decade – acceded just as his father had
wished. Merenptah was, however, already an old man unlikely to
celebrate even one *heb-sed*, and the immediate succession was by
no means obvious. Thanks to Ramesses' combined longevity
and fertility, and his habit of counting the offspring of his
lesser wives among the legitimate royal children, the throne was
surrounded by a sea of ambitious royal grandsons and great-
grandsons all with roughly equal links to the throne. Now these

potential pharaohs started to watch the new king's health with interest. Merenptah was to confound their expectations by reigning for an impressive ten years.

Ramesses the Great was a very hard act to follow. How could anyone hope to compete with Egypt's most prolific builder, her most celebrated warrior and her living god? The Nile Valley was filled with the carved evidence of Ramesses' lengthy rule; everywhere Merenptah looked, he was reminded of his father. Ramesses, already a legend in his own lifetime, had gained increased status with death; copious monuments made worship of the dead pharaoh easy, and his people would continue to revere Ramesses for centuries. As Egypt gradually descended into chaos, his prosperous reign would shine out as a classic golden age.

There is little doubt that Merenptah, a vigorous and effective pharaoh in his own right, has suffered from his close association with 'The Great' king. Historians tend to treat him as an appendage of his father, his reign as an extension of the previous one. This is unfair. Merenptah's rule was to see a dynamism, and an awareness of foreign affairs, that had been lacking for many years. Ramesses had, perhaps inevitably, developed the complacency and introspection of old age. He could no longer envisage a world where Egypt and her gods did not flourish. Merenptah, no youngster himself, realised that events were moving swiftly outside the Nile Valley. If her empire was to survive, Egypt once again needed a warrior king.

The Eastern Mediterranean, for so long blessed with a calm and prosperous unity, was slowly but surely fragmenting into its component, not necessarily friendly, parts. It is hard to pinpoint the onset of this decline but an unfortunate combination of natural disasters, economics and politics played their part. As crop failures led to the collapse of the Mycenaean economy, and famine struck in Greece and Turkey, plague broke out along the Aegean coast. The once prosperous Hittites were running out of food, and the generous Merenptah sent grain to his weakened allies. Massive population movement was inevitable as refugees attempted to escape from a life of poverty and toil and settle in a better land.

As always, Egypt became a prime target. She was not the only one. Once prosperous city-states now experienced an unaccustomed insecurity as vassals broke free of their traditional bonds, and nomadic groups, sensing weakness, started to target their assets. Lawlessness was rife. Even the sea was unsafe; pirates now patrolled the Mediterranean unchecked, causing serious disruption to the international trade networks which financed the great nations.

Egypt was in a fortunate position. She was blessed with abundant natural resources and could, if she had to, survive in isolated self-sufficiency. Nevertheless, the effects of the world-wide recession were starting to make themselves felt. The end of Ramesses' reign had seen a tailing off of his construction projects; was this because everything possible had been built, or was the king suffering from a shortage of raw materials? Many of his later buildings employ recycled materials; again, we must ask why. Was this a commendable thrift, a natural desire to speed up the work (to complete it before the king's death) or a simple lack of resources? Was the apparently endless stream of eastern tribute slowly drying up?

In time-honoured fashion, Egypt's Syrian vassals read the death of Ramesses as a signal to revolt. Merenptah was able to reimpose his authority on the eastern territories with a brief but successful eastern campaign. Potentially more dangerous, however, were the Libyans who were once again menacing the western Delta. The Libyans had teamed up with the 'Sea Peoples'; an unsavoury, ill-defined band of sea-borne itinerants and pirates. Now it seemed that they planned a joint invasion. Repeating tactics first used by the Hyksos against Kamose, the Libyans urged the Nubians to rebel, so that Merenptah's army might be divided and weakened. Eventually the Nubians did indeed revolt, but they acted too late to help their northern allies and were ignominiously crushed by the Egyptians.

In Year 5 the Egyptian army defeated the Libyans. It was a vicious, bloody battle with (or so Merenptah tells us) over 6,000 of the enemy killed, thousands captured and the Libyan chief forced to flee in shame. The details of this victory – the high-point of his reign – were recorded on a stela set in Merenptah's mortuary temple, and at Karnak:

> The vile enemy, the Libyan chief, fled in the dark of night. He went alone, with no plume on his head and no shoes on his feet. His wives were carried away from him, his food supplies were stolen and he had no water to quench his thirst . . .

The optimistic Libyans had crossed the border with their families and chattels, their aim the colonisation of the Delta. In an indirect way, many were to achieve this ambition. Merenptah took vast numbers of prisoners of war; suddenly a substantial number of Libyans were incorporated into the national economy.

Already, work was under way on the west bank where Merenptah was building a mortuary temple (constructed from the remains of Amenhotep III's monuments) and a Valley tomb.

Here, in 1204BC, he was buried. His death signalled the end of the line of strong kings stretching from Horemheb to Merenptah, and the start of the end of the 19th Dynasty. From now onwards Egypt would be ruled by a succession of increasingly ineffectual kings whose names are preserved on the official king lists, but whose deeds go largely unrecorded. Only one pharaoh would come anywhere close to emulating the achievements of Ramesses II. Egypt's golden age was set to end not with a bang, but with a long drawn-out whimper.

Merenptah had not appointed a co-regent but had done the next best thing; he had nominated Seti-Merenptah, his son by his sister-consort Iset-Nofret, as heir. The succession should have been automatic, but something went badly wrong. Perhaps Seti-Merenptah was sick or absent from the palace when his father died, and therefore unable to preside over his funeral? Egyptian tradition decreed that he who buried the pharaoh could take his place, but we do not know how strictly this rule was followed. The official records remain obstinately silent over this matter, and all that we are told is that Egypt's next pharaoh was the hitherto obscure Amenmesse, son of the lady Takhat. Whoever he was, Amenmesse enjoyed a brief, undistinguished reign of less than five years. Understandably, his successor attempted to delete all traces of his rule.

The next pharaoh, Seti II, is almost certainly the thwarted Seti-Merenptah, middle-aged and now extremely bitter about his treatment at the hands of Amenmesse. He adopted a string of impressive military titles but Seti proved ineffectual and, as far as we know, never fought for his country. He died after almost six years on the throne and it was the turn of the minor Ramesses-Siptah to become king under the joint guidance of his stepmother, Queen Twosret, and the 'Chancellor of the

Whole Land' Bay. Soon after his accession the young king changed his name to Merenptah-Siptah.

Siptah's reign saw Egypt plunge into deep recession. Official records gloss over the difficulties; Siptah wished to preserve the official propaganda, projecting himself as a conventional pharaoh ruling over a *maat*-filled land. This, however, was all an illusion. Siptah stands straight and healthy in his portraits, yet we know from his mummy, recovered from the Amenhotep II cache and now stored in Cairo Museum, that Siptah was disabled, his deformed left foot and shortened lower leg a legacy of cerebral palsy. Just as he denied the truth about his own body, so Siptah was able to ignore his faltering economy. The bureaucracy was on the brink of collapse, there was increasing civil unrest and, in the north, Libyan tribesmen were crossing the border to settle in the western Delta in ever increasing numbers.

Siptah went ahead with the construction of a Theban mortuary temple and a tomb in the Valley of the Kings. However, this was no longer a secure environment for Egypt's dead kings. The corrupt and inefficient civil service were unwilling, or unable, to police the west bank and, as official rations were in short supply, the necropolis workforce were both hungry and unhappy. In consequence, the tombs and temples were suffering from sporadic outbursts of looting. This is the era of Paneb, the Deir el-Medina workman whom we last met stealing from the tomb of Seti II. Paneb was by no means the only offender to be caught violating his oath of loyalty.

A strong king might have been able to turn things around. But Siptah was disadvantaged by his youth, his inexperience and perhaps his failing health, and he did not stand a chance. When he died, childless, after six years on the throne, there was again no obvious heir. Dowager Queen Twosret stepped forward to fill the gap. For the first time in 250 years Egypt was, briefly, to be ruled by a woman.

The assumption of a female pharaoh was a sure and certain sign of a dynasty in crisis. Twosret's reign is often compared to that of Hatshepsut, but Twosret was ruling in very different circumstances. While Hatshepsut's reign may be viewed as an indulgence, albeit an indulgence which brought huge benefits to Egypt, Twosret's reign may be interpreted as a necessary political move designed to keep the fragmented 19th dynasty in power. It was a move, however, doomed to fail. Twosret lasted a mere two years; not even long enough to complete her mortuary temple and certainly not long enough to restore *maat* to Egypt. Her death marked the end of the 19th dynasty and the end of the direct line of Ramesses II.

The 20th Dynasty was founded by the mysterious King Sethnakht. We can guess that Sethnakht was in some way connected with the 19th Dynasty pharaohs; how otherwise would he have been accepted as pharaoh? But this is only guesswork, as Sethnakht appears as if from nowhere and volunteers no information, telling us only, on a stela carved at Elephantine, that he came to the throne via a divine oracle. His principal monuments were his two tombs in the Valley of the Kings. The first, (KV 11), breached the tomb of Amenmesse (KV 10), and so Sethnakht usurped Twosret's tomb (KV 14), carefully erasing her name and image from its walls. Sethnakht's principal achievement was to father the next pharaoh, Ramesses III.

Ramesses III came to the throne in 1184BC. By now, with Egypt deep in recession, the golden court of Ramesses II had acquired the status of legend and 'Ramesses' was almost a brand-name, denoting successful Egyptian kingship. Egypt's new pharaoh deliberately and unashamedly modelled himself on Ramesses II. Although they were not, as far as we know, closely related, he copied his hero's name and titles, even naming his own children after the children of Ramesses II. Unfortunately, he was unable to re-create the old Ramesses' prosperity. The new Ramesses lived in very different times. He would be called upon to deal with problems which his famous predecessor had never faced.

The situation in the outside world had become increasingly dangerous. The Sea Peoples, erstwhile allies of the Libyans, had swept into the Near East. This loose confederation of displaced tribes and pirates had achieved the unthinkable and destroyed the Hittite empire. Egypt's greatest ally was gone. The Bronze Age world was on the brink of collapse. The king of Ugarit wrote one last, desperate letter to the king of Alashiya before his country was completely destroyed by the Sea Peoples:

The enemy ships are already here ... there are seven enemy ships that have come and done very great damage ...

City after city fell. The whole economic infrastructure of the Near East was collapsing. Now firmly ensconced in Syria, the Sea Peoples had started to move southwards by land and boat. Their declared goal was the Delta. Ramesses gathered together a great army and prepared to fight. Ramesses II had enjoyed the luxury of campaigns designed to extend the limits of the Egyptian frontiers. Ramesses III had no choice but to fight to repel the invaders who threatened the Nile Delta. Egypt was to be saved by three mighty battles recorded on the wall of the Medinet Habu temple.

The Tjemehu lands united and attacked *en masse*: Libu, Meshwesh and Seped side by side. Their warriors were sure of their plans. They advanced confident that they would do well for themselves, utterly convinced that they would succeed. They intended all sorts of evil and mischief, but their plans were thwarted and went awry, because of what the god willed.

Ramesses' battle inscription tells us that the first campaign was directed against three specific Libyan tribes: the Libu, the Meshwesh and the Seped. Libyan nomads had, from the time of Siptah onwards, been gradually colonising the western Delta. Theirs was a peaceful take-over, but it was not something that Ramesses wanted to encourage. A minor revolt, caused by Ramesses' interference in Libyan politics, gave him an excuse to take action. The battle was short and sweet, and the Libyans, humiliated, retired to lick their wounds.

Year 8 saw a more worrying development; a two-pronged, land and sea assault by the Sea Peoples. Fortunately Ramesses was ready, his troops were in position and his ships were prepared. As the Egyptian army repelled the invaders in Canaan, a desperate sea battle was being fought off the Delta coast:

First I reinforced the Syrian border against them ... Next I fortified the river mouths with an impenetrable wall of warships, galleys and boats. From prow to stern they bristled with heavily armed warriors, crack troops, the very best that Egypt could offer. They were like lions roaring on the mountain path ...
The attackers who reached my borders [overland] will have no descendants, because their hearts and souls were

destroyed for ever. All of the invaders who came from the sea were met with fire at the river mouths, and were hemmed in on the shore by a palisade of spears. They were lured in, rounded up, crowded on to the shore and slaughtered. Their corpses were piled up top to tail, their ships and all their contents sunk beneath the water...

Naturally the heroic Ramesses triumphed over the Sea Peoples, and the Delta was (temporarily) saved. The Sea Peoples, however, were not crushed; they retreated and eventually settled on the Levantine coast, where the Peleset tribe gave their name to the modern land of Palestine.

The Libyans now returned to the fray. In Year 11 they attempted to take the Delta by force. Ramesses stood firm, and another great triumph followed:

I made them turn back from the boundary of Egypt. From those whom my sword spared I took many captives, pinioned like birds before my horses, their women and children in tens of thousands...

*Papyrus Harris*

Finally, Ramesses could relax, his borders secure. Like Ramesses II before him, pharaoh could now turn his attention to internal matters.

Once again, the masons took up their hammers. The capital, Pi-Ramesses, was expanded. At Thebes the Medinet Habu mortuary temple, situated close to the Ramesseum (the mortuary temple of Ramesses II), was provided with a gatehouse built in the style of a *migdol* or Syrian fortress and decorated with traditional scenes of victory over the Nubians and Syrians; the resourceful

Ramesses had 'borrowed' these scenes from the nearby Rames-seum. A successful trading mission to the mysterious land of Punt seemed to herald the economic success of the new regime. Surely Egypt was back on track.

> Year 29, 2nd month of Winter, day 12. They reached the temple, spent the night protesting in its entrance, and then went into it... The district official, Hednakht, and three of the temple's priests came to listen to their demands. And they told them: 'We broke in here because we were starving and dying of thirst. We have no clothes, no oil, no fish and no vegetables. Send a messenger to our good lord, the Pharaoh, asking for them. And send another messenger to our boss, the vizier, [telling him] to provide us with emergency rations.' That same day he issued them with the grain [they were owed] for the month...
>
> *Turin Strike Papyrus*

Appearances were, however, deceptive. No one understood better than the pharaohs how to put on a convincing public display. The truth was grim. Ramesses had inherited a poor country on the brink of civil war. Three military campaigns in seven years had proved expensive. Now foreign tribute was drying up, the harvests were poor and the storehouses were running low. Ineffi-cient land management contributed to the growing sense of crisis; the royal estates had been drastically reduced, and Amen's priesthood now controlled almost a third of the agricultural land. Inflation was causing widespread discontent and, over on the Theban west bank, the workmen were on strike. Mindful of the threat to the royal tombs, Ramesses hurriedly sent officials to negotiate with the ringleaders. All outstanding rations were paid,

267

and the crisis was temporarily averted.

To make things worse, Libyan nomads, sensing weakness, were attacking the Theban settlements. No wonder the Deir el-Medina villagers, isolated and completely dependent upon government rations, were growing uneasy. Soon the workmen were again causing trouble. The Turin Strike Papyrus details the almost unthinkable; thefts from the tombs of Ramesses II and his sons:

> Now Userhat and Pentaweret have stolen blocks of stone from above the tomb of the late King Usermaatre Sete-penre [Ramesses II]... and Kenena son of Ruta did exactly the same thing above the tomb of the royal children of King Usermaatre Setepenre...

After thirty-two years on the throne Ramesses III was losing his grip on his empire, his country and even his family. The king was no longer a godlike being. He was mortal in every way and, like any other vulnerable mortal, he could be killed. For Ramesses III, danger lurked close to home. A series of papyri tell an astonishing tale of palace intrigue:

> The great enemy Paibekamen, was chamberlain at the time. He was charged with siding with Tiy and the other harem women, and conspiring with them. He had dared to carry messages from them, to their mothers and brothers in the outside world, saying, 'Agitate the people and whip up ill-feeling, so that they are ready to rebel against their lord'...
>
> *Turin Judicial Papyrus*

Official records find it difficult to admit that a pharaoh might ever be killed by his people. This was such a grave offence against *maat*, such a threat to the idea of semi-divine kingship, that it was best left unwritten. However, the Turin Judicial Papyrus is one of several legal documents which tell of a harem conspiracy that aimed to assassinate Ramesses III and replace him with Prince Pentaweret, a son born to the lesser queen Tiy. The plotters included six women and thirty-one men, a mixture of harem officials, soldiers and priests. Firstly, the papyri tell us, the conspirators attempted a long-range assassination by means of black magic and wax figurines. When magic failed, a more practical plan was evolved. The assassins would strike while Ramesses celebrated a religious festival at Medinet Habu. The details have not been preserved, but it seems that the king was to be killed with a dagger hidden in a basket. Things went wrong, however, and the conspirators were arrested and put on trial. The punishments meted out to the guilty were, as we would expect, severe:

> And they set him in the presence of the great officials of the Examination Court. They examined his crimes and found him guilty. And his crimes took hold of him, and the officials who examined him caused his punishment to befall him ... Pentaweret. He was charged with plotting with his mother, Tiy, when she was conspiring with the other harem women, and stirring up rebellion against His Majesty. He was brought before the butlers for questioning, and they found him guilty. They left him to his own devices and he committed suicide ...

Further scandal broke when some of the judges were also arrested and convicted of 'consorting' with the untouchable

269

ladies of the harem. Now they, too, were to be punished:

> People were punished by the amputating of their noses
> and ears because they had ignored the instructions given to
> them. The women had gone. They followed them home
> and revelled with them... Their crime caught up with
> them...

Just one crucial piece of evidence is missing. We do not know
whether Ramesses III perished at the hands of his would-be
assassins. The king's mummy shows no obvious sign of a fatal
knife wound but, as it is covered with rock-hard 20th dynasty
bandages, a superficial examination is by no means conclusive.

The imminent end of the New Kingdom loomed over the
remaining 20th dynasty kings. There were to be a further eight
Ramesses (their names assumed at their accession), their reigns
increasingly blighted both by official corruption and by low
Nile levels which led directly to high inflation and civil discontent. History has dealt harshly with these kings whose reigns get
unceremoniously lumped together. None was obviously weak, or
did anything obviously wrong, none was particularly short-lived
and indeed some showed remarkable longevity, yet none was
blessed with the strength needed to deal with Egypt's problems.
Things simply went from bad to worse. Gradually the eastern
empire dwindled away, and slowly but surely royal authority
within Egypt faded as the priesthood of Amen grew corre-
spondingly strong. Eventually the pharaohs were confined to the
north, ruling first from Pi-Ramesse and then from the new city
of Tanis. The south now belonged to Amen.

This was the era of the great Theban tomb robberies. A
collection of legal documents provides us with precise details of

crimes, criminals, suspects and punishments during the reigns of
Ramesses IX and Ramesses XI. They make sorry, if fascinating,
reading. For example, during the reign of Ramesses XI, the
magnificent, once untouchable Ramesseum was targeted by
those who should have known better:

> We paid another visit to the door-jambs together with the
> priest Hori, son of Pakharu, the temple scribe Sedi, and
> the priest Nesamun... We took away 5 *kite* of gold and
> used it to buy barley in Thebes, and split it between
> ourselves...

It was not only the necropolis officials and the residents of the
west bank villages who were turning to crime. Poverty, enhanced
by the government's failure to pay rations, drove honest Thebans
to desperate means. It was not easy to starve surrounded by
gold. Everyone knew of the treasures available on the west bank,
and east bank Thebans started to hire boats and boatmen to
cross the river and rob the temples and tombs. Even the
highest-ranking citizens were in on the act; those who believed
themselves too grand to steal were happy enough to accept their
share of bribes and look the other way.

An official tour of inspection conducted during Year 16 of
Ramesses IX and recorded in a document today known as
Papyrus Abbott found that the tombs of the nobles were now in
a dreadful condition:

> The tombs and graves on the west bank of Thebes, where
> favoured courtiers of the past, noblewomen and free
> citizens had been buried [were checked by the inspectors
> on this date]: it was found that thieves had broken into all

of them. They had tipped the bodies of the tomb owners out of their mummy-cases and coffins and left them lying on the ground. They had then stolen all of the funerary goods buried with them, as well as the gold, silver, and jewellery that had been put inside their mummy cases . . .

Unfortunately, it seemed that Paweraa, mayor of western Thebes, was the godfather of necropolis crime! Paser, the honest mayor of eastern Thebes, attempted to prove his colleague's guilt, but failed, and vanished, leaving Paweraa to continue in his lucrative criminal career.

Ramesses XI, last of the Ramesses, reigned for almost thirty years, spending much of his time in the north. Thebes, still menaced by Libyans, had grown dangerously insecure and was suffering from famine. This was to be remembered as the 'Year of the Hyena'. Years 8 and 9 saw virtual civil war as the High Priest of Amen, Amenhotep, was deposed by an anonymous rival. The king, and the Viceroy of Nubia, Panehsy, took up arms in support of Amenhotep, and Thebes suffered the indignity of Nubian troops fighting in her once sacred streets. With the restoration of Amenhotep came a tentative peace, a peace that was shattered by a Nubian rebellion led by the once-loyal Panehsy. Egypt was able to push back the Nubians, but things would never be the same again.

Ramesses XI was by now king in name only. In the south Egypt was ruled by the new High Priest of Amen, Herihor, while beyond the southern border the disgraced Panehsy retained his grip on Nubia.

In the north Smendes ruled from Tanis; theoretically he deferred to Ramesses as his overlord, but in practice he was founding a new dynasty. It was during these troubled times that

Wenamun, an official of the temple of Amen, set off for Byblos in search of cedar wood to make a magnificent sacred boat for his god.

Wenamun was embarking on a journey which countless royal emissaries had made before him. In the past they had always been received with hospitality, returning to Egypt with ships laden high with valuable wood. This time, however, the trip would be less successful. Arriving in Dor, a town belonging to the Tjeker tribe of Sea People, Wenamun was robbed by one of his crew. Complaints made to the local ruler fell on deaf ears; not unreasonably he refused to make good the stolen property, and merely advised Wenamun to stay in port while he searched for the thief. Wenamun, angry on behalf of his god, grew impatient and set sail, seizing property *en route* from a Tjeker boat.

Wenamun then landed at Byblos. For a whole month the prince of Byblos bombarded Wenamun with messages telling him to leave his land. When Wenamun refused to obey, the prince of Byblos finally agreed to meet him. Perhaps he was going to apologise for his discourtesy? No, the prince simply wanted to make it clear that the traditional roles would no longer be played. If Wenamun wanted wood, he would have to pay for it, just like everyone else. In the prince's own words:

If the ruler of Egypt were my lord, and I were his servant, he would not have to send silver and gold saying, 'Carry out the commission of Amen' ... I am not your servant, and I am not the servant of him who sent you either ...

How times had changed. No one would have dared to speak so bluntly to a messenger of Ramesses II. Eventually, after a bout of prolonged oratory, Wenamun got his timber, the prince of Byblos received a reward (four jars and one vessel of gold, five jars of silver and a variety of garments, hides, ropes and lentils), and Amen eventually received his boat. Everyone appeared happy, although it is obvious that none of Egypt's three rulers had any influence outside their borders. Egypt's empire had ended. The tale of Wenamun may be fiction rather than fact – we have no means of knowing – but its message, of declining Egyptian influence and split rule, remains constant.

Back at Thebes, most of the royal monuments had been violated. The open tombs and looted temples stood vulnerable and exposed, forlorn reminders of Egypt's vanished glories. Ramesses, his sphere of influence confined to the north, was understandably reluctant to commit himself to an insecure Theban burial. Eventually he abandoned his own almost complete Valley tomb (KV 4), and made plans to be buried elsewhere. With no more royal work, Deir el-Medina was abandoned and her workforce resettled at Medinet Habu. Future royal burials were to be incorporated within the northern temple precincts. This system proved very secure. The royal tombs of Tanis were rediscovered during the Second World War. Their treasures, including gold jewellery, gold and silver vessels, *shabti* figures and the spectacular silver coffins of the pharaohs Psusennes and Shoshenk-Hekakheperre, are today housed in Cairo Museum.

In 1070BC the New Kingdom ended with the death of Ramesses XI. Egypt was once again a country of two halves. Smendes, founder of the Third Intermediate Period 21st Dynasty, ruled the north. At the same time the High Priests of Amen, the descendants of Herihor, ruled the south.

It was now that the priests of Amen embarked upon their

rescue mission in the Valley of the Kings. It would be nice – but naive – to imagine that the restoration of the New Kingdom pharaohs was conducted with the purest of motives. In fact, the preservation of the bodies and souls of Egypt's dead kings was a minor consideration. The priests, still paying the costs of victory in the civil war, had recognised that the tombs were an easily exploited source of wealth. Although many, if not all, had already been robbed, the thieves had not been particularly thorough and there were still rich pickings to be had. Now the necropolis officials opened all the royal tombs, emptying them of their contents and cutting open the mummies to extract their amulets and jewels. Only the valueless bodies would survive this savage 'restoration'.

Temporary workshops were set up within the necropolis. Here the exposed mummies were repaired, rebandaged and replaced in their wooden coffins, now stripped of all gold leaf. Although the undertakers took the precaution of labelling both bandages and coffins, confusion was inevitable; Ramesses IX was accidentally stored in the coffin of the Third Intermediate Period Lady Neskhons while the coffin of the 18th dynasty Queen Ahmose Nefertari also held the 20th dynasty Ramesses III.

The kings and queens, in their modern bandages and plain coffins, had little to tempt thieves; the era of the tomb robbers had effectively ended and the priests were left with a collection of long-dead pharaohs. These were put into storage. By the end of the dynastic age there were two principal collections; one in the Pinodjem II family tomb in the Deir el-Bahari cliff, and one in the Valley tomb of Amenhotep II.

The Deir el-Bahari cache was rediscovered by the tomb robber Ahmed abd el-Rassul (brother of Mohammed whom we last met interfering with the Amenhotep II cache) in 1871. For a decade Ahmed and Mohammed exploited the find, selling valuables from the intact Pinodjem burials on the antiquities black market. The New Kingdom mummies, of course, had no valuables left to offer and were ignored. Eventually the Egyptian Antiquities Service learned of the tomb. On 6 July 1881 Mohammed abd el-Rassul revealed the tomb entrance. The mummies were now officially discovered, and Emile Brugsch, the representative of the Antiquities Service, was the first to enter and view the chamber packed with gleaming coffins. His description of this awesome occasion was published in *The Century Magazine* (1887):

> Their gold covering and their polished surfaces reflected my own excited visage so that it seemed as though I was looking into the faces of my own ancestors ... I took in the situation quickly, with a gasp, and hurried to the open air lest I should be overcome and the glorious prize, still unrevealed, be lost to science.

Brugsch made hasty plans for the mummies to travel by boat to Cairo Museum. Once more the New Kingdom pharaohs were to sail on the Nile. Now huge crowds gathered to watch the passing of their long-lost kings. It was a moving occasion. As at a modern funeral, women wept and tore their hair, men fired shots into the air. The pharaohs were, however, sailing from the sublime to the ridiculous. In Cairo the customs official who recorded their arrival classified the royal mummies as dried fish.

# CHAPTER 15

# The Undertaker:
# Travel Agent to the Unknown

> O flesh of the king, do not decay, do not rot, do not stink.
>
> *Old Kingdom Pyramid Text*

Death, and the preparations for death, have loomed large in our account of the New Kingdom empire. This is unavoidable; an unfortunate result of the differential preservation of Egypt's remains. Mud-brick palaces crumble and dissolve; stone-built temples may be dismantled and reassembled as new buildings. Rock-cut tombs, however, are virtually indestructible. They may be emptied, vandalised, flooded and usurped, they can even be lost and rediscovered, but they cannot totally disappear. Many pharaohs – far too many – are principally represented by their mortuary architecture, the empty tomb in the Valley of the Kings being the main evidence of an otherwise (as far as we can tell) uneventful rule. Tutankhamen is a prime example of this phenomenon; his burial has made him world famous yet, if we ignore the spectacular contents of his tomb, we actually know very little about the boy king's reign.

The Egyptian way of death, a tempting mixture of bizarre rituals, unique beliefs and vast quantities of gold, holds a very

277

real fascination for both amateur and professional Egyptologists. In any museum display it is death, and the artifacts of
death, which fill the cases and attract the largest audiences.
Death has therefore become something of an Egyptian cliché;
there is a tendency to focus on death at the expense of all other
aspects of dynastic life. It is important not to get this emphasis
out of proportion; death was only one aspect of Egyptian daily
life.

The economics of Egyptian death appear fairly simple. We
can see, for we have the evidence before us, that a substantial
part of the nation's wealth and resources, not only raw materials
but thought and manpower, was directed towards preparations
for death. We can guess, considering the evidence of tomb
robbery and royal restorations throughout the centuries, that
many of these material resources were eventually recycled,
gradually making their way from the tombs back into the local
economies. Even beyond death the dead influenced the
economy, as they required the living to make regular offerings of
food and drink. The more prudent dead were still landowners,
having established endowments of land to finance the priests
who made the offerings.

Less easy for us to understand is the theology which under-
pinned, and justified, this vast expenditure. Today, as advances in
medical understanding and longevity coincide with a loss of
religious beliefs, many people accept that death is simply the end
of life. As a complete annihilation of the body and soul it is
something to be feared. Death has become the inevitable unmen-
tionable; we do not talk about it, we seldom think about it, and
we rarely make long-term plans for it. As more and more of us
die in hospital, death becomes an increasingly remote rite of
passage. We can forget about it and imagine ourselves immortal

until that uncomfortable moment when reality intervenes.

The Egyptians took a very different, far more practical approach to their own demise. To them, too, death was inevitable and frightening. Death was all around them; accidents, disease and the perils of childbirth ensured that everyone came into contact with the dying and the dead. This could be accepted if not exactly welcomed as part of the natural cycle of life. Just as the Nile swelled, fell and swelled again, or the sun rose, set and rose again, so birth would be followed by life, death and rebirth. Death became a journey like any other. As such it became something which deserved serious planning. By taking control, by ensuring that the correct rituals were applied, the Egyptian could ensure that death was not the end of existence.

This planning was, however, the prerogative of the wealthy. The poor, those who could not afford mummification and elaborate tombs, would continue to be buried unbandaged in simple pit graves cut into the desert sands as they had been for centuries. We do not know their expectations of life beyond death; their thoughts go unrecorded. Of course, there is little reason why the elite, too, could not have been buried in the desert sands. For those with social aspirations, however, this had become unthinkable. The rock-cut tomb was an infinitely desirable goal. Not only did it serve as a comfortable home for the corpse and its grave goods, it acted as a conspicuous status symbol signifying wealth and royal patronage to the living. Elaborate, expensive mummification, too, proclaimed social position. To maintain their social standing, and irrespective of religious belief, the elite were compelled to participate in the expensive rituals of death.

By the beginning of the Old Kingdom, theology had decreed that the survival of the lifelike body (not a mere skeleton) was essential for the survival of the soul. It was well known that bodies could survive death; the occasional desert-burials that were re-exposed in the village graveyards housed naturally dried, shrunken yet essentially lifelike bodies. The trick was to replicate this natural desiccation in the stone-lined tombs of the upper classes. Separation from the hot, sterile desert sands was unfortunately causing Egypt's elite to rot.

The earliest attempts at mummification had involved wrapping the semi-flexed corpse in tight layers of resin-soaked bandages. This was optimistic, and doomed to fail. The 'mummies' simply decomposed beneath their cosmetic wrappings. If it were to be preserved in anything resembling a lifelike form, the body would have to be desiccated before its bandaging. In order to achieve a thorough drying, and to delay the onset of putrefaction, the soft tissue would first have to be removed. Some experimentation must have taken place; unfortunately, by their very nature the failures have not survived. By the end of the Old Kingdom, evisceration of the dead via a slit in the abdomen had become the norm. The undertakers, having discovered the essence of their technique, now sought to perfect their art. This, by the 18th dynasty, they had done. Embalming was now big business.

The technique was not one that was to be shared by the general public. Egypt's embalmers operated a closed shop, exploiting the twilight margin between the living and the dead, the practical and the ritual. The mortician was part priest, part technician. His workshop, part laboratory and part temple, was situated in the no man's land between the living Black- and dead Red-lands. Mummification was undoubtedly messy and distasteful, but it was essentially simple. Anyone, given the knowledge and vast quantities of natron salt and linen, could preserve a body. However, mummification was not merely a physical deed. The transformation of the dead into a latent Osiris – an Osiris who could be reanimated successfully at the entrance to the tomb – was a ritual act. The entire process called for the use of spells, charms, amulets, ritual tools and traditional masks.

In order to protect their market, the undertakers promoted the ritual aspect of their work, operating under a mystical aura of secrecy with traditions being passed by word of mouth from father to son. The mysteries of mummification were never written down by their practitioners. Today we base our understanding of their methods on a combination of modern experimentation, mummy analysis, and the accounts left by the near-contemporary historians Herodotus and Diodorus Siculus:

This is their procedure for the most perfect style of embalming. First of all they draw out the brain through the nostrils using an iron hook. When they have extracted all that they can, they wash out the remnants with an infusion of drugs. Then, using a sharp obsidian stone, they make a cut along the flank. Through this they extract the whole contents of the abdomen. The abdomen is then cleaned, rinsed with palm wine and rinsed again with powdered spices but not frankincense, and stitched up. And when they have done this they heap the body with natron for seventy days, but no longer, and so the mummy is made. After the seventy days are over they wash the body and wrap it from head to toe in the finest linen bandages coated with resin.

*Herodotus:* Histories II: 82

One of them inserts his hand through the wound in the body into the breast and takes out everything except the kidneys and the heart. Another man cleans each of the entrails, washing them with palm wine and with incense. Finally, having washed the whole corpse, they first diligently treat it with cedar oil and other things for thirty days, and then with myrrh, cinnamon and spices.

Diodorus Siculus: Histories I: 7

Herodotus details two cheaper, and therefore less effective methods of embalming. In the first, the undertaker eviscerates the body using dissolving oils:

They do not cut the flesh or extract the internal organs, but introduce the oil through the anus which is then stopped up. Then they mummify the body for the pre-scribed number of days. After this they allow the oil which has been injected to escape. So great is its strength that it carries away all the internal organs in liquid form.

Herodotus: Histories II: 87

Cheapest of all:

The undertakers clean out the abdomen with a purge, mummify the corpse for seven days, then give it back to be taken away.

Herodotus: Histories II: 88

Herodotus and Diodorus Siculus were writing after the classic age of mummification had passed, but their details were essen-tially correct. The undertaker would receive the body soon after death, before it could be attacked by putrefaction and flies. It would be washed in purifying water and then taken to the *Per-Nefer*, the House of Mummification. Here the removal of the soft tissue would start with the extraction of the brain via the nose, and finish with the emptying of the abdomen. The heart would be left in place; it would be needed in the Judgement Hall of Osiris. The stomach, intestines, liver and lungs would be removed, cleaned, preserved and stored for burial with the mummy. The emptied body would then be washed, stuffed with a temporary packing, and covered with powdered natron, a drying agent with mild antiseptic properties which had been used as a ritual purifier for many years. The desiccation of the body would take forty days.

Once dry, the body would be transferred to the *Wabet*, or House of Purification, for bandaging. Emptied of its temporary stuffing, and washed with purifying water, the abdomen was repacked and sewn together. The limbs and face, too, might be stuffed to restore a natural appearance. Any missing body parts would be replaced at this stage. Finally the body might be painted – red for men or yellow for women – and sealed with molten resin. A shroud completed the toilette.

Bandaging a mummy was a time-consuming, labour-intensive operation: the wealthier the client, the more bandages required, the longer the time needed to wrap and, of course, the costlier the process. Royal mummies were wrapped in purpose-woven bandages. Linen, however, was expensive and so we find lesser members of society meeting Osiris dressed in a variety of used cloths ranging from the discarded clothing of sacred statues (expensive) to old sheets and towels (cheap).

The undertakers worked to a deliberate pattern; the order of bandaging, the appropriate amulets and, of course, the correct spells were all pre-ordained and were all important in determining the correct preservation of the soul. Here, if they wanted it, the unscrupulous had the opportunity to rob the deceased. No one would ever see beneath the bandages, now glued in place with molten resin; no one would be able to check that the amulets and jewellery were in place. Equally, no one could ever be certain that the appropriate spells had been spoken over the body or, indeed, that the correct body had been returned to the grieving family. The choice of an honest undertaker was to become a crucial factor in determining the survival of the soul.

Finally the completed mummy was enveloped in a shroud knotted at head and feet and held in place by wide bandages. The mask, an idealised portrait of the deceased, would be fitted over this shroud. The mummy was now complete and awaited reawakening.

The full-scale Theban funeral started on the east bank, in the land of the living, where the extensive mourning ritual unfolded. The body would then make its way, in stately procession by boat and sledge, towards the west bank cemetery. It was accompanied on its final journey by an impressive cortège of priests, friends, family, servants carrying the funerary feast, two women representing the goddesses Isis and Nephthys, and groups of professional female mourners paid to lament the death.

Over on the west bank, if all had gone to plan, the tomb was already complete, decorated and filled with a splendid array of grave goods including a stone sarcophagus and a sturdy door. The tomb was to serve a dual purpose. At its most basic level, it would serve as a permanent home for the deceased and his or her property. At a spiritual level it served as a departure point for the journey into the unknown. It was therefore important that the tomb contained the correct symbolism, and that the necessary texts and scenes were provided to assist the departed on the most difficult of journeys.

The tomb now awaited its occupant. At its entrance the cortège would be met by ritual male dancers and a priest reading aloud from a magical scroll. Here, in the doorway, the Opening of the Mouth ritual was performed. It was this ceremony which transformed the inert mummy into an Osiris: a being capable of rebirth. In preparation, the priest donned the jackal-headed mask of the god Anubis and the mummy was propped upright. Two assistants touched the mouth of the mummy with a variety of sacred objects while spells were recited to ensure that he or she would be able to see, speak, hear, taste and touch in the Afterlife. All ritual over, offerings were made and a sumptuous funeral banquet was eaten in the tomb entrance. The mummy would then be installed in the burial chamber and, as the workmen left, the tomb would be swept ritually clean. The lights would be extinguished, the door shut and sealed, and the mummy left alone to await rebirth with the setting of the sun.

Now, within the sealed tomb, the three separate but linked parts of the soul were free to leave the body. The Ka, the spirit of life, would remain close to the mummy, living off the offerings of food and drink brought to the tomb by the living. The Ba, the spirit of personality, would also haunt the tomb but would be able to make brief visits to the land of the living. Only the Akh, the spirit of immortality, would leave the tomb for ever. Moving in the direction of the western horizon, the Akh would travel towards eternal life.

Entrance to the kingdom of Osiris was never intended to be easy. The deceased had to negotiate a path through a frightening maze of gates and doorways guarded by unhelpful porters who would cross-question the spirit before allowing it to proceed. However, as the living had advanced knowledge of the questions which would be asked *en route*, this was not exactly the frightening ordeal that Osiris had designed. Magical instructions included within the tomb – pyramid texts, coffin texts and, during the New Kingdom, the illuminated scroll known as the Chapters of Coming Forth by Day, or the Book of the Dead – would ensure that the deceased reached the Hall of Judgement in safety.

The true ordeal for the New Kingdom soul came in the Judgement Hall. Here Osiris and his divine tribunal of forty-two assessor-gods would identify the pure in heart; those who had avoided earthly temptation. The deceased would be required to recite the 'negative confession' – a list of offences which he or she had not committed. These ranged from relatively mild social misdemeanours (greed, adultery and indulgence in curious sexual practices) through true crimes (murder and theft) to offences against the king and the gods. No credit was given for leading an actively good life; it was the avoidance of wrongdoing which counted here. Next, the heart of the deceased would be weighed against the feather of *maat*, the symbol of truth and goodness. Thoth, the divine scribe, would deliver the verdict and record it in his scroll.

Those who passed this crucial test would be transfigured. They would be admitted to the Field of Reeds where they would live for ever enjoying a perfect replica of the earthly Egypt, ruled by the dead pharaoh Osiris. Those who failed were denied entry. Their hearts were thrown to Ammit, the 'Eater of the Dead', a compound monster part crocodile, part hippopotamus and part lion, and their souls were doomed to haunt the living for ever.

# Acknowledgements

I would like to thank everyone who has helped, either directly or indirectly, with the production of this book. In particular, at Lion TV I would like to thank Ciara Byrne and Jake Wilson, who were unfailingly enthusiastic at all times, as well as Justin Pollard who wrote the scripts for the film series. At Headline I would like to thank Ian Marshall and Jo Roberts-Miller.

# Sources

The majority of the quotations from contemporary Egyptian documents included in this book are free translations prepared for the television series *Egypt's Golden Empire* by Jake Wilson. The principal relevant published sources for Egyptian texts in English are listed below.

Breasted, J. H., *Ancient Records of Egypt* (5 volumes), New York, 1906.
Cumming, B., *Egyptian Historical Records of the Later Eighteenth Dynasty 1–3*, Warminster, 1982–4.
Davies, B. G., *Egyptian Historical Records of the Later Eighteenth Dynasty (4–6)*, Warminster, 1992–5.
Diodorus Siculus, *Bibliotheca Historica*, translated by C. H. Oldfather and C. L. Sherman, New York.
Erman, A., *The Ancient Egyptians: a sourcebook of their writings*, New York, 1966.
Herodotus, *The Histories*, translated by A. de Selincourt, revised with Introduction and Notes by A. R. Burn, London, 1983.
Kitchen, K. A., *Poetry of Ancient Egypt*, Jonsered, 1999.
—, *Ramesside Inscriptions: Historical and Biographical*, translated and annotated, Oxford, 1968–ongoing.
Lichtheim, M., *Ancient Egyptian Literature I: the Old and Middle Kingdoms*, Berkeley, 1973.
—, *Ancient Egyptian Literature II: The New Kingdom*, Berkeley, 1976.
Moran, W. L., *The Amarna Letters*, Baltimore, 1992.
Parkinson, R. B., *Voices From Ancient Egypt*, London, 1991.
Peden, A. J., *Egyptian Historical Inscriptions of the Twentieth Dynasty*, Jonsered, 1994.
Simpson, W. K. (ed.), *The Literature of Ancient Egypt: an anthology of stories, instructions and poetry*, New Haven and London, 1973.

# Further Reading

The books included in this bibliography have been chosen to provide an accessible, readable introduction to the traditional and social history of New Kingdom Egypt. For this reason preference has been given to books rather than to articles published in academic journals, and to publications written in English. All the works include their own bibliographies which will prove of interest to the more experienced reader.

## Traditional and Social Histories

Baines, J. and Malek, J., *Atlas of Ancient Egypt*, Oxford and New York, 1980.

Brovarski, E. *et al. Egypt's Golden Age: the art of living in the New Kingdom, 1558–1085BC*, Boston, 1982.

Donadoni, S. (ed.), *The Egyptians*, translated by R. Bianchi *et al.*, Chicago and London, 1997.

Gardiner, A. H., *Egypt of the Pharaohs*, Oxford, 1961.

Grimal, N., *A History of Ancient Egypt*, translated by I. Shaw, Oxford and Cambridge, Mass., 1992.

Harris, J. R. (ed.), *The Legacy of Egypt*, Oxford, 2nd edition, 1971.

Hayes, W. C., *The Scepter of Egypt 2: The Hyksos period and the New Kingdom*, New York, 1959.

James, T. G. H., *Pharaoh's People: scenes from life in imperial Egypt*, Oxford, 1984.

Kees, H., *Ancient Egypt: anatomy of a civilization*, London and New York, 1980.

Kemp, B. J., *Ancient Egypt: anatomy of a civilization*, London and New York, 1980.

Redford, D. B., *History and Chronology of the Eighteenth Dynasty: seven studies*, Toronto, 1967.

—, *Egypt, Caanan and Israel in Ancient Times*, Cairo, 1992.

Shafer, B. E. (ed.), *Religion in Ancient Egypt: gods, myths and personal practices*, London, 1991.

Shaw, I., ed., *The Oxford History of Ancient Egypt*, Oxford, 2000.

Stevenson Smith, W., revised and edited by W. K. Simpson, *The Art and*

*Architecture of Ancient Egypt*, New Haven and London, 1981.
Trigger, B. G., *Nubia Under the Pharaohs*, London, 1976.
— *et al.*, *Ancient Egypt: a Social History*, Cambridge, 1983.
Tubb, J. N., *Canaanites*, London, 1998.
Wilson, H., *People of the Pharaohs; from Peasant to Courtier*, London, 1997.


## Foundation (Sekenenre Taa – Tuthmosis III)

Bietak, M., *Avaris; the capital of the Hyksos, recent excavations at Tell el-Daba*, London, 1996.
Dorman, P. F., *The Monuments of Senenmut: problems in historical methodology*, London, 1988.
—, *The Tombs of Senenmut*, New York, 1991.
Hall, E. S., *The Pharaoh Smites His Enemies*, Berlin, 1986.
James, T. G. H., Egypt: from the expulsion of the Hyksos to Amenophis I, in I. E. S. Edwards *et al.* (eds), *The Cambridge Ancient History*, 2.1: pp. 289–312, 3rd Edition, Cambridge.
Naville, E., *The Temple of Deir el-Bahari*, 7 volumes, London, 1895–1908.
Robins, G., *Women in Ancient Egypt*, London, 1993.
Schmitz, F-J., *Amenophis I*, Hildesheim, 1978.
Schulman, A. R., *Military Rank, Title and Organisation in the Egyptian New Kingdom*, Munchner Agyptologische Studien 6, Berlin, 1964.
Shaw, I., *Egyptian Warfare and Weapons*, Princes Risborough, 1991.
Troy, L., *Patterns of Queenship in Ancient Egyptian Myth and History*, Boreas, 1986.
Tyldesley, J. A., *Daughters of Isis: Women of Ancient Egypt*, London, 1994.
—, *Hatchepsut: the Female Pharaoh*, London, 1996.
—, *Judgement of the Pharaoh: Crime and Punishment in Ancient Egypt*, London, 2000.
Waterson, B., *Women in Ancient Egypt*, Stroud, 1991.


## The Risen Sun (Amenhotep II–Horemheb)

Aldred, C., *Akhenaten and Nefertiti*, Brooklyn, 1973.
—, *Egyptian Art*, London, 1980.
—, *Akhenaten, King of Egypt*, London, 1988.
Arnold, D., Green, L. and Allen, J., *The Royal Women at Amarna: Images of Beauty from Ancient Egypt*, New York, 1996.
Brier, B., *The Murder of Tutankhamen*, London, 1998.
Bryan, B. M., *The Reign of Tutmose IV*, Baltimore, 1991.

Carter, H., *The Tomb of Tutankhamen*, London, 3 volumes, 1925; reprinted in I volume, 1972.

Desroches Noblecourt, C., *Tutankhamen: Life and Death of a Pharaoh*, London and New York, 1963.

Fletcher, J., *Egypt's Sun King: Amenhotep III*, London, 2000.

Hart, G., *A Dictionary of Egyptian Gods and Goddesses*, London, 1986.

James, T. G. H., *Howard Carter: the Path to Tutankhamun*, London, 1992.

Kemp, B. J. and Garfi, S., *A Survey of the Ancient City of El-Amarna*, London, 1993.

Kozloff, A. P. and Bryan, B. M., *Egypt's Dazzling Sun: Amenhotep III and his World*, Cleveland, 1992.

Martin, G. T., *A Bibliography of the Amarna Period and its Aftermath*, London, 1991.

O'Connor, D. and Cline, E. H. (eds), *Amenhotep III: Perspectives on his Reign*, Michigan, 1998.

Pendlebury, J. D. S., *Tell el-Amarna*, London, 1935.

Redford, D. B., *Akhenaten: the Heretic King*, Princeton, 1984.

Reeves, M., *Akhenaten: Egypt's False Prophet*, London, 2000.

—, *The Complete Tutankhamun: the King, the Tomb, the Royal Treasure*, London, 1990.

Reeves, N. and Wilkinson, R. H., *The Complete Valley of the Kings*, London, 1996.

Riefstahl, E., *Thebes in the Time of Amunhotep III*, Oklahoma, 1964.

Romer, J., *Valley of the Kings: Exploring the Tombs of the Pharaohs*, London, 1981.

Samson, J., *Amarna, city of Akhenaten and Nefertiti: Nefertiti as Pharaoh*, Warminster, 1978.

Samson, J., *Nefertiti and Cleopatra*, London, 1985, revised 1990.

Thomas, A. P., *Akhenaten's Egypt*, Aylesbury, 1988.

Tyldesley, J. A., *Nefertiti: Egypt's Sun Queen*, London, 1998.

# Divinity and Decay (Ramesses I–Ramesses XI)

Adams, W. Y., *Corridor to Africa*, Princeton, 1984.

Andrews, C., *Egyptian Mummies*, London, 1984.

Breasted, J. H., *The Battle of Kadesh: a study in the earliest known military strategy*, Chicago, 1903.

Brier, B., *Egyptian Mummies: unravelling the secrets of an ancient art*, New York, 1994.

Budge, E. A. W., *The Mummy: a Handbook of Egyptian Funerary Archaeology*, Cambridge, 1925.

Cerny, J., Papyrus Salt 124, *Journal of Egyptian Archaeology* 15: pp. 243–58, 1929.

Cockburn, A. and E., *Mummies, Disease and Ancient Cultures*, Cambridge, 1980.

Corzo, M. A. and M. Afshar (eds), *Art and Eternity: the Nefertari wall paintings conservation project 1986–92*, Getty Conservation Institute, 1993.

Corzo, M. A. (ed.), *Wall Paintings of the Tomb of Nefertari: scientific studies for their conservation*, Cairo, 1987.

David, A. R. (ed.), *The Manchester Museum Project*, Manchester, 1979.

David, A. R. and Tapp, E. (eds), *Evidence Embalmed*, Manchester, 1984.

Desroches Noblecourt, C., *The Great Pharaoh Ramses II and His Time: an exhibition of antiquities from the Egyptian Museum*, translated by E. Mialon, Cairo, 1985.

Freed, R. E. (1987), *Ramesses the Great: His Life and World (an exhibition on the city of Memphis)*, Memphis, 1987.

Gardiner, A. H., *The Kadesh Inscriptions of Ramesses II*, Oxford, 1960.

Goedicke, H. (ed.), *Perspectives on the Battle of Kadesh*, Baltimore, 1985.

Habachi, L., *Features of the Deification of Ramesses II*, Gluckstadt, 1969.

Hasel, M. G., *Domination and resistance: Egyptian Military Activity in the Southern Levant 1300–1185BC*, Leiden, 1998.

Ikram, S. and Dodson, A., *The Mummy in Ancient Egypt*, London, 1998.

Kitchen, K. A., *Pharaoh Triumphant: the Life and Times of Ramesses II*, Warminster, 1982.

McDowell, A. G., *Jurisdiction in the Workmen's Community of Deir el-Medina*, Leiden, 1990.

Menu, B., *Ramesses the Great: Warrior and Builder*, translated by Harry N. Abrams, London, 1999.

Murnane, W. J., *The Road to Kadesh*, Chicago, 1985.

—, *Ancient Egyptian Coregencies*, Chicago, 1977.

Partridge, R. B., *Faces of the Pharaohs: Royal Mummies and Coffins from Ancient Thebes*, London, 1994.

Peet, T. E., *Great Tomb Robberies of the XX Dynasty*, Oxford, 1930.

Reeves, C. N., *Valley of the Kings: the Decline of a Royal Necropolis*, London and New York, 1990.

Smith, G. E., *The Royal Mummies*, Cairo, 1912.

Spencer, A. J., *Death in Ancient Egypt*, London 1982.

Taylor, J. H., *Unwrapping a Mummy*, London, 1995.

Trigger, B. G., *Nubia Under the Pharaohs*, London, 1976.

Tyldesley, J. A., *Ramesses II: Egypt's Greatest Pharaoh*, Viking, London, 2000.

Weeks, K. R., *The Lost Tomb: the Greatest Discovery at the Valley of the Kings since Tutankhamen*, London, 1998.

# Index

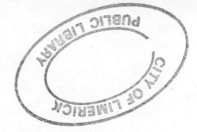